TEA
Exam

SECRETS

Study Guide
Your Key to Exam Success

TEA Test Review for the
Treasury Enforcement Agent Exam

Dear Future Exam Success Story:

First of all, **THANK YOU** for purchasing Mometrix study materials!

Second, congratulations! You are one of the few determined test-takers who are committed to doing whatever it takes to excel on your exam. **You have come to the right place.** We developed these study materials with one goal in mind: to deliver you the information you need in a format that's concise and easy to use.

In addition to optimizing your guide for the content of the test, we've outlined our recommended steps for breaking down the preparation process into small, attainable goals so you can make sure you stay on track.

We've also analyzed the entire test-taking process, identifying the most common pitfalls and showing how you can overcome them and be ready for any curveball the test throws you.

Standardized testing is one of the biggest obstacles on your road to success, which only increases the importance of doing well in the high-pressure, high-stakes environment of test day. Your results on this test could have a significant impact on your future, and this guide provides the information and practical advice to help you achieve your full potential on test day.

Your success is our success

We would love to hear from you! If you would like to share the story of your exam success or if you have any questions or comments in regard to our products, please contact us at **800-673-8175** or **support@mometrix.com**.

Thanks again for your business and we wish you continued success!

Sincerely,
The Mometrix Test Preparation Team

Need more help? Check out our flashcards at: http://MometrixFlashcards.com/TEA

TABLE OF CONTENTS

Introduction

Thank you for purchasing this resource! You have made the choice to prepare yourself for a test that could have a huge impact on your future, and this guide is designed to help you be fully ready for test day. Obviously, it's important to have a solid understanding of the test material, but you also need to be prepared for the unique environment and stressors of the test, so that you can perform to the best of your abilities.

For this purpose, the first section that appears in this guide is the **Secret Keys**. We've devoted countless hours to meticulously researching what works and what doesn't, and we've boiled down our findings to the five most impactful steps you can take to improve your performance on the test. We start at the beginning with study planning and move through the preparation process, all the way to the testing strategies that will help you get the most out of what you know when you're finally sitting in front of the test.

We recommend that you start preparing for your test as far in advance as possible. However, if you've bought this guide as a last-minute study resource and only have a few days before your test, we recommend that you skip over the first two Secret Keys since they address a long-term study plan.

If you struggle with **test anxiety**, we strongly encourage you to check out our recommendations for how you can overcome it. Test anxiety is a formidable foe, but it can be beaten, and we want to make sure you have the tools you need to defeat it.

Secret Key #1 – Plan Big, Study Small

There's a lot riding on your performance. If you want to ace this test, you're going to need to keep your skills sharp and the material fresh in your mind. You need a plan that lets you review everything you need to know while still fitting in your schedule. We'll break this strategy down into three categories.

Information Organization

Start with the information you already have: the official test outline. From this, you can make a complete list of all the concepts you need to cover before the test. Organize these concepts into groups that can be studied together, and create a list of any related vocabulary you need to learn so you can brush up on any difficult terms. You'll want to keep this vocabulary list handy once you actually start studying since you may need to add to it along the way.

Time Management

Once you have your set of study concepts, decide how to spread them out over the time you have left before the test. Break your study plan into small, clear goals so you have a manageable task for each day and know exactly what you're doing. Then just focus on one small step at a time. When you manage your time this way, you don't need to spend hours at a time studying. Studying a small block of content for a short period each day helps you retain information better and avoid stressing over how much you have left to do. You can relax knowing that you have a plan to cover everything in time. In order for this strategy to be effective though, you have to start studying early and stick to your schedule. Avoid the exhaustion and futility that comes from last-minute cramming!

Study Environment

The environment you study in has a big impact on your learning. Studying in a coffee shop, while probably more enjoyable, is not likely to be as fruitful as studying in a quiet room. It's important to keep distractions to a minimum. You're only planning to study for a short block of time, so make the most of it. Don't pause to check your phone or get up to find a snack. It's also important to **avoid multitasking**. Research has consistently shown that multitasking will make your studying dramatically less effective. Your study area should also be comfortable and well-lit so you don't have the distraction of straining your eyes or sitting on an uncomfortable chair.

The time of day you study is also important. You want to be rested and alert. Don't wait until just before bedtime. Study when you'll be most likely to comprehend and remember. Even better, if you know what time of day your test will be, set that time aside for study. That way your brain will be used to working on that subject at that specific time and you'll have a better chance of recalling information.

Finally, it can be helpful to team up with others who are studying for the same test. Your actual studying should be done in as isolated an environment as possible, but the work of organizing the information and setting up the study plan can be divided up. In between study sessions, you can discuss with your teammates the concepts that you're all studying and quiz each other on the details. Just be sure that your teammates are as serious about the test as you are. If you find that your study time is being replaced with social time, you might need to find a new team.

Secret Key #2 – Make Your Studying Count

You're devoting a lot of time and effort to preparing for this test, so you want to be absolutely certain it will pay off. This means doing more than just reading the content and hoping you can remember it on test day. It's important to make every minute of study count. There are two main areas you can focus on to make your studying count:

Retention

It doesn't matter how much time you study if you can't remember the material. You need to make sure you are retaining the concepts. To check your retention of the information you're learning, try recalling it at later times with minimal prompting. Try carrying around flashcards and glance at one or two from time to time or ask a friend who's also studying for the test to quiz you.

To enhance your retention, look for ways to put the information into practice so that you can apply it rather than simply recalling it. If you're using the information in practical ways, it will be much easier to remember. Similarly, it helps to solidify a concept in your mind if you're not only reading it to yourself but also explaining it to someone else. Ask a friend to let you teach them about a concept you're a little shaky on (or speak aloud to an imaginary audience if necessary). As you try to summarize, define, give examples, and answer your friend's questions, you'll understand the concepts better and they will stay with you longer. Finally, step back for a big picture view and ask yourself how each piece of information fits with the whole subject. When you link the different concepts together and see them working together as a whole, it's easier to remember the individual components.

Finally, practice showing your work on any multi-step problems, even if you're just studying. Writing out each step you take to solve a problem will help solidify the process in your mind, and you'll be more likely to remember it during the test.

Modality

Modality simply refers to the means or method by which you study. Choosing a study modality that fits your own individual learning style is crucial. No two people learn best in exactly the same way, so it's important to know your strengths and use them to your advantage.

For example, if you learn best by visualization, focus on visualizing a concept in your mind and draw an image or a diagram. Try color-coding your notes, illustrating them, or creating symbols that will trigger your mind to recall a learned concept. If you learn best by hearing or discussing information, find a study partner who learns the same way or read aloud to yourself. Think about how to put the information in your own words. Imagine that you are giving a lecture on the topic and record yourself so you can listen to it later.

For any learning style, flashcards can be helpful. Organize the information so you can take advantage of spare moments to review. Underline key words or phrases. Use different colors for different categories. Mnemonic devices (such as creating a short list in which every item starts with the same letter) can also help with retention. Find what works best for you and use it to store the information in your mind most effectively and easily.

Secret Key #3 – Practice the Right Way

Your success on test day depends not only on how many hours you put into preparing, but also on whether you prepared the right way. It's good to check along the way to see if your studying is paying off. One of the most effective ways to do this is by taking practice tests to evaluate your progress. Practice tests are useful because they show exactly where you need to improve. Every time you take a practice test, pay special attention to these three groups of questions:

- The questions you got wrong
- The questions you had to guess on, even if you guessed right
- The questions you found difficult or slow to work through

This will show you exactly what your weak areas are, and where you need to devote more study time. Ask yourself why each of these questions gave you trouble. Was it because you didn't understand the material? Was it because you didn't remember the vocabulary? Do you need more repetitions on this type of question to build speed and confidence? Dig into those questions and figure out how you can strengthen your weak areas as you go back to review the material.

Additionally, many practice tests have a section explaining the answer choices. It can be tempting to read the explanation and think that you now have a good understanding of the concept. However, an explanation likely only covers part of the question's broader context. Even if the explanation makes sense, **go back and investigate** every concept related to the question until you're positive you have a thorough understanding.

As you go along, keep in mind that the practice test is just that: practice. Memorizing these questions and answers will not be very helpful on the actual test because it is unlikely to have any of the same exact questions. If you only know the right answers to the sample questions, you won't be prepared for the real thing. **Study the concepts** until you understand them fully, and then you'll be able to answer any question that shows up on the test.

It's important to wait on the practice tests until you're ready. If you take a test on your first day of study, you may be overwhelmed by the amount of material covered and how much you need to learn. Work up to it gradually.

On test day, you'll need to be prepared for answering questions, managing your time, and using the test-taking strategies you've learned. It's a lot to balance, like a mental marathon that will have a big impact on your future. Like training for a marathon, you'll need to start slowly and work your way up. When test day arrives, you'll be ready.

Start with the strategies you've read in the first two Secret Keys—plan your course and study in the way that works best for you. If you have time, consider using multiple study resources to get different approaches to the same concepts. It can be helpful to see difficult concepts from more than one angle. Then find a good source for practice tests. Many times, the test website will suggest potential study resources or provide sample tests.

Practice Test Strategy

If you're able to find at least three practice tests, we recommend this strategy:

1. Take the first test with no time constraints and with your notes and study guide handy. Take your time and focus on applying the strategies you've learned.
2. Take the second practice test open-book as well, but set a timer and practice pacing yourself to finish in time.
3. Take any other practice tests as if it were test day. Set a timer and put away your study materials. Sit at a table or desk in a quiet room, imagine yourself at the testing center, and answer questions as quickly and accurately as possible.
4. Keep repeating step 3 on a regular basis until you run out of practice tests or it's time for the actual test. Your mind will be ready for the schedule and stress of test day, and you'll be able to focus on recalling the material you've learned.

Secret Key #4 – Pace Yourself

Once you're fully prepared for the material on the test, your biggest challenge on test day will be managing your time. Just knowing that the clock is ticking can make you panic even if you have plenty of time left. Work on pacing yourself so you can build confidence against the time constraints of the exam. Pacing is a difficult skill to master, especially in a high-pressure environment, so **practice is vital**.

Set time expectations for your pace based on how much time is available. For example, if a section has 60 questions and the time limit is 30 minutes, you know you have to average 30 seconds or less per question in order to answer them all. Although 30 seconds is the hard limit, set 25 seconds per question as your goal, so you reserve extra time to spend on harder questions. When you budget extra time for the harder questions, you no longer have any reason to stress when those questions take longer to answer.

Don't let this time expectation distract you from working through the test at a calm, steady pace, but keep it in mind so you don't spend too much time on any one question. Recognize that taking extra time on one question you don't understand may keep you from answering two that you do understand later in the test. If your time limit for a question is up and you're still not sure of the answer, mark it and move on, and come back to it later if the time and the test format allow. If the testing format doesn't allow you to return to earlier questions, just make an educated guess; then put it out of your mind and move on.

On the easier questions, be careful not to rush. It may seem wise to hurry through them so you have more time for the challenging ones, but it's not worth missing one if you know the concept and just didn't take the time to read the question fully. Work efficiently but make sure you understand the question and have looked at all of the answer choices, since more than one may seem right at first.

Even if you're paying attention to the time, you may find yourself a little behind at some point. You should speed up to get back on track, but do so wisely. Don't panic; just take a few seconds less on each question until you're caught up. Don't guess without thinking, but do look through the answer choices and eliminate any you know are wrong. If you can get down to two choices, it is often worthwhile to guess from those. Once you've chosen an answer, move on and don't dwell on any that you skipped or had to hurry through. If a question was taking too long, chances are it was one of the harder ones, so you weren't as likely to get it right anyway.

On the other hand, if you find yourself getting ahead of schedule, it may be beneficial to slow down a little. The more quickly you work, the more likely you are to make a careless mistake that will affect your score. You've budgeted time for each question, so don't be afraid to spend that time. Practice an efficient but careful pace to get the most out of the time you have.

Secret Key #5 – Have a Plan for Guessing

When you're taking the test, you may find yourself stuck on a question. Some of the answer choices seem better than others, but you don't see the one answer choice that is obviously correct. What do you do?

The scenario described above is very common, yet most test takers have not effectively prepared for it. Developing and practicing a plan for guessing may be one of the single most effective uses of your time as you get ready for the exam.

In developing your plan for guessing, there are three questions to address:

- When should you start the guessing process?
- How should you narrow down the choices?
- Which answer should you choose?

When to Start the Guessing Process

Unless your plan for guessing is to select C every time (which, despite its merits, is not what we recommend), you need to leave yourself enough time to apply your answer elimination strategies. Since you have a limited amount of time for each question, that means that if you're going to give yourself the best shot at guessing correctly, you have to decide quickly whether or not you will guess.

Of course, the best-case scenario is that you don't have to guess at all, so first, see if you can answer the question based on your knowledge of the subject and basic reasoning skills. Focus on the key words in the question and try to jog your memory of related topics. Give yourself a chance to bring the knowledge to mind, but once you realize that you don't have (or you can't access) the knowledge you need to answer the question, it's time to start the guessing process.

It's almost always better to start the guessing process too early than too late. It only takes a few seconds to remember something and answer the question from knowledge. Carefully eliminating wrong answer choices takes longer. Plus, going through the process of eliminating answer choices can actually help jog your memory.

Summary: Start the guessing process as soon as you decide that you can't answer the question based on your knowledge.

How to Narrow Down the Choices

The next chapter in this book (**Test-Taking Strategies**) includes a wide range of strategies for how to approach questions and how to look for answer choices to eliminate. You will definitely want to read those carefully, practice them, and figure out which ones work best for you. Here though, we're going to address a mindset rather than a particular strategy.

Your chances of guessing an answer correctly depend on how many options you are choosing from.

How many choices you have	How likely you are to guess correctly
5	20%
4	25%
3	33%
2	50%
1	100%

You can see from this chart just how valuable it is to be able to eliminate incorrect answers and make an educated guess, but there are two things that many test takers do that cause them to miss out on the benefits of guessing:

- Accidentally eliminating the correct answer
- Selecting an answer based on an impression

We'll look at the first one here, and the second one in the next section.

To avoid accidentally eliminating the correct answer, we recommend a thought exercise called **the $5 challenge**. In this challenge, you only eliminate an answer choice from contention if you are willing to bet $5 on it being wrong. Why $5? Five dollars is a small but not insignificant amount of money. It's an amount you could afford to lose but wouldn't want to throw away. And while losing $5 once might not hurt too much, doing it twenty times will set you back $100. In the same way, each small decision you make—eliminating a choice here, guessing on a question there—won't by itself impact your score very much, but when you put them all together, they can make a big difference. By holding each answer choice elimination decision to a higher standard, you can reduce the risk of accidentally eliminating the correct answer.

The $5 challenge can also be applied in a positive sense: If you are willing to bet $5 that an answer choice *is* correct, go ahead and mark it as correct.

Summary: Only eliminate an answer choice if you are willing to bet $5 that it is wrong.

Which Answer to Choose

You're taking the test. You've run into a hard question and decided you'll have to guess. You've eliminated all the answer choices you're willing to bet $5 on. Now you have to pick an answer. Why do we even need to talk about this? Why can't you just pick whichever one you feel like when the time comes?

The answer to these questions is that if you don't come into the test with a plan, you'll rely on your impression to select an answer choice, and if you do that, you risk falling into a trap. The test writers know that everyone who takes their test will be guessing on some of the questions, so they intentionally write wrong answer choices to seem plausible. You still have to pick an answer though, and if the wrong answer choices are designed to look right, how can you ever be sure that you're not falling for their trap? The best solution we've found to this dilemma is to take the decision out of your hands entirely. Here is the process we recommend:

Once you've eliminated any choices that you are confident (willing to bet $5) are wrong, select the first remaining choice as your answer.

Whether you choose to select the first remaining choice, the second, or the last, the important thing is that you use some preselected standard. Using this approach guarantees that you will not be enticed into selecting an answer choice that looks right, because you are not basing your decision on how the answer choices look.

This is not meant to make you question your knowledge. Instead, it is to help you recognize the difference between your knowledge and your impressions. There's a huge difference between thinking an answer is right because of what you know, and thinking an answer is right because it looks or sounds like it should be right.

Summary: To ensure that your selection is appropriately random, make a predetermined selection from among all answer choices you have not eliminated.

Test-Taking Strategies

This section contains a list of test-taking strategies that you may find helpful as you work through the test. By taking what you know and applying logical thought, you can maximize your chances of answering any question correctly!

It is very important to realize that every question is different and every person is different: no single strategy will work on every question, and no single strategy will work for every person. That's why we've included all of them here, so you can try them out and determine which ones work best for different types of questions and which ones work best for you.

Question Strategies

Read Carefully

Read the question and answer choices carefully. Don't miss the question because you misread the terms. You have plenty of time to read each question thoroughly and make sure you understand what is being asked. Yet a happy medium must be attained, so don't waste too much time. You must read carefully, but efficiently.

Contextual Clues

Look for contextual clues. If the question includes a word you are not familiar with, look at the immediate context for some indication of what the word might mean. Contextual clues can often give you all the information you need to decipher the meaning of an unfamiliar word. Even if you can't determine the meaning, you may be able to narrow down the possibilities enough to make a solid guess at the answer to the question.

Prefixes

If you're having trouble with a word in the question or answer choices, try dissecting it. Take advantage of every clue that the word might include. Prefixes and suffixes can be a huge help. Usually they allow you to determine a basic meaning. Pre- means before, post- means after, pro - is positive, de- is negative. From prefixes and suffixes, you can get an idea of the general meaning of the word and try to put it into context.

Hedge Words

Watch out for critical hedge words, such as *likely, may, can, sometimes, often, almost, mostly, usually, generally, rarely,* and *sometimes.* Question writers insert these hedge phrases to cover every possibility. Often an answer choice will be wrong simply because it leaves no room for exception. Be on guard for answer choices that have definitive words such as *exactly* and *always.*

Switchback Words

Stay alert for *switchbacks.* These are the words and phrases frequently used to alert you to shifts in thought. The most common switchback words are *but, although,* and *however.* Others include *nevertheless, on the other hand, even though, while, in spite of, despite, regardless of.* Switchback words are important to catch because they can change the direction of the question or an answer choice.

Face Value

When in doubt, use common sense. Accept the situation in the problem at face value. Don't read too much into it. These problems will not require you to make wild assumptions. If you have to go beyond creativity and warp time or space in order to have an answer choice fit the question, then you should move on and consider the other answer choices. These are normal problems rooted in reality. The applicable relationship or explanation may not be readily apparent, but it is there for you to figure out. Use your common sense to interpret anything that isn't clear.

Answer Choice Strategies

Answer Selection

The most thorough way to pick an answer choice is to identify and eliminate wrong answers until only one is left, then confirm it is the correct answer. Sometimes an answer choice may immediately seem right, but be careful. The test writers will usually put more than one reasonable answer choice on each question, so take a second to read all of them and make sure that the other choices are not equally obvious. As long as you have time left, it is better to read every answer choice than to pick the first one that looks right without checking the others.

Answer Choice Families

An answer choice family consists of two (in rare cases, three) answer choices that are very similar in construction and cannot all be true at the same time. If you see two answer choices that are direct opposites or parallels, one of them is usually the correct answer. For instance, if one answer choice says that quantity *x* increases and another either says that quantity *x* decreases (opposite) or says that quantity *y* increases (parallel), then those answer choices would fall into the same family. An answer choice that doesn't match the construction of the answer choice family is more likely to be incorrect. Most questions will not have answer choice families, but when they do appear, you should be prepared to recognize them.

Eliminate Answers

Eliminate answer choices as soon as you realize they are wrong, but make sure you consider all possibilities. If you are eliminating answer choices and realize that the last one you are left with is also wrong, don't panic. Start over and consider each choice again. There may be something you missed the first time that you will realize on the second pass.

Avoid Fact Traps

Don't be distracted by an answer choice that is factually true but doesn't answer the question. You are looking for the choice that answers the question. Stay focused on what the question is asking for so you don't accidentally pick an answer that is true but incorrect. Always go back to the question and make sure the answer choice you've selected actually answers the question and is not merely a true statement.

Extreme Statements

In general, you should avoid answers that put forth extreme actions as standard practice or proclaim controversial ideas as established fact. An answer choice that states the "process should be used in certain situations, if..." is much more likely to be correct than one that states the "process should be discontinued completely." The first is a calm rational statement and doesn't even make a definitive, uncompromising stance, using a hedge word *if* to provide wiggle room, whereas the second choice is a radical idea and far more extreme.

Benchmark

As you read through the answer choices and you come across one that seems to answer the question well, mentally select that answer choice. This is not your final answer, but it's the one that will help you evaluate the other answer choices. The one that you selected is your benchmark or standard for judging each of the other answer choices. Every other answer choice must be compared to your benchmark. That choice is correct until proven otherwise by another answer choice beating it. If you find a better answer, then that one becomes your new benchmark. Once you've decided that no other choice answers the question as well as your benchmark, you have your final answer.

Predict the Answer

Before you even start looking at the answer choices, it is often best to try to predict the answer. When you come up with the answer on your own, it is easier to avoid distractions and traps because you will know exactly what to look for. The right answer choice is unlikely to be word-for-word what you came up with, but it should be a close match. Even if you are confident that you have the right answer, you should still take the time to read each option before moving on.

General Strategies

Tough Questions

If you are stumped on a problem or it appears too hard or too difficult, don't waste time. Move on! Remember though, if you can quickly check for obviously incorrect answer choices, your chances of guessing correctly are greatly improved. Before you completely give up, at least try to knock out a couple of possible answers. Eliminate what you can and then guess at the remaining answer choices before moving on.

Check Your Work

Since you will probably not know every term listed and the answer to every question, it is important that you get credit for the ones that you do know. Don't miss any questions through careless mistakes. If at all possible, try to take a second to look back over your answer selection and make sure you've selected the correct answer choice and haven't made a costly careless mistake (such as marking an answer choice that you didn't mean to mark). This quick double check should more than pay for itself in caught mistakes for the time it costs.

Pace Yourself

It's easy to be overwhelmed when you're looking at a page full of questions; your mind is confused and full of random thoughts, and the clock is ticking down faster than you would like. Calm down and maintain the pace that you have set for yourself. Especially as you get down to the last few minutes of the test, don't let the small numbers on the clock make you panic. As long as you are on track by monitoring your pace, you are guaranteed to have time for each question.

Don't Rush

It is very easy to make errors when you are in a hurry. Maintaining a fast pace in answering questions is pointless if it makes you miss questions that you would have gotten right otherwise. Test writers like to include distracting information and wrong answers that seem right. Taking a little extra time to avoid careless mistakes can make all the difference in your test score. Find a pace that allows you to be confident in the answers that you select.

Keep Moving

Panicking will not help you pass the test, so do your best to stay calm and keep moving. Taking deep breaths and going through the answer elimination steps you practiced can help to break through a stress barrier and keep your pace.

Final Notes

The combination of a solid foundation of content knowledge and the confidence that comes from practicing your plan for applying that knowledge is the key to maximizing your performance on test day. As your foundation of content knowledge is built up and strengthened, you'll find that the strategies included in this chapter become more and more effective in helping you quickly sift through the distractions and traps of the test to isolate the correct answer.

Now it's time to move on to the test content chapters of this book, but be sure to keep your goal in mind. As you read, think about how you will be able to apply this information on the test. If you've already seen sample questions for the test and you have an idea of the question format and style, try to come up with questions of your own that you can answer based on what you're reading. This will give you valuable practice applying your knowledge in the same ways you can expect to on test day.

Good luck and good studying!

Part I. Why am I Taking this Test?

What is the TEA Exam?

If you are reading this guide, chances are that you have probably already heard about the Treasury Enforcement Agent (TEA) Exam. However, you may still be wondering what is the TEA Exam? This is actually a relatively easy question to answer as the TEA Exam is simply a standardized test that is required for an individual to obtain a position in several different federal law enforcement agencies. The TEA Exam is designed by the Office of Personnel Management (OPM) and administered by either the OPM or by the specific agency to which you are applying. This exam is designed to determine whether you have the basic skills, knowledge, and experience necessary to function as a federal law enforcement officer. In other words, if you are interested in becoming a federal law enforcement officer, you may be required to take the TEA Exam.

Who requires the TEA Exam?

There are three federal departments that require the TEA Exam; these include the Department of Homeland Security, the Department of Justice, and the Department of the Treasury. Within these three federal departments, there are five different agencies that require the TEA Exam. The five agencies that require an individual to take the TEA exam in order to obtain a position are the Bureau of Alcohol, Tobacco, and Firearms (ATF), the Immigration and Customs Enforcement Agency (ICE), the Internal Revenue Service (IRS), the United States Marshals Service, and the United States Secret Service (USSS.)

What does an employee of the Bureau of Alcohol, Tobacco, and Firearms actually do and am I qualified to work for the ATF?

The Bureau of Alcohol, Tobacco, and Firearms (ATF or BTAF) is a division of the Department of Justice that is designed to prevent and investigate crimes related to alcohol, arson, tobacco, explosives, and firearms. The ATF employs over 4,500 people with each of the agency's employees performing the duties associated with one of a number of different positions. The positions offered by the ATF include Auditor, Examiner, Intelligence Analyst, Inspector, Special Agent, and a variety of other related positions. Each position within the ATF, as is the case in most organizations, has its own distinct set of duties and responsibilities associated with it.

ATF Auditors are entrusted with the responsibility to audit businesses that sell alcohol, explosives, firearms, or tobacco in order to confirm that these businesses are adhering to the appropriate federal regulations and that each business is paying the appropriate excise taxes. ATF Auditors are also responsible for investigating cases of confirmed arson or potential arson. ATF Examiners, who are more commonly referred to as Firearms Examiners, Toolmarks Examiners, or Forensic Chemists are required to use a variety of different techniques to collect, preserve, and examine evidence from crime scenes. ATF Examiners usually focus on firearms and the markings on bullets that can be used to confirm that a weapon was used for a particular crime. ATF Examiners are also often required to testify in court in order to explain their findings. ATF Intelligence Analysts use a variety of different techniques to research information, examine documents, and analyze evidence. Intelligence Analysts are also responsible for developing reports that provide other individuals within the ATF as well as other agencies with information about their findings, their professional opinion on what each piece of evidence indicates, and their advice on how to proceed.

ATF Inspectors, also known as Industry Operations Investigators, are responsible for examining industrial records and reports in order to determine if an individual or business is conducting illegal activities related to alcohol, explosives, firearms, or tobacco. ATF Inspectors are also required to examine the alcohol, explosives, firearms, and tobacco that businesses manufacture and sell in order to ensure that these products meet federal regulations, are stored according to federal regulations, and are sold according to federal regulations. ATF Special Agents, also known as ATF Criminal Investigators, are required to perform a number of different functions including, but not limited to, arresting individuals who have violated the federal laws related to firearms and explosives, arresting individuals who have violated the federal regulations related to the manufacture and taxing of alcohol and tobacco, conducting suspect interviews, conducting witness interviews, executing searches, obtaining valid search warrants, performing surveillance activities, raiding locations suspected of housing illegal weapons or explosives, and raiding locations suspected of housing illegal alcohol or tobacco operations.

There are certain basic requirements that most ATF positions require you to meet in order to be eligible for the position. First, you must be a U.S. citizen over the age of 21 but under the age of 37 at the time you take up the position, and you must have a valid driver's license. Second, you must pass a thorough medical examination, pass a drug test, meet the hearing and vision requirements established by the ATF, and meet the height/weight requirements of the ATF. It is important to note that the height and weight requirements established by the ATF are based on whether an individual's weight is proportional to his or her height rather than determining a specific weight limit at which people are prohibited from receiving a position. Third, you must pass a polygraph test, pass a full background check, get through a full panel interview, and pass an ATF special agent assessment test. Finally, you must meet the education and experience requirements established by the ATF and pass the Treasury Enforcement Agent Exam.

What does an Agent of the Immigration and Customs Enforcement Agency actually do and am I qualified to be a Customs Agent?

The Immigration and Customs Enforcement (ICE) Agency is a division of the Department of Homeland Security that is designed to prevent and investigate crimes related to people and goods entering, traveling through, and leaving the United States. ICE employs over 20,000 people with most of their employees working as Special Agents. The Special Agents that make up ICE, who are usually referred to as Customs Agents or Immigration Enforcement Agents depending on the specific duties of the Agent, are required to perform a variety of different functions. These functions include, but are not limited to, coordinating their activities with the investigations of other agencies, establishing relationships with informants, examining bank records and other similar records, executing searches, interviewing suspects, obtaining valid search warrants, performing surveillance activities, and using information from informants to identify suspects. ICE is specifically responsible for enforcing the federal laws and regulations that are designed to prevent crimes such as customs fraud, illegal immigration, illegal pornography, money laundering, smuggling, and other similar illegal activities.

In order to become an ICE Special Agent, you must meet certain basic criteria. First, you must be a U.S. citizen under the age of 37 with a bachelor's degree in any field or have three years of experience in criminal investigation or law enforcement. If you do not have a bachelor's degree or three years of experience, you may still be eligible to apply for a position as an ICE Special Agent if you have a combination of experience and education that is comparable to ICE's experience and/or education requirements. Second, you must pass a medical examination, pass a drug test, and meet the basic health requirements for the position established by ICE. Finally, you must pass a full background check, and you must pass a written exam. It is extremely important to note that the written exam you must pass in order to become an ICE Special Agent may or may not be the Treasury Enforcement Agent Exam. This is because ICE currently uses the Treasury Enforcement Agent Exam to test the skills and knowledge of its applicants, but this may change in the future as ICE is considering the possibility of using other exams that are more agency-specific.

What does an employee of the Internal Revenue Service actually do and am I qualified to work for the IRS?

The Internal Revenue Service (IRS) is a division of the Department of the Treasury that is designed to prevent and investigate financial crimes and to ensure that federal taxes are collected. Some of the positions offered by the IRS include Computer Specialist, Internal Auditor, Internal Security Inspector, Internal Revenue Agent, Internal Revenue Officer, Special Agent for Computer Crime, Special Agent for the IRS Criminal Investigation Division, Tax Specialist, Tax Resolution Representative, and a long list of other related positions. The IRS employs over 112,000 people and each position within the organization has its own distinct set of duties and responsibilities.

IRS Computer Specialists are responsible for creating and managing the computer systems that keep track of each taxpayer's tax account and for generating reports that can be used to issue bills and refund checks. Internal Auditors are responsible for conducting audits of every division of the IRS in order to ensure that each division is using its funds appropriately and that each division is keeping the taxes paid to the federal government separate from the agency's own funds. Internal Security Inspectors are responsible for verifying the background of potential employees and investigating the actions of current employees that are suspected of crimes in the workplace. Internal Revenue Agents are responsible for checking each tax return in order to determine that the return is filled out correctly and that the individual has calculated and paid the appropriate amount of taxes. Internal Revenue Officers are responsible for tracking down individuals who have not filed a tax return or paid their taxes and are responsible for collecting tax returns and taxes that are past due from these individuals.

The Special Agents of the IRS who specifically investigate computerized financial crimes, also known as Computer Investigators, are required to use a variety of different techniques to track the trail of computer records left behind by individuals who commit financial crimes, retrieve information that has been encrypted or hidden in order to cover up financial crimes, and provide information to other divisions of the IRS and other agencies that can be used to prove that a particular individual is guilty of committing a specific crime. The Special Agents that investigate all financial crimes for the IRS, also known as IRS Criminal Investigation Special Agents or IRS Criminal Investigators, are required to perform a variety of different functions including, but not limited to, examining financial records, obtaining financial records, performing undercover operations, recovering missing financial records, and tracking electronic exchanges that may be related to computerized financial crimes. The Criminal Investigation Division of the IRS, which consists of over 4,000 employees, is specifically responsible for enforcing and/or helping other agencies to enforce the federal laws and regulations that are designed to prevent crimes such as corruption, drug trafficking, embezzlement, fraud, international money laundering, organized crime, and tax evasion.

Tax Specialists perform a number of different functions related to helping taxpayers who are filing their taxes, including functions such as providing information to taxpayers about sensible accounting practices, providing instructions to taxpayers on how to file taxes, and providing assistance to or answering questions for taxpayers who are having difficulty filling out their tax forms. Tax Specialists are also required to use surveys and other similar evaluation techniques to determine whether each method that the IRS is using to help taxpayers is actually working or not.

Tax Resolution Representatives, also known as Contact Representatives, offer a number of services to taxpayers related to correcting problems with a specific individual's tax account. These services include developing payment plans for individuals who are having difficulty paying their taxes, correcting errors related to the individual's tax account, and offering information on how to handle other similar problems.

The specific requirements that you must meet in order to work for the IRS depend on the specific position for which you are applying and these requirements can vary greatly from position to position. However, there are certain basic requirements that most positions will require you to meet. First, in order to apply for most IRS positions, you must be a U.S. citizen. If you are applying for a law enforcement position, you must be under the age of 37 and have a valid driver's license. Second, you must have a bachelor's degree in any field, a Certified Public Accountant (CPA) certificate, or three years of experience in business or accounting. If you do not have a bachelor's degree, a CPA, or three years of experience, you may still be eligible to apply for a position with the IRS if you have a combination of experience and education that is comparable to the Internal Revenue Service's education and/or experience requirements. If you are applying for an IRS Criminal Investigator position, you will also be required to complete at least 9 semester hours of business law, economics, finance, money and banking, tax law, or 9 semester hours from another similar field and at least 15 semester hours of accounting before applying for the position. Other positions within the IRS may have similar accounting requirements that range anywhere from 6 – 30 semester hours of accounting courses depending on the specific position for which you are applying. Third, you may be required to pass a medical examination and a drug test, and you must meet the basic health requirements established for the position by the IRS if specific requirements exist. Finally, you must pass a full background check and pass the Treasury Enforcement Agent Exam if it is required for the specific position that you are pursuing.

What does a Marshal of the United States Marshals Service actually do and am I qualified to be a U.S. Deputy Marshal?

The United States Marshals Service is a division of the Department of Justice that is designed to carry out the basic operations that are necessary to ensure that the federal judicial system can continue to function. The United States Marshals Service currently employs approximately 4,800 employees and most of the individuals hired into the agency begin as Deputy U.S. Marshals. Deputy U.S. Marshals are required to perform a variety of different functions including, but not limited to, apprehending fugitives, managing and selling seized property, managing the housing and care of federal prisoners, protecting federal judges and jurors, protecting federal courts, protecting witnesses, serving court documents, and transporting federal prisoners.

In order to become a U.S. Deputy Marshal, there are certain basic requirements that you must meet. First, you must be a U.S. citizen over the age of 21 but under the age of 37 at the time you take up the position and have a valid driver's license and a relatively clean driving record. Second, you must have a bachelor's degree in any field or three years of experience in criminal investigation, law enforcement, business management, teaching, working in a correctional facility or in any facility working with prisoners, or in any other workplace that required you to use your leadership abilities and make decisions on your own. If you do not have a bachelor's degree or three years of experience, you may still be eligible to apply for a position as a U.S. Marshal if you have a combination of experience and education that is comparable to the U.S. Marshals Service's experience and/or education requirements. Third, you must pass a thorough medical examination, pass a drug test, meet the hearing and vision requirements established by the U.S. Marshals Service, and pass a fitness test. The fitness test will measure your percentage of body fat and will test your ability to sit and reach, your ability to do push-ups and sit-ups, and your ability to run. Finally, you must pass a full background check, get through a structured interview, and pass the Treasury Enforcement Agent Exam.

What does an employee of the United States Secret Service actually do and am I qualified to work for the Secret Service?

The United States Secret Service (USSS) was originally a division of the Department of the Treasury that was designed to prevent and investigate counterfeiting within the United States. However, the USSS is now a division of the Department of Homeland Security and is designed to not only handle the investigations and law enforcement activities related to counterfeiting and other similar crimes but to protect the leaders of our country and their families, protect potential leaders during a campaign, and protect the leaders of foreign governments while they are visiting the United States. The USSS currently employs over 4,500 individuals who carry out the duties and responsibilities associated with a number of different positions. Some of the law enforcement positions offered by the USSS include Forensic Examiner, Physical Security Specialist, Special Agent, and Uniformed Division Officer.

Secret Service Forensic Examiners are required to use a variety of different techniques to examine documents, fingerprints, identification, and other similar types of evidence in order to identify forgeries, confirm the fraudulent use of a credit card, confirm the fraudulent use of a form of identification, and provide information that can be used to track down and convict individuals that forge documents or defraud other individuals. Secret Service Physical Security Specialists are responsible for identifying potential threats to the safety of individuals under the protection of the Secret Service and developing countermeasures that can be used to protect these individuals from the threats that have been identified. Secret Service Physical Security Specialists are required to perform threat analyses, fire surveys, life safety surveys, and other similar evaluations to determine which threats are of concern for the specific individual that the Secret Service is protecting. Secret Service Physical Security Specialists are also required to install systems to detect intruders, monitor the area in question and control access, eliminate or reduce the risk of injury or death due to a fire or explosion, and eliminate or reduce the risk of injury or death due to a chemical or biological attack.

The Special Agents of the U.S. Secret Service are required to perform a variety of different functions including, but not limited to, analyzing and tracking counterfeit currency, analyzing and tracking counterfeit government-issued identification, identifying forgeries, identifying counterfeit bills, providing security for the President and Vice President, providing security for the immediate family of the President and Vice President, providing security for former presidents and their spouses, providing security for presidential and vice-presidential candidates and the spouses of those candidates, and tracking electronic exchanges related to crimes involving financial institutions. Uniformed Division Officers are responsible for providing security for the President and Vice President, providing security for the President-elect (or in other words, a Presidential candidate who has been elected to office but is not yet in office), providing security for the Vice President-elect (or in other words, a Vice Presidential candidate that has been elected to office but is not yet in office), providing security for foreign leaders visiting the United States, and providing security for major government buildings, such as the White House and the Main Treasury Building.

The specific requirements that you must meet in order to work for the United States Secret Service depends on the specific position for which you are applying, and these requirements can vary greatly from position to position. However, most Secret Service positions will require you to meet several basic requirements. First, you must be a U.S. citizen over the age of 21, but under the age of 40 at the time you take up the position. Secondly, you must pass a thorough medical examination,

- 19 -

pass a drug test, meet the basic vision and hearing requirements established by the U.S. Secret Service for the specific position for which you are applying, and meet the basic health requirements established for the specific position by the U.S. Secret Service. Third, you must pass a polygraph test, a full background check, and get through several thorough interviews. If you are applying for a Secret Service Agent position, you must have a bachelor's degree in any field or three years of experience in criminal investigation or law enforcement. If you do not have a bachelor's degree or three years of experience, you may still be eligible to apply for a position as a Secret Service Special Agent if you have a combination of experience and education that is comparable to the United States Secret Service's experience and/or education requirements. You will also have to pass the Treasury Enforcement Agent Exam in order to be considered for a position as a Secret Service Special Agent.

Important Note: The ATF, ICE, IRS, United States Marshals Service, and the United States Secret Service all use the Treasury Enforcement Agent Exam. However, it is important to note that these agencies do not require the TEA Exam for every position and the requirements that an individual must meet in order to be eligible for a particular position can vary greatly from position to position and from agency to agency. As a result, you should check the requirements for the specific position that you are pursuing prior to beginning the application process. It is also important to note that the positions mentioned in this section are not necessarily the only positions offered by these agencies and other positions may have education and experience requirements that are very different from those mentioned here.

Why should I take the TEA Exam?

By now, you probably have a general idea of what the TEA Exam is and the functions of organizations that use the TEA Exam. If you don't know what the TEA Exam is or what these organizations do, you can find out by reading the information contained in the previous sections. However, even with this information, you may still be wondering "why should I take the TEA Exam?" The obvious answer to this question is of course that you have decided to become a Special Agent for one of the five government agencies that uses the TEA Exam, but that still doesn't answer "why would someone want to join one of these agencies?" This is actually an important question to consider as there are a number of different reasons for an individual to seek a position with one of these organizations.

The first and most obvious reason to seek a position within one of these government agencies is that these organizations offer employees better salaries than most other employers. This is because an individual can expect to make between $25,000 and $42,000 a year as soon as he or she obtains a position within any of these organizations. In addition, an individual may be able to start at a pay rate even higher that this starting rate if he or she has completed additional education, has additional experience, has achieved a high GPA, has obtained additional certifications, or has made other similar academic achievements. These pay rates will also increase over time as the individual moves up the pay scale, and an individual may receive additional pay to compensate for the cost of living in the area in which he or she works. As a result, the average salary of a full-time permanent federal employee is approximately $57,000 a year.

Another reason that many people seek positions within these agencies is that these organizations usually offer better benefits than most other employers. Individuals working within these agencies will typically receive 10 paid holidays, 13 sick days that can be carried over from year to year, and vacation time that can be carried over from year to year up to a maximum of 240 hours. These vacation days will be distributed so that each individual will receive a set number of vacation days a year, but the specific number of vacation days that the individual will receive is based on the number of years that the individual has been with the agency. Individuals working within these agencies will also usually be able to choose a health plan from a long list of different health plans and different insurers, to receive low-cost life insurance, and to take part in a 401k plan or another similar retirement plan.

The third and final reason that many people seek positions within one of these five government agencies is that they simply want to work in federal law enforcement. There are a number of different reasons that people decide that federal law enforcement is the right career for them, so the specific reason that an individual wants to work for one of these agencies can vary greatly from person to person. However, some individuals have always dreamed of being a Special Agent for the Secret Service, or a U.S. Marshal. Others have always had a strong desire to protect other individuals, been excited about tracking down criminals, or had any of a long list of other similar desires or interests that have drawn them to federal law enforcement. In other words, certain individuals may seek positions within these federal agencies not only for the competitive salary and benefits but also for the sense of satisfaction that the individual will receive when he or she obtains a career in federal law enforcement.

Keeping Your Eye on the Prize

If you've read or skimmed over the information in this guide that describes the TEA Exam, the bureaus and agencies that use the TEA Exam, and the reasons people take the TEA Exam, you're probably thinking "all of this information is interesting but what does any of this have to do with passing the TEA Exam?" In fact, it may seem to some people that this information has nothing to do with passing the exam at all as it isn't related to what's actually on the exam. However, the fact of the matter is that this information has more to do with passing the TEA Exam than it might seem. This is because this information is related to what the exam is and, more importantly, why *you* are taking the exam. This is important because you need to know what the test is and what you hope to accomplish by taking the test in order to make sure that you know what you are getting yourself into and make sure that you are studying for the TEA Exam in as effective a manner as possible.

It is essential that you understand what you are getting yourself into with the TEA Exam because many people consider the exam to be an extremely difficult test. It is important for you to understand the purpose of the test because this will help you to determine the best way for you to study the information and make sure that you're prepared. In other words, everyone learns differently, so a method of studying that one person finds to be extremely helpful may not be nearly as helpful for someone else. You also need to understand what you are getting yourself into if you take a position with one of the agencies that uses the TEA Exam because each of these agencies requires an individual to perform many different functions. If you're not prepared to perform these functions, or if you simply don't want to perform these functions on a daily basis, then you may be looking at the wrong career and, therefore, the wrong exam.

It is also extremely important for you to understand what you hope to accomplish by taking the exam because this will help you to stay motivated. There's a lot of information to study for the TEA Exam, and the TEA Exam is timed, so you need to know that information pretty well. If you can't stay motivated, you'll be much more likely to procrastinate, which will make it extremely difficult for you to get a basic understanding of all of the information covered on the TEA Exam, and you will have a much more difficult time with the test. It may sound clichéd, but it is important for you to keep your eye on the prize because one of the best motivational tools you can use is simply to focus on what *you* are attempting to achieve by taking the exam.

How to Set Your Study Goals

A study goal can be defined as an objective that an individual hopes to achieve while he or she is studying or an objective that an individual hopes to achieve as a result of his or her studying. If you are taking the Treasury Enforcement Exam, your primary study goal is of course to pass the exam. This is simply because passing the exam allows you to move one step closer to achieving your overall goal of obtaining a position within one of the five agencies or bureaus that uses the TEA Exam as an evaluation tool. Yet, in order for you to pass the exam, there are a number of other goals that you will have to accomplish on the way. These goals can vary greatly from person to person as each person has his or her own distinct strengths and weaknesses. However, there are certain steps that an individual should take in order to determine which goals he or she needs to accomplish.

First, before you begin studying the material on the exam, you should try to get an idea of what you know and what you don't know. One of the best ways to do this is to read over what is covered in each section of the exam (each section of the exam is described later in this guide) and try to identify any material that looks confusing or unfamiliar. This will allow you to identify the material that you don't fully understand, which is also the material that you should focus on while you are studying. This is important because there's never enough time to study everything, so you need to focus on the material that you don't understand first.

Second, once you have identified the topics that you need to focus on, you should set a series of goals that you need to accomplish in order to gain a better understanding of each topic. For example, if you are having trouble with the arithmetic portion of the exam, you may decide that you need to focus on the problems related to interest, the problems related to profit and loss, and the problems related to taxation because these are the sections with which you are having the most trouble. You may then decide to study the material and practice answering some questions related to the interest problems the first night you study, study the material and practice answering some questions related to the profit and loss problems the next night, and study the material and practice answering some questions related to the taxation problems on the third night. This allows you to separate the material you need to learn into a series of specific goals that you can spread out over the time you have available instead of attempting to learn everything all at once.

Third, when you are attempting to set your study goals, you should make sure that each goal is a valid goal. In other words, if you plan on establishing a series of study goals, you need to make sure that each goal is something that you can actually achieve and that there is some way for you to tell that you have actually achieved that goal. In order to make sure that a goal is valid, you should make sure that you clearly describe the objective that you want to achieve and set a specific deadline for that goal. This will help to keep you motivated because you know that you need to accomplish a certain amount by a certain time. Each goal should also be something that you can realistically accomplish within the time allowed and something that is measurable.

For example, learning all of the material for the TEA Exam on the night before the exam is probably not a realistic goal, but studying the material for one section each night for several weeks before the exam might be something that you can actually accomplish. Learning all of the material for the TEA Exam is also a difficult goal to measure unless you break it down into smaller goals. Studying one section each night, on the other hand, is a relatively easy goal to measure because you can determine whether you have accomplished your goal or not based on how many paragraphs or pages are left for you to study in a particular section. It is important for you to be able to measure how close you are to accomplishing a particular goal because each goal will act as an accomplishment milestone that allows you to measure your total progress as you to continue to study the material.

Finally, once you have established all of your goals, it is important to remember that your goals should not necessarily be set in stone. This is because there are many events beyond your control that may affect the amount of time that you have available, which may in turn affect your ability to actually accomplish your goals. As a result, it may be necessary for you to change your goals if you are no longer able to accomplish everything in the time that you have because something else has changed. It is important to note that this does not mean that you should give up if you are running out of time on a goal, but instead, that you should alter your other goals to compensate for lost time if you are unable to achieve a specific goal.

It is also important to note that even though a study goal should be relatively specific, it is not necessary for every study goal to be related to how much studying you have left to accomplish. In other words, it may actually be a good idea to establish a series of major goals such as learning all of the information in the arithmetic section of the exam, learning all of the information in the verbal reasoning section of the exam, and learning all of the information in the problems for investigation section of the exam. These goals represent major goals that you are attempting to achieve in order to pass the TEA Exam, so it can be useful to keep these goals in mind. These goals are difficult to measure, however, as it is usually very difficult to measure how much you have actually learned about a particular subject. Therefore, it is usually a good idea to have several major goals that can be split into smaller goals that are easier to measure, such as reading a certain amount or studying a certain section.

How to Accomplish Your Study Goals

In order to study all of the information included on the TEA exam, you need to set a series of study goals. Each of these goals should help you to stay motivated and allow you to measure your progress as you study. However, a set of study goals alone is not necessarily enough for you to succeed on the exam as each goal is simply an objective that you have identified as something that you hope to accomplish. As a result, it is important for you to make sure that you are actually progressing towards accomplishing a particular goal each time you study. The best way to do this is to follow a few simple steps.

First, you should try to identify anything that may affect your ability to accomplish your goals. This means that you should identify anything that might distract you, anything that you will need to do in order to continue functioning (such as eating and sleeping), and anything else that might prevent you from accomplishing one of your goals. Once you have identified each of the factors that may be a potential distraction, you should try to identify ways to eliminate or reduce the effects of these factors. For example, you may decide to study in the afternoon and to eat before you study because then you won't be walking around in search of food, and you probably won't be falling asleep.

Second, if you have set a large goal that seems to be too overwhelming or a goal that you keep putting aside, it is usually a good idea to break the goal down into two or more smaller goals. For example, instead of studying the entire arithmetic section of the TEA exam in one night, you may decide to study a certain number of topics tonight, the same number of topics tomorrow night, and continue studying a small number of topics each night until you have studied all of the information in the section. This allows you to take a single, large, overwhelming task and split it into several smaller, less difficult tasks, which makes it easier for you to accomplish the overall goal.

Finally, while you are studying for the TEA Exam, you should try to focus on achieving one goal at a time. This is because focusing on too many tasks at once can be distracting and/or overwhelming, which can make it much more difficult for you to study the material. An individual that is too distracted and/or too overwhelmed by the material that he or she is attempting to study will be much more likely to procrastinate. As a result, an individual who tries to focus on too many goals at once will not be able to accomplish as much as someone who focuses on a single goal at a time. This means that it is important for you to try to focus on one specific goal at a time, accomplish that goal and then move on to the next goal so that you can accomplish as many goals as possible.

Part II. What's on the TEA Exam?

TEA Exam Overview

The TEA Exam consists of four main sections: a verbal reasoning section, an arithmetic section, a problems for investigation section, and an applicant experience questionnaire. The verbal reasoning section of the exam includes a series of multiple-choice questions that examine your reading comprehension skills. The arithmetic reasoning section of the exam includes a series of multiple-choice questions that examine your grasp of basic mathematical concepts and the practical application of those concepts. The problems for investigation questions on the exam are a series of multiple-choice questions that are related to identifying how specific pieces of information can be used to draw conclusions and/or how effective a specific piece of information will be if it is used to prove a specific fact in court. The applicant experience questionnaire includes a series of multiple-choice questions that examine an individual's achievements and how his or her personality fits with the position for which he or she is applying.

Verbal Reasoning Section

The first section of the TEA Exam, which is referred to as Part A, is the verbal reasoning section. This section of the exam is designed to examine your ability to read, analyze, and comprehend a written passage. There are a total of 25 multiple-choice questions in this section of the exam, and each of these questions will present you with a passage that you must read in order to answer the question. These passages may be related to any of a long list of different topics from virtually any field, and each question will ask you to identify the main idea of the passage, identify a statement that the passage appears to support, identify a specific piece of information provided in the passage, define a term from the passage based on the context in which the term is used, or draw a conclusion from the information provided in the passage. You will have 50 minutes to complete the verbal reasoning section of the TEA Exam.

Arithmetic Reasoning Section

The second section of the TEA Exam, referred to as Part B, is the arithmetic reasoning section. This section of the exam is designed to examine your knowledge of basic mathematical concepts and your knowledge of how to apply those concepts. There are a total of 20 multiple-choice questions in this section of the exam, and each question is related to basic algebra, the distance traveled or the amount of gas that is required to travel a certain distance, interest, the length of time it would take to perform a certain amount of work, payroll, profit and loss, proportions, ratios, and/or taxation. These questions may ask you to identify the choice that correctly solves the problem or simply to identify the choice that indicates the correct way to find the answer for the problem. For example, you may be presented with a problem such as "A team of 14 trained workers working at the same speed can erect an entire house in 168 hours, how many hours would it take for a single trained worker to erect a house?" The exam would then present you with five choices, and one of those choices provides the solution to the problem (2,352 hours) or the correct formula to find the solution (168 * 14.) You will then have to choose the option that identifies the correct solution or formula. You will have 50 minutes to complete the arithmetic reasoning section of the TEA Exam.

Problems for Investigation Section

The third section of the TEA Exam, referred to as Part C, is the problems for investigation section. This section of the exam is designed to examine an individual's ability to analyze a series of statements related to a particular situation. The multiple-choice questions in this section of the exam are split into sets, and each set of questions will present you with a short passage and a series of short statements that are related to the passage. Each passage will describe a specific situation that is being investigated, and each statement will describe the information that has been collected during the investigation. Each question will then either ask you to identify the statement that indicates that a particular piece of information is true or to identify a specific type of statement. For example, a question might ask you "which statement should be considered hearsay?" while another question might ask you to identify a statement that indicates that a specific individual may be responsible for the crime. You will have 60 minutes to complete the problems for investigation section of the exam, and there are 30 multiple-choice questions within this section.

Applicant Experience Questionnaire

The fourth and final section of the TEA Exam, which is known as the applicant experience questionnaire, is split into two separate parts and these parts are referred to as Part D and Part E. This section of the exam is actually very different from the other sections of exam as it is not testing your knowledge of a particular topic or your ability to comprehend and apply information. Instead, this section of the exam examines your experience, your achievements, your personality characteristics, you skills, and your interests. This means that this section of the exam is probably not something you would typically see on your average exam at all as this section is more of a personality test than a standard set of questions. However, even though the questions in this section are related specifically to your own experiences and education rather than what you know, it is important to realize that these questions may still be extremely important. This is because the agency to which you are applying may use your answers to these questions when they are attempting to determine whether you should receive a particular position or not. Agencies use these questions because they make it easier for the agency to compare your personality, skills, and interests with the personality, skills, and interests of other candidates for the position and with other individuals that have already succeeded in a similar position.

Each question in this section of the exam will ask you to choose the option that best describes your own background. These questions will ask you to provide information about your extracurricular activities, you grades, your favorite and least favorite subjects, how regularly you attended classes, how regularly you called out of work, how well you performed at work, what do you think other people would say about you, and information related to a number of other similar elements of your background. It is important to note, however, that there is not one single correct answer for any of the questions in this section of the exam and it is usually best to answer each question as truthfully as possible. The exact amount of time that you will have to answer the questions in this section can vary from agency to agency, but you will usually have to answer 40 - 70 questions in 15 – 30 minutes in order to complete the section.

Verbal Reasoning Questions

There are five different types of questions in the verbal reasoning section of the TEA Exam, and each of these questions will require you to read a short written passage. The five types of questions that are included in this section of the exam are questions that ask you to identify the main idea of the passage, questions that ask you to identify a statement that is supported by the passage, questions that ask you to identify a specific piece of information presented in the passage, questions that ask you to define a term based on how it is used in the passage, and questions that ask you to draw a conclusion based on the information included in the passage.

Main Idea Questions

One type of question that you will encounter in the verbal reasoning section of the exam is the main idea question. These questions will ask you to identify the topic that the passage is discussing or identify the specific opinion that the author is attempting to defend. These questions may begin with phrases such as "The writer believes that," "The author believes that," "The best summary of the argument is," "Which of the following best sums up the author's attitude," and "The passage best supports the statement that." It is important to note that these questions will only ask you for what the passage or author is actually saying and not for what you or someone else believes to be true. This can be an important distinction to make because there may be passages on the exam that are attempting to defend opinions that you may disagree with or that are presenting conclusions that are outright incorrect.

Supported Statement Questions

Another type of question that you may encounter in the verbal reasoning section of the exam is the supported statement question. These questions will ask you to identify a statement that the passage appears to indicate or prove. These questions are often very similar to the main idea questions on the exam and/or the questions on the exam that ask you to draw conclusions as the information you are looking for is usually related to applying or identifying an opinion that is suggested within the passage but may or may not be stated outright. In other words, these questions will ask you to choose the statement that appears to match with what the author of the passage believes or matches with the author's point of view even if the author doesn't explicitly state his or her view in this way. These questions may begin with phrases such as "The author would probably agree that," "With which of the following statements is the author most likely to agree," "The author would most likely oppose," and "The passage best supports the statement that." It is important to note that these questions will only ask you for what the passage supports and not necessarily for what you actually know to be true.

Identifying Specific Information Questions

Another type of question that you will encounter in the verbal reasoning section of the exam is the identifying specific information question. These questions will ask you to choose a statement that the passage indicates to be true. These questions are somewhat similar to the main idea questions on the exam except that these questions are not necessarily looking for a statement that indicates the main topic of the passage but rather a statement that simply states a fact presented within the passage. These questions may begin with phrases such as "The passage best supports the statement that" or "The passage best supports that." The best way to distinguish these questions from the main idea questions on the exam is to read each of the options that are available and see if they describe the main topic of the passage or not. It is also important to note that these questions will only ask you to identify information that is actually stated in the passage, and they will not ask you to use any information other than what is specifically stated.

Definition Questions

The fourth type of question that you will encounter in the verbal reasoning section of the exam is the definition question. These questions will ask you to choose a statement that defines a word or concept that is used in the passage. These questions may begin with a phrase that contains the word "definition," the word "define," or begins with the phrase "The passage best supports the statement that." If the question begins with the phrase "The passage best supports the statement that," each of the choices offered will usually begin with a phrase such as "A(n) [insert term here] refers to" or "A(n) [insert term here] is." The definition questions on the exam are designed so that you should be able to determine the meaning of the word from the context in which it is used. Some of the definition questions on the exam will state the correct answer outright in the passage, so you may be able to determine the answer without looking too closely. However, most of the definition questions require you to look at how the word fits into the sentence and how the word fits into the rest of the passage in order to determine its meaning. As a result, it may be necessary for you to read the passage very closely in order to determine the correct meaning for each term.

Drawing Conclusion Questions

The fifth and final type of question that you will encounter in the verbal reasoning section of the exam is the drawing conclusion question. These questions will ask you to choose a statement that describes something that isn't directly stated within the passage, but appears to be true according to the information provided in the passage. In other words, these questions will ask you to analyze the information included in the passage and then take that information one step further by applying that information to an example or describing the underlying meaning that the passage appears to be implying. These questions may begin with phrases such as "The passage suggests that," or "The passage best supports the statement that." In order to answer these questions, you will usually have to read the passage very closely and look for any information that may indicate that the passage actually supports the conclusion presented in a particular option.

Important Note: You may have noticed that each of the question types described above may begin with the phrase "The passage best supports the statement that." This is because most of the verbal reasoning questions on the TEA Exam will begin with this phrase. In fact, there are some versions of the exam in which the verbal reasoning questions will **only** begin with the phrase "The passage best supports the statement that." This means that it may be difficult for you to determine what the question is looking for from the statement at the beginning of the question alone. As a result, it is usually a very good idea to read each option before reading the passage because the wording that is used in each option is usually a good indication of the type of answer that the question requires.

Arithmetic Reasoning Questions

There are nine different types of questions in the arithmetic reasoning section of the TEA Exam, and each of these questions will require you to solve a mathematical problem or identify the formula that an individual could use to solve the problem. The nine different types of questions that are included in this section of the exam are basic algebra questions, distance/fuel required questions, interest questions, payroll questions, profit and loss questions, proportion questions, ratio questions, taxation questions, and work/time required questions.

Basic Algebra Questions

One of the types of questions you will encounter in the arithmetic reasoning section of the TEA Exam is the basic algebra question. These questions will present you with a word problem that uses variables rather than specific terms. In other words, these questions describe a situation in terms of letters rather than numbers. For example, you may be presented with a question such as "If Jack has x apples, Jill has y apples, and Jane has z apples, how many apples do Jack and Jill have in total? The question will then present you with five options that have different formulas using the variables presented in the problem such as $x + y$, $x + z$, $z + y$, $x + z + y$, or none of these. You will then have to choose the answer that identifies the correct formula to find the total. The correct answer for this particular example is simply $x + y$ because the total number of apples owned by Jack and Jill

- 28 -

can be determined by adding the number of apples Jack has (x) with the number of apples that Jill has (y.)

Distance/Fuel Required Questions

Another type of question that you will encounter in the arithmetic reasoning section of the TEA Exam is the distance/fuel required question. Each of these questions will present you with a word problem that asks you to determine the total distance that an individual, group of individuals, or a vehicle would be able to travel in a specific amount of time, the amount of time that it would take to travel a certain distance, the rate at which an individual or vehicle would have to travel in order to travel a certain distance in a certain amount of time, or the amount of fuel that would be required for a vehicle to travel a certain distance. These questions typically present you with the distance that the traveler needs to travel and the rate at which the traveler is traveling or the rate at which the vehicle uses fuel, the time that the traveler spent traveling and the rate at which the traveler traveled or the rate at which the vehicle uses fuel, or the distance that the traveler traveled and the time that the traveler spent traveling. In other words, each of these problems will present you with the distance, rate of travel, rate of fuel consumption, and/or the time traveled and you will have to determine the distance traveled, the rate that the traveler traveled at, the amount of fuel consumed, or the time that the traveler spent traveling.

For example, you may be presented with a question such as "If a train from Boston and a train from New York are traveling towards each other on the same 225-mile long track, how long will it take for the two trains to meet each other if the train from Boston is traveling at 80 miles per hour, and the train from New York is traveling at 70 miles per hour?" This question would then present you with five options with different lengths of time before the two trains meet, such as 1 ½ hours, 2 hours, 2.8 hours, 3 hours, or none of these and you will have to choose the option that identifies the length of time that it would take for the two trains to meet. This may appear to be incredibly complicated, but the correct answer for this particular example is 1 ½ hours. This is because the length of time before the two trains meet is equal to the length of the track (225 miles) divided by the rate that the first train is traveling plus the rate that the second train is traveling (80 miles per hour + 70 miles per hour.)

Interest Questions

The third type of question that you will encounter in the arithmetic reasoning section of the TEA Exam is the interest question. Each of these questions will present you with a word problem that asks you to determine the amount of interest that will be paid for a certain amount of money over a certain period of time, the amount of money that an individual would have to invest to earn a certain amount of interest over a certain period of time, the interest rate that an account with a specific amount of money must have in order to earn a certain amount of interest over a certain period of time, or the time that a certain amount of money will have to remain in an account or investment in order to earn a certain amount of interest. These questions will typically present you with the amount of money that was invested or saved, the interest rate, the time that the money remains in the account, and/or the amount of interest earned or paid for that investment or account.

For example, you may be presented with a question such as "How much interest would an individual earn from an account with an annual interest rate of 5.5% if the individual invested $1000 in the account for a period of 2 years?" This question would then present you with five options that each identify different amounts of interest that the account might earn over that period, such as $11, $55, $110, $220, or none of these. You will then have to choose the option that

- 29 -

identifies the amount of interest that the account would earn, which is $110 for this particular example. This is because the interest earned from an investment or account is equal to the amount invested ($1000) times the interest rate (5.5% or .055 a year) times the period of time that the amount was invested for (2 years.)

Payroll Questions

The fourth type of question that you will encounter in the arithmetic reasoning section of the TEA Exam is the payroll question. Each of these questions will present you with a word problem that will ask you to determine the total pay that an individual will earn for working a specific number of hours in a single week, the amount of tax that needs to be withheld from an individual's paycheck for a given week, and/or the amount that the individual will actually take home once all of the taxes are deducted from his or her check. These questions will typically present you with the individual's base salary, the amount that the individual gets paid for overtime and whether the individual is eligible for overtime pay or not, any bonuses or commissions that the individual may be entitled to receive, and/or the information necessary to determine the amount of taxes that needs to be withheld from the individual's check. If a question requires you to determine the amount of tax that needs to be withheld from a particular paycheck, the question will usually present you with a table or a group of tables that you can use to determine the federal, state, or other similar type of tax simply by finding the appropriate line on the table.

For example, you may be presented with a question such as "A security guard who typically works 40 hours a week receives time and a half for overtime and double time for holidays. If the security guard is normally paid $20.00 an hour, how much would the security guard earn before taxes for working 52 hours, including 8 hours that were worked on a holiday, in a single week? This question would then present you with five options that each identify different amounts that the security guard might have earned for that 52 hour week, such as $1,040; $1,160; $1,320; $1,560; or none of these. You will then have to choose the option that identifies the amount that the security guard would earn, which in this particular case is $1,320. This is because the security guard's pay is equal to his or her regular pay ($20.00) multiplied by the number of hours that he or she received regular pay for (40 hours – 8 hours of holiday pay or 32 hours) plus his or her holiday pay ($20.00 * 2 or $40.00) multiplied by the number of hours that he or she worked on a holiday (8 hours) plus his or her overtime pay ($20.00 * 1.5 or $30.00) multiplied by the number of hours he or she worked overtime (52 hours – 40 hours or 12 hours.) This means that the security guard's pay is equal to 32 * 20.00 + 8 * $40.00 + 12 * $30.00 or $1,320.

Profit and Loss Questions

Another type of question that you will encounter in the arithmetic reasoning section of the TEA Exam is the profit and loss question. Each of these questions will present you with a word problem that will ask you to determine the profit made from selling a particular item or offering a particular service, the amount lost from selling a particular item or offering a particular service, the price at which a particular item was sold or a service was offered, the cost of manufacturing and/or acquiring the item for sale or the cost of performing the service, the percentage of profit associated with the sale of a particular item or service, or the percentage of loss associated with the sale of a particular item or service. These questions will typically present you with the profit earned, the loss incurred, the percentage of profit, the percentage of loss, the cost of manufacturing/acquiring the item for sale or the cost of performing the service, any expenses associated with manufacturing/selling the item or performing the service other than what is directly related to the production of the item or the performance of the service itself, the price at which the item or service was actually sold, the price at which the item or service was listed or marked, and/or any discounts

- 30 -

associated with the item or service. In other words, each of these problems will present you with the profit or loss, the listing price, the selling price, the cost price, any overhead costs, and/or any discounts, and you will have to determine the profit or loss, the selling price, or the cost price.

For example, you may be presented with a question such as "If a coin shop purchased 10 rare silver coins from a collector and paid $15.00 for each coin, how much would the coin shop have to sell each coin for to make a 50% profit?" The question would then present you with five options that would each indicate a different selling price that the coin shop could sell each coin for, such as $1.50, $7.50, $15.00, $22.50, or none of these. You would then have to choose the option that identifies the price that the coin shop would have to sell the coin for in order to make a 50% profit. In this particular case, the coin shop would have to sell each coin for $22.50 because the selling price is equal to the cost price of the item ($15.00) plus the profit (50% or .5) * the cost price ($15.00.) This means that the selling price of the coin is equal to $15.00 + $7.50 or $22.50.

Proportion Questions

The sixth type of question that you may see in the arithmetic reasoning section of the TEA Exam is the proportion question. Each of these questions will present you with a word problem that will indicate a specific ratio and ask you to determine a specific length, amount, or number related to another similar ratio. In other words, each of these questions will be written in a form similar to "If a certain amount of this is equal to a certain amount of that, how much of that will you have if you have this amount of this?" For example, you may be presented with a question such as "The owners of an apple farm have determined that they will need 50 barrels for every 3 acres of land in order to pick all of the apples. How many barrels will the owners of the apple farm need if they have 15 acres of land?" The question will then present you with five options that each indicate a different number of barrels that the farm might need, such as 45 barrels, 50 barrels, 150 barrels, 250 barrels, or none of these. You would then have to choose the option that identifies the number of barrels that the farm would need. In this particular case, the farm would need a total of 250 barrels because the farm needs 50 barrels for every 3 acres (50 / 3) so the number of barrels that the farm would need for 15 acres is equal to the number of barrels required for every 3 acres (50) multiplied by the number of acres (15) divided by 3. This means that the number of barrels required is equal to 50 * 15 / 3 or 250.

Ratio Questions

The seventh type of question that you may come across in the arithmetic reasoning section of the TEA Exam is the ratio question. Each of these questions will present you with a word problem that will provide you with a specific ratio, and you must either simplify that ratio or apply that ratio in order to determine the solution to the problem. In other words, most of these questions will be written in a form similar to "If you sold this portion for this amount, how much would you have received if you sold everything?" For example, you may be presented with a question such as "The owners of an apple farm have decided to sell some of their land to another farm. However, 3/5 of the apple farm's land is not suitable for the other farm's use. If the farm sold 1/3 of the land that is suitable for the other farm's use for $3,000, what is the value of all of the land that the apple farm owns?" The question will then present you with five options that each indicate a different amount that the land might be worth, such as $6,000; $7,500; $9,000; $15,000; or none of these. You would then have to choose the option that identifies the value of **all** of the land that the farm owns, which in this case is $15,000. This is because 1/3 of 2/5 (5/5 – 3/5) is equal to 3/15 (1/3 * 2/5) or 1/5. Since all of the land that the farm owns is equal to 5/5, the value of the land is equal to $3,000 (the value of 1/5) times 5 or $15,000.

- 31 -

Taxation Questions

The eighth type of question that you may encounter in the arithmetic reasoning section of the TEA Exam is the taxation question. Each of these questions will present you with a word problem that will ask you to determine the amount of taxes owed on a certain amount of money at a certain tax rate, the tax rate that must be charged in order to receive a certain amount of tax from a certain amount of money, or the amount of money that must be taxed in order to receive a certain amount of tax at a certain rate. These questions will typically present you with the amount of money that is being taxed and the tax rate, the amount of taxes and the amount of money that is being taxed, or the tax rate and the amount of taxes. For example, you may be presented with a question such as "If a taxpayer paid $2,250 in taxes on $15,000 of income, what rate was the taxpayer's income taxed at?" The question will then present you with five options that identify different tax rates that the money may have been taxed at such as 10%, 15%, 20%, 25%, or none of these. You would then have to choose the option that identifies the tax rate that the taxpayer's income would have to be taxed at in order for the taxpayer to pay $2,250 in taxes on $15,000 of income, which in this case is 15%. This is because the tax rate is equal to the taxes assessed to the taxpayer (2,250) divided by the taxpayer's income ($15,000), which means that the tax rate is .15 or 15%.

Work/Time Required Questions

The ninth and final type of question that you will encounter in the arithmetic reasoning section of the TEA Exam is the work required question. Each of these questions will present you with a word problem that will ask you to determine the amount of work performed by a particular worker or group of workers in a specific time period, the amount of time that is required for a particular worker or a group of workers to complete a particular job, or the number of workers required to finish a particular job in a specific amount of time. These questions will typically provide you with the number of workers that are working, the amount of work that each worker can perform in a specific amount of time, the time that the workers have available to work on the job, and/or the time that it will take the workers to complete the work related to the job.

For example, you may be presented with a question such as "Two trained laborers and two untrained laborers can unload 8 trucks in an hour. The two untrained laborers work at the same speed, but each of the trained laborers works three times as fast as the untrained laborers. How long would it take for one of the untrained laborers to unload a single truck?" The question will then present you with five options and each option will indicate a different amount of time that it may take the untrained laborer to unload the truck, such as 7 ½ minutes, 15 minutes, 1 hour, 8 hours, or none of these. You would then have to choose the option that identifies the amount of time that it took the untrained laborer to unload the truck, which would be 1 hour for this particular example. This example may appear to be relatively complicated as it has workers working at different speeds. However, the answer to this question can be determined simply by determining how many untrained laborers are equivalent to the two trained laborers (2 * 3.) You can then add that number to the number of untrained laborers (2) in order to determine the total number of untrained laborers that would be equivalent to the staff that is working on the job (6 + 2 = 8 workers.) This means that 8 untrained laborers working at the same speed can unload 8 trucks in an hour, so 1 untrained laborer would be able to unload 8 trucks in 8 hours (1 hour * 8 laborers) or 1 truck in 1 hour (8 trucks / 8 hours.)

Important Note: You may have noticed that all of the examples related to the arithmetic section of the TEA Exam end with the option "none of these." This is because all of the arithmetic questions on the actual exam will offer this option as the "E" choice. However, it is important to note that, even though this option is offered as a possible answer for every question in the arithmetic section

- 32 -

of exam, this doesn't necessarily mean that this option will be correct or incorrect more often than any other option. In other words, you may have to choose the "none of these" option in order to answer some of the questions on the exam correctly, but you should make sure that the other options are incorrect before choosing the "none of these" option. Unfortunately, this can sometimes be difficult as you will not be allowed to use a calculator on the exam. As a result, you will have to double check your calculations on scrap paper before choosing the "none of these" option.

Problems for Investigation Questions

There are three different types of questions in the problems for investigation section of the TEA Exam. The three types of questions in this section of the exam include fact verification questions, evidence reliability/usefulness questions, and statement type identification questions. Each of these questions is somewhat different from the other types of questions found on the exam as the questions in this section are organized into sets with each question related to a passage about an investigation. Each passage is then followed by a list of 8 – 15 statements, and each of the questions related to that passage will identify 5 statements or 5 pairs of statements from that list. You will then have to choose the option that identifies the correct statement or statements.

Fact Verification Questions

The first type of question that you will encounter in the problems for investigation section of the TEA Exam is the fact verification question. Each of these questions will ask you to identify a statement that indicates or proves that a particular piece of information is true. These questions will typically be written in a format similar to "Which one of the following statements best indicates that this event occurred?," "Which one of the following statements indicates that a specific individual may have committed the crime?," "Which one of the following statements best links this event to this event?," or "Which one of the following statements best indicates that a particular fact is true?" For example, you may be presented with a passage describing an unusual car accident and there are 8 statements that follow the passage. One of the questions related to the passage may be a question such as "Which one of the following statements best indicates that the damage to the car was intentional?" The question would then be followed by five options, and each option would identify the number of a statement that may indicate that the damage to the car was intentional. For example, the question might offer options such as Statement 1, Statement 2, Statement 4, Statement 6, and Statement 8. You would then need to choose the option that indentifies a statement that indicates that the damage to the car may have been intentional. This may be a statement such as "The insurance adjuster on the scene determined that the vehicle was not moving when it was hit and that there was damage on both the left and right sides of the vehicle's hood but no damage to the center of the vehicle's hood" because this statement may indicate that the vehicle was hit twice.

Evidence Reliability/Usefulness Questions

Another type of question that you will encounter in the problems for investigation section of the TEA Exam is the evidence reliability/usefulness question. Each of these questions will ask you to identify a statement that indicates that a particular piece of evidence is reliable, unreliable, or useful in court. These questions will typically be written in a format similar to "Which of the following statements would be the least likely statement to be used in proving the case?," "Which two of the following statements corroborate each other?," "Which of the following statements appears to provide the most useful information for solving the case?," "Which of the following statements should not be used to prove the suspect's guilt?," "Which of the following statements appears to offer a reasonable alibi?," and "Which of the following statements is an opinion rather than a fact?"

For example, you may be presented with a passage describing an unusual car accident and there are 8 statements that follow the passage. One of the questions related to the passage may be a question such as "Which of the following statements would be the least likely statement to be used in proving the case?" The question would then be followed by five options and each option would identify the number of a statement that may be useless or unreliable. For instance, the question might offer options such as Statement 1, Statement 3, Statement 5, Statement 7, and Statement 8. You would then need to choose the option that identifies the most unreliable statement or the statement that is the most irrelevant. This could be a statement such as "Mrs. Stevens, the driver of the red sports car, said she was a skilled driver who had been driving for nearly 25 years." This statement, regardless of whether it is true or not, is irrelevant to proving who was responsible for the accident or what actually happened, so it would not be useful for proving the case in court.

Statement Type Identification Questions

The third and final type of question that you may encounter in the problems for investigation section of the TEA Exam is the statement type identification question. Each of these questions will ask you to identify a specific statement based on the type of information that the statement offers. These questions are somewhat similar to the evidence reliability/usefulness questions and the fact verification questions on the exam. However, each of these questions will ask you to identify a specific type of statement rather than a statement that presents a specific fact or the most reliable/unreliable statement. These questions will typically be written in a format similar to "Which of the following statements should be considered hearsay?," "Which of the following statements presents circumstantial evidence?," and "Which of the following statements appears to offer a motive?"

For example, you may be presented with a passage describing an unusual car accident and there are 8 statements that follow the passage. One of the questions related to the passage may be a question such as "Which of the following statements should be considered hearsay?" The question would then be followed by five options, and each option would identify the number of a statement that might be considered hearsay. For instance, the question might offer options such as Statement 1, Statement 2, Statement 4, Statement 5, and Statement 7. You would then need to choose the option that identifies a statement that should be considered hearsay. This could be a statement such as "Mrs. Jacobs stated that she heard from a friend that Mrs. Stevens had never driven a day in her life before the accident." This statement would be considered hearsay because Mrs. Jacobs did not actually have first-hand knowledge or the information, but instead, heard the information from an indirect source.

Applicant Experience Questionnaire

The questions in the applicant experience questionnaire section of the exam are not actually designed to test your knowledge but rather to gather information about your background. It is nearly impossible for an individual to study for these questions because there is no right or wrong answer to any of the questions in this section. However, you can prepare for these questions by getting an idea of your high school and college grades, GPAs, class ranks, and other similar information. This is because some of these questions will ask you to identify a range into which each of your grades, GPAs, class ranks, and other similar rankings fall. It is also important to note that you should try to answer each of the questions in this section of the exam as honestly as possible because you won't have a lot of time to think about the answer for each question, and the agency that you are applying to will have the ability to double-check your high school, college, and other similar records in order to determine whether you were telling the truth or not. This doesn't necessarily mean that you have to know your exact high school GPA or be certain of the grade that you received for every class that you ever took but rather that you need to have a basic idea of how well you performed in each school and/or type of class. For example, if you just barely got through high school with a 2.0 average, you may raise some red flags with the agency you are applying to if you indicate that you graduated with a 4.0 on one of the questions in the applicant experience questionnaire section of the exam.

Part III. How do I Pass this Test?

Passing the TEA Exam Overview

If you have read Parts I and II of this guide, then you probably already know that the TEA Exam is designed to determine whether you have the basic skills, knowledge, and experience necessary to become a federal law enforcement officer with the ATF, ICE, IRS, U.S. Marshals Service, or the U.S. Secret Service. You also probably know that the TEA Exam, in order to assess your skills, knowledge, and experience, contains a number of different questions that are designed to evaluate your reading skills, your mathematical skills, your critical thinking skills, your ability to analyze information, and your background. In fact, if you have read the second part of this guide, you probably have a good idea of what's covered in each section of the exam as well. However, regardless of whether you have read the first two parts of this guide or not, you may have already realized that knowing what's on the exam may not necessarily be enough to pass the exam. This is because it is not only important for you to be aware of the topics that the exam covers, but also for you to know how to answer all of the questions related to those topics as well. In other words, in order for you to pass the TEA Exam, you need to know what sorts of questions are on the exam and, more importantly, how to answer those questions in a short period of time.

Understanding the Format

In order to study for the TEA Exam in the most effective way possible, you need to understand how the exam is setup. This is actually important for two distinct reasons. First, if you understand the setup of the exam, you will have a better idea of what to expect when you actually take the exam. This is important because the exam is timed, and you don't want to be wasting time trying to figure out what you are supposed to be doing while you are taking the exam. Secondly, if you understand the setup of the exam, it will be easier for you to practice for the exam. This is because you can practice answering questions within time limits similar to the time constraints you will have to deal with on the actual exam. This can be extremely important because you will only have a limited amount of time to answer each question. As a result, you need to be prepared to answer each of the questions on the exam in the amount of time that you have available.

The setup of each part of the TEA exam is discussed briefly in the second part of this guide. However, you may want to get an idea of how each of these parts fits together to establish the setup of the exam as a whole. The TEA Exam consists of four main sections that are split into five parts. The first three parts of the exam are the verbal reasoning section, the arithmetic reasoning section, and the problems for investigation section. Part A, which is the verbal reasoning section of the exam, consists of 25 reading comprehension questions. Part B, which is the arithmetic reasoning section of the exam, consists of 20 word problems related to basic mathematics. Part C, which is the problems for investigation section, consists of 30 questions related to analyzing information. These three sections of the exam make up a total of 75 questions. The final two parts of the exam consist of a total of 40 – 70 questions that ask for information about your own personal background. These two parts are referred to as Part D and Part E or as the Applicant Experience Questionnaire section of the exam. Each part of the exam is timed and you will only have 50 minutes to answer the questions in Part A, 50 minutes to answer the questions in Part B, 60 minutes to answer the questions in Part C, 15 minutes to answer the questions in Part D, and 15 minutes to answer the questions in Part E. If you complete a section before time has run out, it is important to note that you will not be able to start the next section of the exam until the time limit has elapsed for the previous section. It is also important to note that you will not be able to go back to a section once you have reached the time limit for that section.

How do I Answer the Verbal Reasoning Questions?

The verbal reasoning section of the TEA Exam consists of 25 multiple-choice questions that are designed to test your ability to read and comprehend the information within a written passage. In other words, the questions in the verbal reasoning section of the exam are designed to test your reading comprehension skills. These questions assess your reading comprehension by asking you to identify the main idea of the passage, identify a statement that is supported by the passage, identify a specific piece of information provided in the passage, define a term, or draw a conclusion based on what you have learned from the passage. These questions may sound as if they are very similar to the reading comprehension questions found on many other standardized exams as the types of answers that the questions ask for are similar. However, there are several key differences between the reading comprehension questions on the TEA Exam and what you would typically see on other exams. As a result, there are a few things that you might want to keep in mind.

First, it is always a good idea to read each question and the options associated with that question before reading the passage. This is because reading each question and the options related to that question will allow you to identify what you should be looking for before you read the passage. The passages in this section of the exam are relatively short as each passage is only 50 – 100 words long. It is important to remember, however, that time is still a concern even though the passages are short because you will only have around 2 minutes to determine what the question is looking for and identify the correct answer to the question. It is also important to note that determining what a question is looking for may be more difficult than you anticipate. This is because most, if not all, of the reading comprehension questions on the TEA Exam will begin with the phrase "The passage best supports the statement that." This means that it may be nearly impossible for you to tell what the question is looking for by reading the question alone.

Second, it is important to remember that this section of the exam is testing your reading comprehension skills and **not** your knowledge of any specific topic. This is important to remember because each of the questions in this section of the exam may be related to any of a number of different topics from a variety of different fields. This means that you may be tempted to answer a question based on what you actually know about the subject. However, this is exactly what you shouldn't do in this particular section of the exam. Each of these questions is designed to try to trick you into providing a response that seems correct but in reality has nothing to do with the passage itself. In order to answer the question correctly, you must answer it based on the information provided and not on what you know. This is especially important for any of the passages that offer an opinion or a hypothesis as the information that these passages are presenting may actually be incorrect, but you are still being tested on what the passage says and not on what you actually know to be true.

Third, while you are reading each passage, keep an eye out for words or prefixes that may negate something in the phrase such as "no," "not," and "nowhere" and words that begin with "in" or "un." These words can easily change the meaning of a sentence, and each of the questions in this section of the exam are designed to offer you options that appear to be similar to what the passage stated but which are actually stating something entirely different. This means that a passage may contain a statement such as "If the safe is not locked, someone will take the money," and one of the options following the question that goes with the passage may have an answer that states "If the safe is locked, someone will take the money." These two statements are very similar, but they have completely different meanings because of the word "not."

- 37 -

Fourth, while you are reading each passage, you should also keep an eye out for quantity words. Quantity words describe how much of something is present, describe the number of things that the statement applies to, or describe how often an event occurs. Quantity words include words such as "some," "all" "none," "nothing," "many," "much," "any," "several" "every," "always," "sometimes," and "never." You should also keep an eye out for conditional words such as "might," "may," "should," "could," "usually," and "probably." These words, like the words and prefixes that negate, can easily change the meaning of a sentence. As a result, some of the questions in the verbal reasoning section of the TEA Exam may present you with options that appear to be correct but do not actually agree with the information presented in the passage. For example, a passage may contain a statement that says "If the safe is not locked, someone may take the money," and one of the options following the question that goes with the passage may have an answer that states "If the safe is not locked, someone will take the money." These two statements are very similar, but the first statement makes it clear that it is possible that someone **may** take the money if the safe is not locked while the second statement makes it clear that it is guaranteed that someone **will** take the money if the safe is not locked.

Finally, it is important to remember that even though the test is timed, it is usually a good idea to read each passage twice. This is especially true if you encounter a question that you are having difficulty answering or if you encounter a question that requires you to identify a specific fact presented in the passage. This is important because the questions in this section of the TEA Exam are specifically designed to trick you. This means that certain questions will offer you choices that are related to the topic that is discussed in the passage but have nothing to do with what the passage itself actually stated or choices that are related to statements from the passage that are taken out of context. In order for you to choose the correct answer, you need to make sure that you actually read the passage correctly.

Finding the Main Idea

Some of the questions in the verbal reasoning section of the TEA Exam will require you to identify the main idea of a passage. This may seem relatively straightforward, but you may want to keep a few simple things in mind. First, it is important to realize that the first sentence of a passage may state the main idea of the passage, but it doesn't necessarily state it. This means that you may find the main idea of the passage stated in the first sentence of the passage or you may find it stated in the second sentence, the third sentence, the fourth sentence, or somewhere else within the passage. Therefore, in order for you to find the main idea of a particular passage, you will usually have to read the entire passage very carefully.

Second, some passages may state their main ideas outright while others will only imply them. This can be an extremely important thing to keep in mind if you are looking for a statement that states the main idea because you may be looking for something that doesn't exist. However, this doesn't mean that you should panic if the main idea isn't stated outright. If the passage doesn't have a single statement that makes its topic clear, try to identify what all of the statements in the passage have in common. This common element could be a central opinion that all of the statements are defending, a topic that all of the statements are discussing, or a hypothesis that the statements are attempting to prove.

Finally, if you are having trouble finding the main idea for a particular passage, read each of the options and the passage again carefully. While you read the passage, think about the statements offered in each option and try to answer the question "Is this passage discussing this statement?" If the passage appears to be discussing that statement, then the option that identifies that statement is probably the correct answer. If the passage doesn't seem to have anything to do with the statement, or if some parts of the passage appear to be related to the statement, but other parts of the passage appear to be unrelated, then the answer is probably incorrect.

Identifying a Supported Statement

Some of the questions in the verbal reasoning section of the TEA Exam will require you to identify a statement that is supported by a passage. These questions are often very similar to the questions that ask you to identify the main idea of a passage and/or the questions that ask you to draw a conclusion based on the information included in a passage. However, there are some key differences between the supported statement questions and some of the other questions in the verbal reasoning section of the exam that you may want to keep in mind.

First, it is important to realize that each of the supported statement questions on the exam will require you to identify the main idea of a passage and then take that main idea one step further. This means that you are not only looking for the main idea of the passage but that you are also attempting to understand exactly how the author feels about the topic in order to draw a conclusion. For example, you may be presented with a passage that discusses how the author of the passage feels about a new forensic technique. In the passage, the author explains that the technique is unreliable and often results in the contamination of evidence. The statements that follow the passage each describe different situations in which the author might use the new technique.

In order to answer the question, you would then need to choose the statement that best matches with what you know about the author's opinion on the technique. In this particular case, this means that you might choose a statement such as "It is unlikely that the author would use this particular forensic technique during an investigation" because you know that the author considers the technique to be unreliable and potentially detrimental to an investigation. All of the supported statement questions in the verbal reasoning section of the exam will be set up in the same way as this example, and they will ask you to make a judgment on what the author would think or do in a particular situation based on what he or she said in the passage. In other words, each of the supported statement questions in this section of the exam are a combination of a main idea question and a drawing conclusion question as each of these questions will require you to identify the author's opinion and draw a conclusion based on that opinion.

Secondly, if you are having difficulty with a supported statement question, try reading each of the statements that the question offers with a phrase similar to "If the author believes this then..." For instance, you might use the statement from the example above to create a phrase like "If the author believes that the technique is unreliable and often results in contamination then it is unlikely that the author would use this particular forensic technique during an investigation." This allows you to compare the statement with what the author said in order to determine whether the statement is something with which the author would agree or disagree. If the statement makes sense when placed into a sentence with the author's opinion, then the statement is probably the correct answer. As a result, the phrase in the above example proves that the statement is probably correct because the opinion and the statement make sense together. However, it is important to note that if the statement does not make sense when placed into a sentence with the author's opinion, then the statement is probably incorrect.

Finding Specific Information

Some of the questions in the verbal reasoning section of the TEA Exam will require you to identify a specific fact that is presented by a passage. These questions are usually easier to answer than the other types of questions found in the verbal reasoning section of the exam as they are just looking

- 39 -

for one specific piece of information that is located somewhere in the passage. However, like most of the questions throughout this section, these questions are still designed to trick you. As a result, you need to know how to avoid some of the common tricks that the exam's designers will try to use.

First, most of the options for these questions will look similar to something you read in the passage, but the way that the options are worded may change the meaning. In other words, you may have an option that is phrased so that it looks similar to what the passage said, but the phrase in the option actually means something completely different or is saying something completely different from what the passage actually stated. For example, when the phrase "The fact that you are looking for can be found in the first sentence of a passage" and the phrase "The fact that you are looking for can be found in the second sentence of a passage" are placed side by side, it is pretty obvious that the two sentences are different. However, if the first sentence was included in a passage and the second sentence was located in the options that followed a question associated with that passage, the difference between the two sentences might not be as obvious. As a result, it is always a good idea to read or skim the passage both before and after you have chosen an answer in order to make sure that the answer you have chosen is actually correct.

Second, some of the options for these questions will combine two facts from the passage together into one phrase. These options can be confusing because the information in each option looks familiar even though it isn't necessarily correct. This is because the two facts are from the passage, but the phrase combines them in a way that the facts do not actually state the same thing as the passage originally stated. For example, a passage might state that "The amount of current in a circuit will decrease as the resistance increases" and "The amount of current in a circuit will increase as the voltage increases." The question following the passage might then offer an option that "The amount of resistance in a circuit will increase as the voltage increases." This statement looks familiar because the passage discussed resistance and voltage in a similar way. However, this statement isn't actually stating the same thing that the passage stated because the passage stated that the **current** would increase as the voltage increased and not that the **resistance** would increase as the voltage increased.

It is important to note, however, that this does not necessarily mean that an option is incorrect simply because it combines two facts from the passage. Some of the questions on the exam will offer you a statement that combines two facts together so that the statement states the same information as the passage, but it states that information in a different way. For example, you might have a passage that provides the phrases from the example in the above paragraph "The amount of current in a circuit will decrease as the resistance increases and "The amount of current in a circuit will increase as the voltage increases." The question following the passage might then offer an option that "The current in a circuit will decrease as the resistance increases and increase as the voltage increases." This statement is actually stating the same thing as the two phrases offered in the passage, so it is correct even though it combines the information from two separate sentences.

Third, some of the options for these questions may provide statements that are true, but are still considered to be incorrect because the information found in the statement is not included in the passage. In other words, some of the options for the finding specific information questions will provide you with accurate facts related to the topic covered in the passage, but these facts are not discussed in the passage. Since all of the questions in this section of the exam are asking you for the statement that the passage best supports or what the passage indicates, the correct answer must be something that you found in the passage or can logically base on something in the passage. As a result, you need to make sure that the information for the answer that you choose is at least discussed in the passage. It is important to remember that if the information in a particular statement is not discussed and/or there is no way to draw the conclusion that the statement makes based on the information provided, that statement is incorrect.

Finally, if you have read the introduction at the beginning of this section on how to answer the verbal reasoning questions on the exam, you know that some of the options for these questions may provide information that you know is incorrect, but the option is still considered to be correct for the purposes of the TEA exam because the passage stated the information. This is especially important for the finding specific information questions on the exam as some of the passages on the exam will provide information that you disagree with or information that is outright incorrect. This means that it is essential for you to focus on what the passage says and not on what you know. These questions are designed to make the incorrect options look correct because they sound more reasonable or, in some cases, are more reasonable than what the author actually stated. However, in order to answer these questions correctly, you have to identify statements that describe information presented in the passage or statements that are based on the information in the passage.

Defining a Term

Some of the questions in the verbal reasoning section of the TEA Exam will require you to define a term based on the information provided. These questions may appear to be relatively difficult as they require you to define a strange or unfamiliar word. However, in most cases, these questions are not as difficult as they seem. This is because these questions do not require you to *know* the meaning of each word, but instead require you to *determine* the meaning of each word based on how each word is used in the passage. As a result, it is essential for you to know how to find the meaning of a word based on its context. In order to find the correct meaning of a word based on its context, there are a few things you should keep in mind.

First, in order to determine what a word means based on its context, you need to look at the underlining meaning of the sentence and how the term you need to define fits into that sentence. In other words, you need to look at the entire sentence and ask yourself "what is this sentence talking about?" For example, if a passage includes the sentence "There are a myriad of different ways that an individual can approach a reading comprehension question," you should be able to tell that the sentence is discussing how many different reading comprehension approaches exist. If the question associated with that passage then requires you to define the word "myriad," you can use the meaning of the sentence to determine the meaning of the word by looking at how that word fits into the meaning of the sentence. This means that, in this particular case, the word "myriad" comes right before the phrase "of different ways" so "myriad" must be referring to a specific number of ways or a large number of ways because it is being used to describe how many different ways there are. As a result, it is relatively safe to assume that "a myriad" probably refers to "a lot" or "a large number."

Second, if you are having trouble determining the meaning of a term, you may want to try reading the sentence without the term or read the sentence as if the sentence contained a blank where the term is supposed to be. For example, the sentence from the above paragraph "There are a myriad of different ways that an individual can approach a reading comprehension question" would become "There are a __ of different ways that an individual can approach a reading comprehension question." This allows you to fill in the blank with a word or phrase that seems to complete the sentence. This method can be extremely helpful because a word or phrase that seems to make sense and fits with what the sentence is saying will usually define the term. For instance, you could fill in the blank in this particular example with words such as "number," "variety," and "lot," which could all be used to define the word "myriad." On the other hand, if you try to place words such as

- 41 -

"none," "very few," "few," "several," or "some" into the blank in this particular example, it is pretty easy to see that these words don't fit because the sentence doesn't make sense when you read it.

Third, if you are still having difficulty determining the meaning of a term after you have read the sentence without the term or with a blank, you may want to try reading the rest of the passage in order to determine how that sentence fits into the passage as a whole. For example, if the sentence from the above example "There are a myriad of different ways that an individual can approach a reading comprehension question" is followed by the sentence "These approaches include reading the question first, reading each passage sentence by sentence and comparing each sentence to the statements offered, breaking the passage down into facts and subtopics, and many other similar methods," you can look at both sentences to determine the meaning of the term. This is because the second sentence makes it clear that there are "many methods" that can be used so the word "myriad" must refer to a large number of methods.

Finally, if you are familiar with a term that you need to define in order to answer one of the definition questions, it is important that you look at the context that the word appears in **before** you mark your answer. This is true even if you are certain that you know what the word means because some words have multiple meanings and the exam's designers will try to trick you by providing statements that use alternate meanings and statements that use the meanings of other similar words. For instance, the word "myriad" can refer to a large number or it can specifically refer to ten thousand. If you are asked to define the term "myriad" as it appears in a passage that includes the sentence "There are a myriad of different ways that an individual can approach a reading comprehension question," there may be an answer that indicates "a myriad refers to ten thousand" and an answer that indicates that "a myriad refers to a large number." However, the correct answer for this particular example would be a large number as a myriad does not necessarily refer to ten thousand in this sentence, and ten thousand does not fit the context of the sentence or the information we have from the passage.

The exam's designers may also use the definitions of words that have similar spellings and/or similar sounds to the word that you are attempting to define in order to trick you into choosing the wrong answer. For example, if you are asked to define the term "myriad," you may be presented with statements that define the words "mirid," "mired," and "mured." These statements are of course incorrect as a "mirid" is a type of bug, the word "mired" is a verb meaning to drag into the mud or become stuck in the mud, and the word "mured" is a verb meaning to surround with a wall. It may seem obvious that these answers are incorrect as they don't fit in the context of the sentence or the passage. However, these options can be a problem if you read the passage quickly or if you ignored the passage entirely because you were certain that you had seen the word before. These words allow the exam's designers to trick you into thinking that you have seen the word before because you see a familiar definition even though that definition is for a completely different word. As a result, you need to make sure that you are choosing an answer that fits with what the sentence and with what the passage is stating in order to answer the question correctly.

Drawing Conclusions

There are some questions on the TEA Exam that will ask you to make a conclusion based on the information provided instead of asking you to identify a specific idea, detail, or definition. These questions are usually more difficult to answer than the other questions in the verbal reasoning section of the exam because each of these questions requires you to take a concept or fact presented in the passage and expand on it. The answers to most of the questions in the verbal reasoning section of the exam can be found simply by reading the passage carefully. However, the drawing conclusion questions often require some additional thought so there are some things you may want to keep in mind.

First, in order to answer each of the drawing conclusions questions on the exam, you will have to look at a piece of information from the passage and take that information one step further. The drawing conclusion questions on the exam are designed so that you can't answer them simply by identifying a specific fact in the passage, which means that these questions are designed to make you think about what the information actually means. This is an important thing to keep in mind because you will not find the specific answer to any of the drawing conclusion questions stated in the passage no matter how hard you look. You will, however, always find a sentence or a group of sentences in the passage that are related to the statements offered in the options following the question. These sentences will allow you to use the information presented in the passage to determine the correct answer.

For example, you may be given a passage that states "Assuming that the pressure does not change, the volume of a gas will decrease as the temperature increases." The question associated with that passage would then provide you with a series of options and one of those options might contain a statement such as "The pressure exerted on a gas has some effect on how the volume of that gas changes when the temperature changes." The passage in this example didn't actually state that the pressure affects how the volume of the gas changes, but it did state that the volume will decrease as the temperature increases **assuming** that the pressure does not change, so we can logically conclude that the pressure has some effect on how the volume of gas changes in relation to the temperature.

Second, you should never assume anything unless you can base your assumption on what is actually stated. This is important because the exam will try to trick you with options that appear to be logical, but the statements offered by the options cannot be deduced from what was actually said in the passage. For example, if you take the sentence from the example in the above paragraph "Assuming that the pressure does not change, the volume of a gas will decrease as the temperature increases," you can assume that the pressure has some effect on the volume. However, you cannot assume exactly what the effect of the change in pressure might be as the example never stated that the volume would increase as the temperature increases if the pressure changed, that the volume would decrease as the temperature increases and increase as the pressure increased, that the volume would remain the same if the pressure was changing all the time, or that another similar type of change would take place. Therefore, you need to make sure that your assumption follows the logic established in the passage.

Third, if you read the introduction at the beginning of this section on how to answer the verbal reasoning questions on the exam, you know that you need to watch out for words such as "no," "not," "some," "all," "none," "several," "every," "could," "might," and "may" because these words can change the meaning of an entire statement. This is something that is especially important for you to keep in mind when you are attempting to draw a conclusion because these words can change the logic of a particular statement and, in turn, change what you can logically conclude based on that particular statement. For example, if a passage stated that "According to most people, every element is affected by the temperature, but research has shown that this is not the case" it may be safe to assume that "**some** elements **are not affected** by the temperature." It is not safe to assume, however, that "**no** element **is affected** by the temperature" or that "**some** elements **are affected** by the temperature." This is because this statement makes it clear that every element is not necessarily affected by the temperature, but it never states that there are elements that **are affected** by the temperature or that there are **no elements that can be affected** by the temperature.

While you are attempting to answer the drawing conclusion questions, you should also look out for the prefixes mentioned in the introduction at the beginning of this section as prefixes such as "in" or "un" can change the meaning of an entire statement as well. For instance, if you take the statement from the example in the above paragraph "According to most people, every element is affected by the temperature, but research has shown that this is not the case" you can conclude that "some elements are unaffected by changes in temperature." If, on the other hand, that statement was changed so that it read "According to most people, every element is unaffected by the temperature, but research has shown that this is not the case," it is safe to assume that "some elements are affected by the temperature," but it is not safe to assume that "some elements are unaffected." This is because the "un" prefix in front of the word "affected" along with the phrase "this is not the case" creates a double negative, which makes it so the sentence is actually stating that "every element is **not unaffected**."

Finally, in order to answer any of these questions correctly, you have to focus on what the passage says and not on what you know. This may seem strange as these questions are asking you to draw a conclusion. However, it is important to remember that these questions are looking for a conclusion that can be logically drawn from what the passage says and not from what you know about the subject. The exam's designers have very carefully designed each of these questions so that they offer options that may actually be accurate, but they are not related to the information in the passage, so they are incorrect for the purposes of the TEA exam.

For example, the sentence that was discussed earlier "Assuming that the pressure does not change, the volume of a gas will decrease as the temperature increases," is actually incorrect. In fact, the question following the passage in this example may offer an option that states that the "The volume of a gas will increase as the temperature increases if the pressure remains constant," which is accurate because the volume of a gas will **increase** as the temperature **increases**. Unfortunately, this sort of option is actually a trick answer because the passage stated that "the volume decreases as the temperature increases" and you are being tested on your ability to make a logical conclusion off of what you have read. As a result, this cannot be the correct answer to the question even though it is accurate because it isn't related to what the passage stated.

How do I Answer the Arithmetic Reasoning Questions?

The arithmetic reasoning section of the TEA Exam consists of 20 multiple-choice questions that are designed to test your basic mathematical skills. Each of these questions will assess your basic accounting and arithmetic knowledge by asking you to solve a word problem related to one of nine different topics. These nine topics include basic algebra, the distance that can be traveled/the fuel required to travel a certain distance, interest, payroll, profit and loss, proportions, ratios, taxes, and the amount of work that can be performed in a specific period of time/the amount of time that is required to complete a specific job. If you are unfamiliar with any of these topics or if it has been some time since you have solved a word problem, this section may appear to be daunting. In fact, the arithmetic reasoning section is often considered to be the most difficult section of the TEA Exam. However, this section is actually not as difficult as it seems, and there are certain things that you can do to make these questions much easier.

First, in order to answer each of the questions in this section correctly, you should read the entire problem and identify the question that the problem is asking you to answer before you start making any calculations. This is important because it can be easy to misread or misunderstand a question if you don't read the entire problem or if you try to solve the problem before you have all of the necessary information. Each problem in this section not only identifies the numbers that you need to use, but also places those numbers into a context, and you need to understand that context in order to understand the question. Each question will almost always appear in the final sentence of the problem, but you will usually not be able to understand the question until you have read the rest of the problem.

Second, once you have read the entire problem and identified the question that you need to answer, you may want to circle the question in the test booklet, underline the question in the test booklet, mark the question in the test booklet, or rewrite the question on a piece of scrap paper. Marking or rewriting the question is usually a good idea because it makes it easier for you to look back at the question if you get confused or if you think you've made a mistake. Marking or rewriting the question can also make it much easier for you to check your answer after you have arrived at a solution because you can look back at the question and ask "Does this answer make sense?" and "Does this answer actually answer the question?" This can be an extremely useful technique to use because some of the problems in this section are written so they appear to be much more complicated than they actually are. This can make it much easier for you to lose sight of what the problem is actually asking you to do.

Third, once you have established what the problem is asking for, you need to decide how you are going to solve the problem. Usually, this means that you need to look at the question, look at the options, and decide on how you can use the information that you have available to get an answer that looks like the options provided. There are usually a number of different methods that you can use to determine the answer to any given problem and some methods will be much easier to use than others. Some of the easier methods that you can use to answer each type of question in the arithmetic reasoning section will be covered later in this section. However, in order to do well in this section of the exam, you must make sure that the method that you choose to use for a particular problem will help *you* to find the correct answer.

Fourth, it is important to remember that you will not be allowed to use a calculator to answer the questions in the arithmetic reasoning section, but you will be allowed to use scrap paper. This is an important thing to keep in mind while you are preparing for the exam because you should practice using scrap paper rather than a calculator. This is because practicing with scrap paper allows you to get an accurate idea of what you need to do in order to answer a question, how difficult it will be to answer each question, and how long it will take you to answer each question. Practicing with a calculator, on the other hand, will not give you an accurate idea of exactly what you have to do, how difficult each question is, or how much time it will take you to answer a particular question because you will not be able to use a calculator on the actual exam and a calculator will make it easier for you to answer each question. As a result, even though it would probably be much easier to answer each question with a calculator, you should practice using scrap paper because you won't be able to use the calculator when you take the exam.

Fifth, scrap paper may not be as easy to use as a calculator, but it can be more useful than you think. In fact, you may be thinking that you're savvy enough about math that you can just answer the problems without using the scrap paper at all, but this is usually not a good idea. This is because each of the questions in this section, just like the questions in the verbal reasoning section, are designed to trick you, and the exam's designers have intentionally designed the problems so that they sound more confusing than they actually are. This means that it is much easier to make a mistake on a question in this section because it is harder to understand the information presented in the question. However, writing the numbers from the problem down on a piece of scrap paper can make it much easier to understand the information and make it much easier for you to determine the answer to the problem without making a mistake.

Sixth, it is important to remember that the exam's designers may try to trick you by placing information in a problem that has nothing to do with actually solving the problem. In other words, some of the problems in this section of the exam may contain numbers that you don't need to use. For example, you may be presented with a question such as "A stamp collector purchased 15 rare stamps from a stamp dealer for $50.00 each. If the stamp dealer originally paid $35.00 for each rare stamp, how much profit did the stamp dealer make on each stamp?" The problem in this example gives you three numbers, which includes the number of stamps sold, the selling price of each stamp, and the cost price of each stamp. In order to solve the problem, however, you only need to know the selling price and the cost price of each stamp. This is because the question is asking you to find the profit the dealer made on **each** stamp so it doesn't matter whether the dealer sold 15 stamps or 115 stamps. This means that, in order for you to answer the question, you will need to separate the important information from the irrelevant information.

Seventh, it is also important to remember that the exam's designers will try to trick you by offering you the opportunity to choose answers that you might have arrived at if you made a mistake. In other words, the incorrect options for each question in this section are designed so that they identify solutions that you would reach if you made a common mathematical error, used the wrong formula, or misread the question. For example, you might be presented with the question from the above example "A stamp collector purchased 15 rare stamps from a stamp dealer for $50.00 each. If the stamp dealer originally paid $35.00 for each stamp, how much profit did the stamp dealer make on each stamp?" The question would then present you with five options such as $15; $50; $225; $715; or none of these. The correct answer would be the first option as the profit on each stamp is equal to the selling price ($50.00) minus the cost price ($35.00) or $15 (50.00 - $35.00.)

The other options offered for this particular example, on the other hand, are incorrect because they each offer an answer that you might arrive at if you misread the problem. The option that identifies $50 as the answer is incorrect because it is simply the selling price of the stamp and not the profit. The option that identifies $225 as the answer is incorrect because it identifies the total profit that the stamp dealer made from selling all 15 stamps and not the profit that the dealer made from each stamp. The option that identifies $715 as the answer is incorrect because it identifies the total profit that the stamp dealer would have made from selling all 15 stamps if the stamp dealer only paid $35 for all the stamps. As this example shows, three out of the five options for each question will usually be designed to trick you so you should double-check your answer to each problem before marking your answer on the exam.

Eighth, even though the questions on the exam are designed to trick you, each question is designed so that you can answer it in a limited amount of time. This means that there is almost always an easy way to determine the solution to a problem even if it appears that that the problem requires you to use a complicated formula. This is because the exam's designers understand that you only have about 2 ½ minutes to answer each question in the arithmetic reasoning section of the exam without the aid of a calculator. As a result, each question will only require you to make relatively simple calculations. If you encounter a question that appears to require a complicated formula, you should try to look for a shortcut because there will almost always be one that you can use.

Ninth, you may be tempted to estimate your answers for some of the problems in this section of the exam in order to conserve as much time as possible. Unfortunately, it is not a good idea to estimate in this section of the TEA Exam because each problem in the arithmetic reasoning section of the exam offers the option "none of these." The "none of these" option makes it very easy for an estimated answer to trick you into choosing the incorrect answer. This is because an estimated answer that is too far from the correct answer may lead you to choose the "none of these" option when it is incorrect or choose a different option when the "none of these" option is actually the correct answer. In order to answer each question correctly, you need to determine your solution in the most accurate way possible.

Finally, there is always a chance that you will encounter a problem that seems to be incredibly complicated or a problem that you just can't seem to figure out. If you encounter a problem that seems overwhelming, try to break the problem down into separate parts. In order to do this, look at each sentence, and write down the numbers or variables included in each sentence on a piece of scrap paper. You should also make sure to include a word, symbol, or short phrase that describes what each number or variable represents, such as 15 stamps or $715. Once you have written down all of the numbers and/or variables, look at the question and the answers that follow that question to get an idea of what the question is asking. Then, once you have an idea of what the question is looking for, look at each number and determine whether you need that number to solve the problem or not. This allows you to look at the problem piece by piece so that you can identify the information that you have available, identify the question that you need to answer, and identify the information that is actually relevant to the question. Breaking the problem down will usually make it much easier for you to solve the problem because it allows you to look at each component that makes up the problem instead of looking at the problem as a whole.

Arithmetic Reasoning Terminology

The following section discusses a series of methods that can be used to answer each type of question in the arithmetic reasoning section of the TEA Exam. However, it is essential for you to know some of the terms related to the topics covered in this section of the exam in order to understand each of these methods. Knowing these terms will help you to identify and understand the underlying components that make up each type of question in this section and may help you to better understand some of the problems on the exam. As a result, you may want to be at least somewhat familiar with each of the following terms:

Commission: a type of pay in which an individual receives a percentage of the money that the individual's employer has earned as a result of the individual's work.

Compound interest: a type of interest that is calculated based on the principal *plus* the interest from the previous interest period.

Cost/Cost price: the amount that an individual or business paid to obtain a specific product or to obtain the equipment or personnel necessary to perform a specific service that the individual or business plans to sell.

Discount: the amount that an individual or business deducts from its price or the amount that a bank deducts from the value of a promissory note because the note has not yet matured.

Double time: a type of pay in which an individual receives twice his or her standard rate of pay for each hour worked. It is typically paid for Sundays, holidays, to individuals on-call when called into work, and for other similar situations in which it may be difficult to get an individual to agree to work.

Fraction: A portion of a larger whole. For example, if an individual has ½ of an apple, ½ is a fraction indicating that the individual has a portion of the apple equal to 50% of the entire apple.

Gross pay: the amount of money that an individual will earn for performing a particular task or group of tasks before taxes have been taken out.

Interest: the amount of money that an individual or business must pay in order to use money that belongs to another individual or business. In other words, the term interest refers to the amount of money that an individual must pay to a lender on top of the money that the individual actually borrowed.

Interest rate: the amount of interest that an individual or business must pay for a specific period. The interest rate is usually described in terms of a percentage that an individual or business pays each year.

List price: price that an individual or business is advertising for a particular item or service.

Loss: amount that an individual or business has lost due to the sale of a particular item or service. A loss may be described in terms of a percentage or in terms of the amount of money lost.

Maturity date: the date on which a bank or other institution must pay the full amount for a promissory note, bond, or other similar financial obligation.

Net pay: the amount of money that an individual will earn for performing a particular task or group of tasks after taxes have been taken out.

Overhead: the amount that a business must pay in order to continue operating that is not related to the costs associated with acquiring each specific part or product. This includes expenses such as rent, salaries, lighting, heating, maintenance, etc.

Overtime: type of pay in which an individual receives an additional percentage of his or standard pay for working more than his or her scheduled hours. An individual receiving overtime pay will typically receive 1 ½ times their standard rate for each hour worked over his or her scheduled hours.

Percent: portion of a larger whole described in terms of number of parts out of 100. For example, 50% of an apple is equal to ½ of that apple.

Period: specific length of time between payments. For example, if you pay interest annually, each interest period is 1 year.

Principal: amount of money that an individual or business must pay interest on due to a loan or other similar financial obligation.

Profit: amount that an individual or business has gained due to the sale of a particular item or service. A profit may be described in terms of a percentage or in terms of the amount of money gained.

Promissory note: written agreement to pay a specific amount to another individual or business on the date that the promissory note matures.

Proportion: relationship of four amounts in which the first amount divided by the second amount is equal to the third amount divided by the fourth amount. In other words, a proportion describes the relationship between two equal ratios.

Ratio: relationship between two or more amounts that is described by how many times the first amount appears compared with how many times the second amount appears. For example, if two events occur at a rate of 3 to 5, this means that for every 3 times the first event occurs, the second event will occur 5 times. Ratios can be expressed in the format 3 to 5, 3:5, or 3/5.

Salary: specific amount that an individual is paid for a specific period.

Selling price: price that an individual or business actually sold a product or service for after any discounts or other markdowns.

Simple interest: type of interest that is calculated based on the principal *rather than* the combination of the principal and the interest from the previous period.

Straight time/standard time: type of pay in which an individual receives his or her standard rate of pay.

Standard pay/base pay: amount that an individual normally earns for working a specific period. Standard Pay is typically described in terms of the amount that an individual will earn each hour, or in other words, in terms of the individual's hourly rate.

Surtax: an extra tax that is applied after something has already been taxed.

Time: the specific length of the period in which a certain activity occurs.

Variable: letter or symbol that represents any one value from a group of values. In other words, a letter or symbol that represents an unspecified number. For example, the variable x in the formula "$x + 5 = z$" may represent 1, 2, 3, 4, 5, or any other number.

Withholding tax: the amount of money that is taken directly from an individual's pay to go towards the individual's income taxes.

Solving Basic Algebra Problems

The basic algebra problems in the arithmetic reasoning section of the exam will present you with a word problem that contains a series of variables and/or numbers. These problems usually appear to be much more difficult than they actually are because most people find variables to be confusing. However, there are a couple of techniques that you can use to solve these problems without too much difficulty.

First, if you are having difficulty understanding the problem because of the variables, one method that you may want to use is to replace each variable with a number. For example, you might be presented with a problem such as "Jay is having a barbecue with x people. If Jay needs to purchase y hamburgers for every z people, how many hamburgers will Jay need to purchase?" This question may look confusing because it uses letters instead of numbers to represent each amount, but you can make this problem much less confusing by plugging numbers into the problem. For instance, you may decide that x = 10, y = 5, and z = 2. This means that Jay is having a barbecue with 10 people, and he needs to purchase 5 hamburgers for every 2 people. As a result, the number of hamburgers Jay would need to purchase is equal to the number of people coming (10) divided by the number of people per group of burgers (2) times the number of hamburgers each group of people needs (5) or 10 / 2 * 5. In order to determine the answer to the original problem, you just need to plug the variables back into the formula that you used to solve the problem. As a result, the correct answer for this particular problem would be that the number of hamburgers Jay's needs to purchase is equal to $x / z * y$.

It is important to note, however, that this method will only work if you plug in the same number that you have chosen for a particular variable every time that variable shows up in a formula or shows up in the problem. For example, if you have a formula such as y = (x + x) / (z + z) and you decide that x = 10, y = 5, and z = 2, each *x* in the equation must be equal to 10 and each *z* in the equation must be equal to 2. This means that the equation must be 5 = (10 + 10) / (2 + 2) if you plug these numbers into the equation. If you do not consistently plug the same number in for the same variable, you will not be able to determine the correct answer. For example, plugging different numbers in the place of each x or z as would be the case if 5 = (10 + 5) / (2 + 4) will not yield the correct answer.

Another method that you can use to solve a basic algebra problem is to place the variables into an equation based on how they are described in the problem. For example, you may be presented with the same problem that was mentioned above that stated "Jay is having a barbecue with *x* people. If Jay needs to purchase *y* hamburgers for every *z* people, how many hamburgers will Jay need to purchase?" You would then take the variables from that problem and place them into an equation based on the phrases or words that describe each variable. This means that if *x* people are coming, and Jay needs to purchase *y* hamburgers for every *z* people, you can write the equation as y / z * x because the words "for every" between the *y* hamburgers and the *z* people signify that you can divide the two variables to determine how many hamburgers each person needs. Since there are *x* people attending the barbecue, you can then multiply the number of people attending by the number of hamburgers each person needs in order to determine the total number of hamburgers that Jay needs to purchase. This means that the number of hamburgers Jay needs to purchase is equal to y / z * x.

You may have noticed that the formula from the second method is set up differently from the formula that was determined using the first method. This is because it is possible for the same algebraic equation to be written in several different ways. This means that you may need to choose an option that has a formula similar to the formula that you determined using one of these methods or another similar method. In order to double-check whether a formula is similar or not, you may want to plug numbers into your equation and into the option that you believe is correct. If your equation and the option end up with the same answer when you plug in the same numbers for the variables, then that option is probably the correct answer. For example, if you take the equations that were determined using the two different methods that were mentioned above "x / z * y" and "y / z * x" and you establish that x = 10, y = 5, and z = 2, then the first equation becomes 10 / 2 * 5 or 25, and the second equation becomes 5 / 2 * 10 or 25. Since both equations equal the same amount when the same numbers are plugged into each equation, the two equations should continue to arrive at the same answer even though they are written differently.

Going the Distance

The distance problems in the arithmetic reasoning section of the exam will present you with a word problem that contains information about the distance that needs to be traveled, the rate at which an individual or vehicle is traveling, and/or the period of time that an individual spends traveling. Each of these questions will ask you to find the distance traveled, the fuel required, the rate at which something traveled, or the time that it would take to travel a certain distance. Many people consider these questions to be the most confusing questions in the arithmetic reasoning section of the exam because each question takes a relatively simple concept and writes it in a way that seems incredibly complicated. In fact, even though you may not realize it, you have probably seen or heard about a distance problem before. This is because the famous word problem that begins "Two trains, one from City A and one from City B are traveling in the same direction" is actually a distance problem that is typically used in movies, literature, and other popular culture as an example of an incredibly difficult problem on an exam. However, even though these problems are stereotypically seen as difficult to solve, they can actually be much easier to solve than they seem as long as you know how to approach them.

- 50 -

One Individual or Vehicle

First, if you need to find the time that it will take an individual or a vehicle to travel a certain distance, you can determine the answer by using the formula time = distance / rate or $t = d / r$. In other words, the time it takes to travel a certain distance is equal to the distance divided by the rate. For example, you might be presented with the problem "A train from Boston needs to travel 225 miles to reach New York. How long will it take the train to reach New York if the train is traveling at 75 miles per hour?" The correct answer to this problem would be 3 hours because the time it would take the train to travel to New York is equal to the distance that needs to be traveled (225 miles) divided by the rate at which the train is traveling (75 miles per hour.) Therefore, the time it would take the train to reach New York is equal to 225 miles / 75 mph or 3 hours.

Second, if you need to find the rate at which an individual or vehicle must travel to travel a certain distance in a certain amount of time, you can determine the answer by using the formula rate = distance / time or $r = d / t$. In other words, the rate at which an individual or vehicle must be traveling is equal to the distance that the individual or vehicle must travel divided by the time that the individual or vehicle spent traveling. For instance, you might be presented with a problem similar to the example above except that this problem states "A train from Boston needs to travel 225 miles to reach New York. How fast must the train travel to reach New York in 5 hours?" The correct answer to this problem is 45 mph because the rate at which the train must travel to reach New York in 5 hours is equal to the distance that needs to be traveled (225 miles) divided by the time that the train spent traveling (5 hours.) As a result, the train was traveling at a speed equal to 225 miles / 5 hours or 45 mph.

Third, if you need to find the distance that a particular individual or vehicle traveled in a specific amount of time, you can determine the answer by using the formula distance = rate * time or $d = r * t$. In other words, the distance that an individual or vehicle can travel in a specific amount of time is equal to the rate at which the individual or vehicle was traveling multiplied by the time that the vehicle spent traveling. For example, you might be presented with a problem such as "A train from Boston is heading towards New York at 50 mph. How far will the train travel in 4 ½ hours?" The correct answer is 225 miles because the distance that the train can travel in 4 ½ hours is equal to rate at which the train is traveling (50 mph) multiplied by the time the train has spent traveling (4 ½ hours.) This means that the distance the train traveled is equal to 50 mph * 4.5 hours or 225 miles.

Fourth, if you need to find the distance that a vehicle can travel with a certain amount of fuel, the rate of fuel consumption for a particular vehicle, or the amount of fuel it will take to travel a certain distance, you can determine the answer by using the appropriate formula from above with the rate of fuel consumption as the r in the formula, the t as the number of gallons, and the distance traveled as the d. This means that you can determine the distance that can be traveled with a certain amount of fuel by using the formula distance traveled = rate of consumption * number of gallons or $d = r * t$, or you can determine the rate of fuel consumption by using the formula rate of fuel consumption = distance traveled / number of gallons used or $r = d / t$. You can also determine the amount of gas that will be consumed if a vehicle travels a certain distance by using the formula number of gallons required = distance traveled / rate of consumption or $t = d / r$.

For example, you might be presented with the problem "If a train can travel approximately 15 miles using a single gallon of gasoline, how far will the train be able to travel with 5 gallons of gasoline?" In order to determine the answer to this problem, you need to use the formula for distance, which is $d = r * t$. This means that the train can travel 15 mpg * 5 gallons or 75 miles. Another example of a fuel problem would be a problem that stated "If a train can travel 125 miles on 5 gallons of gasoline, how many miles can the train travel per gallon?" In order to determine the answer to this problem, you need to use the formula $r = d / t$ because this is the formula that you need to use in order determine the rate of consumption. In other words, the train's rate of fuel consumption is equal to 125 divided by 5 or 25 mpg.

By this point, you have probably realized that each of the distance problems on the exam will require you to use one of three different formulas. However, what you may have not realized yet is that in order to use any of these formulas the individuals or vehicles involved must be traveling at a constant rate or using fuel at a constant rate. This is because each of these formulas is only designed to include a single rate of travel or fuel consumption. Since this is the case, and these formulas will not work with individuals or vehicles that change speeds, you may be wondering "what do I do if I have a problem that has an individual or vehicle that starts out at one speed, but that speeds changes as the individual or vehicle continues to travel?"

This type of problem is where the average rate of travel comes into play because any problem in which the speeds are not constant will usually ask you to determine the average rate at which an individual or vehicle is traveling. This type of problem is actually very simple to solve if the individual spent the same amount of time traveling at each rate. This is because you can determine the average rate of travel by adding all of the rates that the individual or vehicle travels at together and dividing that number by the number of different rates. For example, you might be presented with the problem "A train from Boston heading for New York travels at 45 mph for the first hour, 55 mph for the second hour, and 65 mph for the third hour. What is the train's average speed?" The answer to this question is 55 mph because the average rate of travel for the train from Boston is equal to the speed it traveled at for the first hour (45 mph) plus the speed it traveled at for the second hour (55 mph) plus the speed it traveled at for the third hour (65 mph) divided by the number of different rates (3), or in other words, 45 mph + 55 mph + 65 mph = 165 mph and 165 mph / 3 rates = 55 mph.

Unfortunately, this method will only work if the individual or vehicle spent the same amount of time traveling at each rate. If the individual or vehicle spent a different amount of time traveling at each rate, you will have to find the time that the individual or vehicle spent traveling at each rate before you can find the average rate of travel. For example, a problem might state "A train traveled from Boston to New York at a speed of 50 mph and then traveled from New York to the station it had left from in Boston on the same track at a speed of 75 mph. What was the train's average speed for the entire trip?" Since the train is traveling the same distance at two different speeds, it is safe to assume that the time the train spent traveling in each direction is different. This is because it must have taken the train longer to go from the station in Boston to the station in New York at a speed of 50 mph than it did for the train to go from New York back to the same station in Boston at a speed of 75 mph.

In order to determine the time it took for each speed, you can make up a distance that is easy to work with and divide that distance by the speed. For instance, if you chose a distance of 150 miles, it would have taken the train 3 hours (150 miles / 50 mph) to complete the first part of the trip and 2 hours (150 miles / 75 mph) to complete the second part of the trip. Once you have determined the time it would take the train to travel the distance you chose, you can determine the average rate of travel by taking the total distance traveled and dividing that by the total number of hours spent traveling. This means that for this particular example, the average speed of the train for the entire roundtrip is equal to 300 miles (150 miles + 150 miles) divided by 5 hours (3 hours + 2 hours) or 60 mph (300 miles / 5 hours.) It is important to note that the specific distance that you use in order to solve the problem doesn't really matter as any distance will provide the correct answer.

However, certain distances will be easier to use than others because certain distances will give you the exact answer while others will require you to approximate.

It is also important to note that some of these problems on the exam may actually provide you with different rates, different times, **and** different distances. In order to solve a problem that provides you with different distances and different rates, you can use a method very similar to the above method except that you must use the distances provided by the problem instead of using a made-up distance. For example, you might see a problem that states "A train experiencing major engine problems traveled 150 miles at 75 miles per hour, 100 miles at 50 miles per hour, and 150 miles at 37.5 miles per hour before it finally reached its destination. What was the average speed of the damaged train?" In order to determine the time it took the train to travel each distance at each speed, you need to divide each distance by the speed. This means that it took the train 2 hours (150 miles / 75 mph) to travel the first 150 miles, 2 hours (100 / 50 miles) to travel the next 100 miles, and 4 hours (150 miles / 37.5 mph) to travel the last 150 miles. Once you have determined the time that was spent traveling at each rate, you can determine the average rate of travel by taking the total distance traveled and dividing that by the total number of hours spent traveling. This means that for this particular example, the average speed of the damaged train for the entire trip is equal to 400 (150 miles + 100 miles + 75 miles) divided by 8 hours (2 hours + 2 hours + 4 hours) or 50 mph (400 miles / 8 hours.)

Two Individuals or Vehicles

Now, after looking at the formulas that were discussed above, you may be thinking "Alright, I get the idea. These problems are pretty simple, but the problems here aren't the same as that distance problem with the two trains that everyone is always talking about." Well, if you are thinking this, you're absolutely right as these problems aren't exactly the same as the type of distance problem that everyone usually uses as an example of a truly difficult problem. However, these problems have more in common with the "two trains traveling towards each other" problem than you might think as the hardest part of solving a distance problem is actually determining what you need to do with each of the numbers. This is why the two trains traveling at different speeds causes so many problems as the speed of the second train is an additional number in the problem that tends to confuse people.

Nevertheless, these problems are actually much simpler than they seem. This is because all you need to do in order to solve a problem with two trains traveling towards each other is to add their speeds together before you calculate the time. For example, you might be presented with a version of the familiar problem "A train from Boston and a train from New York have just started traveling towards each other from the ends of the same 225-mile track. If the train from Boston is traveling at a speed of 30 miles per hour, and the train from New York is traveling at a speed of 45 mph, how long will it take for the two trains to meet?" In order to determine the answer to this problem, you need to use the formula $t = d / r$ because this is the formula that you need to use to determine the time it takes to travel a certain distance. However, as you have probably noticed, there are two trains traveling at two different speeds, so you need to do something about the two different rates in order to use this formula, but what do you do with the two rates?

The answer is that, as long as the two trains are heading towards each other, you combine the two rates. This is because the speed at which two individuals or vehicles are traveling towards each other is in effect equal to the sum of the two individuals' or vehicles' speeds. In other words, you can determine the speed at which two individuals or vehicles are approaching each other by adding the speed of the first individual or vehicle to the speed of the second individual or vehicle. This means that the rate at which the two trains are approaching each other can be determined by

- 53 -

adding the speed of the train from Boston (30 mph) to the speed of the train from New York (45 mph.) This will give you the rate at which the two trains are, in effect, traveling, so in order to find the time it would take the trains to meet, you need to divide the distance (225 miles) by the combined speed of the two trains (30 mph + 45 mph or 75 mph.) Therefore, it would take 3 hours for the two trains to meet (225 miles / 75 mph.)

As you can probably see from this example, these problems are actually much simpler than they appear at first glance because you can determine the time that it will take two individuals or vehicles traveling in the same direction to meet simply by dividing the distance by the combined speed of the two individuals or vehicles. However, there is another version of the famous train problem that you may be more familiar with that has the two trains traveling in *opposite directions*. This type of problem may sound incredibly confusing, but it is actually just as easy to answer as the problem with the trains going in the same direction. This is because all you need to do in order to solve a problem with two trains traveling in the opposite direction is to add their speeds together before you calculate the distance.

For example, you may be presented with another version of the famous train problem that states "Two trains, Train A and Train B, are leaving New York traveling in opposite directions. Train A is traveling at 50 mph and Train B is traveling at 75 mph. If both trains left New York at the same time, how far apart will the two trains be at the end of 4 hours?" In order to determine the answer to this problem, you need to use the formula $d = r * t$ because this problem is asking you to find the distance. You may have already noticed, however, that you have the same issue with this problem that you had with the problem with the two trains traveling in the same direction as there are two speeds and you need to have a single speed in order to solve the problem. Fortunately, you can use the same approach that you used in the other train problem because two individuals or vehicles traveling in the opposite direction are, in effect, covering a distance equal to the combination of their two speeds. This means that you can determine the speed at which they are moving apart by adding the speed of the first individual or vehicle to the speed of the second individual or vehicle. As a result, the trains are, in effect, traveling at a speed of 125 mph (50 mph + 75 mph), which means that the train could travel 125 mph * 4 hours or 500 miles.

As you can probably see from these two examples, these problems are actually relatively simple to solve. This is because you can solve these problems simply by adding the speeds of each individual or vehicle together and plugging that combined speed into the appropriate formula. This method will work if you need to determine the time it will take a pair of individuals or vehicles moving towards each other to travel a certain distance or if you need to determine the distance that a pair of individuals or vehicles moving away from each other can travel in a certain amount of time. Unfortunately, this method will not work if you have two individuals or vehicles that are traveling the same direction from the same starting point. That being said, what do you do if you have a problem in which an individual or vehicle is trying to catch up with another individual or vehicle that has a head start?

This type of problem, like many of the other distance problems on the exam, may appear to be overwhelming, but you can solve this problem simply by finding the distance that the faster individual makes up for each specific period of time. For example, you might be presented with a problem such as "The engineers of two trains from New York, Train A and Train B, have decided to have a race on two separate tracks heading in the same direction. Train A is older than Train B so Train A has been given a 2 hour head start. If train A is traveling at 30 mph and Train B is traveling at 50 mph, how long will it take Train B to catch up with train A?" In order to solve this problem, the first thing that you need to do is use the formula $d = r * t$ to determine how far Train A has traveled in 2 hours, which is 60 miles (30 mph * 2 hours.) This is the distance that Train B needs to

- 54 -

makeup. You then need to subtract the speed of the slower Train from the speed of the faster train, which for this particular problem gives you 20 mph (50 mph – 30 mph.) This is how much distance Train B makes up each hour. Finally, you need to divide the distance that Train A has traveled by the distance that Train B catches up each hour, which means that it will take 60 miles / 20 mph or 3 hours for Train B to catch up.

Earning Interest

The interest problems in the arithmetic reasoning section of the exam will present you with a word problem that identifies the amount of principal, the amount of interest, the interest rate, and/or the period of time in which a particular individual or business has paid or been paid interest. Each of these questions will then require you to determine the principal, interest, interest rate, or the time period for which the principal has been earning interest. The interest questions on the exam are usually relatively straightforward as most of these questions can be answered just by plugging the appropriate numbers into the appropriate formula. However, you will need to know how to calculate simple interest, compound interest, and the discounts associated with a promissory note that has been cashed before its maturity date in order to answer all of the interest questions that you may see on the exam. As a result, there are a number of formulas that you will need to keep in mind.

First, if you need to calculate the amount of interest that has been earned or the amount of interest that an individual or business will earn, you can determine the answer to the problem by using the formula interest = principal * interest rate * time or $I = p * r * t$. However, there are actually two different types of interest that the exam may ask you to calculate so you need to know how to put this formula to use. The first type of interest that you may be asked to find is known as simple interest. Simple interest, as the name suggests, is relatively simple to calculate as you only need to plug the numbers from the problem into the equation.

For example, you might be presented with the problem "Becky deposited $600 into an investment account that earns 2.5% on the original principal annually. How much interest will Becky earn in 3 years?" In this particular case, this question is asking you to compute the simple interest because the problem states that the interest is calculated "on the original principal" and it does not state that the interest is compounded at any point. In order to determine the answer to this problem, you simply need to plug each of the numbers from the problem into the formula

$I = p * r * t$. Therefore, the amount of interest that Becky will earn in 3 years is equal to $600 * .025 * 3 years or $45.

The second type of interest that you may be asked to find is known as compound interest. Compound interest is a little more complicated to calculate than simple interest as compound interest adds the interest earned from the previous period to the principal and then calculates the interest for the next period based on the new principal amount. For example, you might be presented with the problem "Becky deposited $600 into a savings account that earns 2.5% compounded annually. How much will be in Becky's savings account after 3 years?" In this particular case, this question is asking you to determine the compound interest because the problem states that the interest is "compounded annually." In order to determine the compound interest, you must determine how much interest is earned during the first interest period by using the formula $I = p * r * t$. For this particular example, the amount of interest for the first period would be equal to $600 * .025 * 1 year or $15. Once you have determined the interest for the first interest period, you must then add the interest from the first period to the principal and use that principal to calculate the interest for the second interest period. This means that the interest on

- 55 -

Becky's account for the second period would be equal to ($600 + $15) * .025 * 1 or 15.375. You must then continue this process until you have calculated the interest for each period that occurs during the length of time described in the problem, which in this case is 3 periods because each period is a yearlong (compounded annually) and you are trying to determine the amount of interest for three years. As a result, the interest for the final period is equal to ($615 + $15.375) * .025 * 1 or 15.759, which means that the account will contain $630.375 + 15.759 or $646.13 (Rounded to the nearest cent) after 3 years.

It is important to note that some of the questions on the exam may ask you to take a problem like the example above one step further and determine the compound interest rather than the total amount in the account or investment. If you need to determine the amount of compound interest that will be earned by the end of a certain length of time rather than the total amount in a compounding account after a certain length of time, you need to calculate the total amount that would be in the account at the end of the time period and subtract the principle. For instance, if you look at the example presented in the above paragraph, Becky's account actually contained $646.13 at the end of the 3-year period. In order to determine the amount of interest that was earned, you simply need to subtract the principal ($600.00) from the amount in the account ($646.13), which means that Becky's account earned $46.13 in interest (646.13 - $600.00.)

Second, if you need to calculate the interest rate at which a certain amount of money must be invested to earn a certain amount of interest in a certain time period, you can determine the answer to the problem by using the formula rate = Interest / principal * time or $r = I / p * t$. For example, you might be presented with a problem such as "Bill is planning on placing $5000.00 into a savings account to save up for college. If Bill wants to earn $150 over the next 2 ½ years, what interest rate must the savings account have?" In order to determine the answer to this problem, you need to divide the amount of interest ($150.00) by the principal ($5,000) multiplied by the time (2 ½ years.) Therefore, the savings account must have an interest rate equal to $150.00 / $5000 * 2.5 years, which is equal to .075 or 7.5%.

Third, if you need to calculate the amount of money that must be invested to earn a certain amount of interest, or in other words the principal, you can determine the answer to the problem by using the formula principal = Interest / rate * time or $p = I / r * t$. For example, you might be presented with a problem such as "Bill is looking at an investment account that is expected to earn 5% annually. If Bill decides to invest in this account, how much money will he need to invest to earn $70.00 in 3 ½ years?" In order to determine the amount of principal for this particular example, you need to divide the amount of interest ($70.00) by the rate (5%) multiplied by the time (3 ½ years.) This means that Bill will have to invest $70.00 / .05 * 3.5 years or $400.00 in order to earn $70.00 in interest from the account after 3 ½ years.

Fourth, if you need to determine the amount of time for which a specific amount of money needs to be invested in order to earn a certain amount of interest at a given rate, you can determine the answer to the problem by using the formula time = Interest / principal * time or $t = I / p * r$. For example, you might be presented with a problem such as "Bill is planning on investing $600.00 in an investment account that is expected to earn 5% annually. How long will it take for Bill's investment to earn $75.00 in interest?" In order to determine the length of time it will take $600.00 to earn $75.00 in interest, you need to divide the amount of interest ($75.00) by the principal ($600.00) multiplied by the rate (5%). This means that the money will have to remain in the account for a length of time equal to $75.00 / $600.00 * .05 or 2.5 years in order for the investment to earn $75 in interest.

Finally, some of the problems on the exam may ask you to determine the value of a promissory note that has been cashed before its maturity date. These questions are based on the fact that most promissory notes can be cashed at any time, but the promissory note will only be worth its full value on its maturity date. If a promissory note is cashed before its maturity date, the bank will assess a discount to the promissory note and pay the individual cashing the note the total value of the note minus the discount. In order to answer a question related to a promissory note, you will need to be able to calculate a bank discount.

If you encounter a problem where you need to calculate a bank discount, you can use the formula discount = principal * time remaining before the maturity date * discount rate or $D = p * t * r$. For example, you might see a problem on the exam that states "Becky has a $600 180-day promissory note that was written on April 29, 2007. If Becky cashes the promissory note on August 16, 2007 at a bank that charges a 5 ½ % discount rate on promissory notes, how much money will she receive?" In order to determine the amount that the promissory note is worth, you need to multiply the principal ($600.00) by the time remaining before the maturity date (April 29th to August 16th is 108 days so the time before the maturity date is 180 days – 108 days, which is equal to 72 days or 1/5 of a year) and multiply that by the discount rate (5.5%). This means that the discount that the bank is assessing to Becky's promissory note is equal to $600.00 * .2 * .055 or $6.60 and the promissory note is worth $600.00 - $6.60 or $593.40.

Important Note: You may have noticed that each of the examples related to the interest problems on the TEA exam discusses the time in terms of years and states that the interest is calculated every year, or in other words, calculated annually. This is because each interest formula requires the length of time to be described in years. However, some of the interest questions on the actual exam may describe the time using different terms, units, or different interest periods. If a question asks you to find the interest for a certain number of days or months, you must determine the percentage or fraction of a year that each number of days or months presented in the problem equals. For example, 3 months or 90 days is equal to ¼ of year, 6 months or 180 days is equal to ½ of a year, 9 months or 270 days is equal to ¾ of a year, and 12 months or 360 days is equal to 1 year.

Problems with Payroll

The payroll problems in the arithmetic reasoning section of the exam will present you with the number of hours an individual has worked, the standard rate that the individual is paid, the rate that the individual receives for overtime, and/or the rate that the individual receives for holidays or Sundays. Some of these questions may also provide you with information that you can use to determine the taxes or other fees that need to be withheld from a particular paycheck. Each of these questions will require you to determine the total amount that an individual will receive for a particular pay period before taxes, the taxes that need to be withheld from a particular paycheck, or the total amount that an individual will receive for a particular pay period after taxes. Most of the payroll questions on the exam will only require you to perform some simple multiplication, addition, and/or subtraction. However, you will need to know how to handle all of the different types of pay that an individual may receive and you will need to know how to read a withholding table in order to answer all of the payroll questions that may appear on the exam. This means that, since each type of pay is calculated differently, there are several things that you may want to keep in mind.

First, if a problem asks you to determine the amount that a particular individual earned during a specific period and that individual **is not entitled** to any special pay, you can determine the answer simply by multiplying the number of hours worked by the individual's hourly pay. For example, you might see a problem that states "Joe is paid on a biweekly basis and he worked 36 hours this

- 57 -

week and 40 hours last week. If Joe earns a standard hourly rate of $10.00, how much did Joe earn during this pay period?" In order to solve this problem, you simply need to multiply the number of hours worked during the period, which is 76 hours (40 + 36), by the hourly rate of $10.00. Therefore, the answer is that Joe earned $760.00 during the period.

Second, if a problem asks you to determine the amount that a particular individual earned during a specific period and that individual **is entitled** to special pay, you must determine the number of hours for which the individual should receive special pay and the number of hours for which the individual should receive his or her standard pay. For example, you might see a problem that states "Joe works for a computer company that pays on a weekly basis with a standard workweek consisting of 40 hours. Joe receives a standard rate of $12.00 per hour and time and a half for overtime. How much will Joe earn if he works 48 hours during a single week?" In order to solve this problem, you need to determine how many hours are considered to be standard time and how many hours are considered to be overtime by subtracting the number of hours in a standard workweek, which in this case is 40 hours, from the total number of hours that Joe worked, which in this case is 48 hours. In other words, the amount of overtime that Joe worked is equal to 48 hours – 40 hours of standard time or 8 hours.

You can then calculate the total amount that Joe earned from his standard pay by multiplying the number of hours Joe worked at standard time, which is 40 hours, by his standard rate of $12.00. This means that Joe earned $480 (40 hours * $12.00) from his standard pay during the period. After you have calculated the total amount that Joe earned from his standard pay, you can calculate the total amount that Joe earned from his overtime pay by multiplying his standard rate of $12.00 by his overtime rate, which is 1.5 times, by the number of overtime hours Joe worked, which is 8 hours. This means that Joe earned $144 ($12.00 * 1.5 times * 8 hours) from his overtime pay during the period. Once you have calculated both the standard pay and the overtime pay, you can then determine the total amount that the individual earned for the week by adding the individual's total overtime pay to the individual's total standard pay. This means that Joe earned a total of $624 ($480 + $144) for the work he performed during this particular workweek.

Third, if a problem asks you to determine the amount that a particular individual earned during a specific period and that individual is entitled to more than one type of special pay, you must determine the number of hours for which the individual should receive each type of special pay and the number of hours for which the individual should receive standard pay. For example, you might see a problem that states "Joe works for a computer company that pays on a weekly basis with a standard workweek consisting of 40 hours. Joe receives a standard rate of $12.00 per hour, time and a half for overtime, and double time for Sundays and holidays. If Joe worked 48 hours in a single week including 8 hours on a Sunday, how much would Joe earn for the entire week?" In order to solve this problem, you need to determine how many hours are considered standard time, how many hours are considered overtime, and how many hours are considered double time. If you are dealing with both overtime and holiday/Sunday double time, you can determine the overtime by subtracting the hours in a standard workweek (40 hours) from the total number of hours worked (48 hours.) You can then determine the *standard time* by subtracting the number of holiday or Sunday hours worked (8 hours) from the total number of hours worked at standard time (40 hours.) In other words, for this particular example, Joe worked 48 hours – 40 hours or 8 hours of overtime, the 8 hours of double time stated in the problem, and 40 hours – 8 hours or 32 hours of standard time.

You can then calculate the total amount that Joe earned from his standard pay by multiplying the number of hours considered to be standard time, which is 32 hours, by his standard rate of $12.00 per hour. This means that Joe earned $384 (32 hours * $12.00) from his standard pay for the week.

- 58 -

Once you have calculated the standard pay, you can calculate the overtime pay by multiplying Joe's standard rate of $12.00 by his overtime rate, which is 1.5 times, by the number of overtime hours Joe worked, which is 8 hours. This means that Joe earned $144 ($12.00 * 1.5 * 8 hours) from his overtime pay for the week. You can then calculate the double time pay by multiplying Joe's standard rate of $12.00 by 2 by the number of double time hours Joe worked, which means that Joe earned $192 ($12.00 * 2 * 8 hours) from his double time pay for the week. Once you have calculated the amount that the individual will receive from each different type of pay, you can determine the total amount that the individual earned for the week by adding all of the different types of pay together. This means that Joe earned a total of $720 ($384 + $144 + $192) for the work he performed during this particular workweek.

Fourth, some of the payroll problems on the exam will ask you to determine the pay for an individual who is paid on commission or an individual who receives a commission in addition to his or her salary. The commission pay that an individual is entitled to can be determined simply by multiplying the individual's sales by the commission rate that the individual receives. However, if you are asked to determine the amount that an individual earned for a specific period and that individual receives both a commission and a salary, you must determine the amount of commission pay that the individual earned, determine the salary that the individual earned, and add the commission pay to the salary in order to determine the individual's total pay.

For example, you might see a problem that states "Hailey receives $10.00 an hour and a 5% commission from the pet store where she works. A standard workweek at the pet store is considered to be 40 hours and the store pays time and a half for overtime. How much would Hailey earn if she made a total of $3,000 in sales during a week in which she worked 35 hours?" In order to solve this problem, you must determine the amount that the individual earned from his or her commission by multiplying the total value of the individual's sales for the week ($3,000) by the percentage that the individual earns from his or her commission (5%.) This means that Hailey earned $150 ($3,000 * .05) from her commission pay. You can then determine the standard pay that Hailey earned by multiplying the number of hours Hailey worked (35 hours) by her standard rate of $10.00 per hour, so Hailey earned $350 from her standard pay. Since Hailey did not work any overtime during this particular week, her total pay for the week is equal to $150 + $350 or $500.

It is also important to note that some of the problems on the exam may present you with more than one commission rate, so you will have to determine which sales are eligible for each rate. For example, you might see a problem that states "Sarah receives a $500 salary in addition to her commission each week. Sarah's commission is 5% for the first $1,000 worth of sales, 10% for sales between $1,001 to $3,000, and 15% for anything above $3,000. How much would Sarah earn during a week in which she made a total of $3,000 in sales?" In order to determine the answer to this problem, you must determine the amount of sales eligible for each rate. According to the problem, any amount under $1,001 is eligible for the 5% rate in this particular example, so the amount that is eligible for the 5% rate is $1,000 because Sarah made over $1,000 in sales. This means that Sarah earned $50 ($1,000 * .05) for the first $1,000 in sales. Any amount from $1,001 to $3,000 is eligible for the 10% rate in this particular example so you can determine the amount that is eligible for the 10% rate by taking the total number of sales or $3,000 (whichever is lower) and subtracting $1,000. This means that Sarah made $200 ($2,000 * .1) for the second $2,000 in sales. Any amount *over* $3,000 is eligible for the 15% rate, but Sarah didn't make any sales over $3,000 so there are no sales eligible for the highest commission rate in this particular example. As a result, the total amount that Sarah earned for the week is equal to her salary ($500) plus her commission at the first rate ($50) plus her commission at the second rate ($200) plus her commission at the last rate ($0) or $750.

Finally, some of the questions on the exam will ask you to determine the amount of a particular deduction or the total amount that an individual will earn for a specific period after all of the deductions have been taken out. In order to answer these questions, you will need to determine the amount that needs to be withheld for income taxes, the amount of Social Security Tax or FICA Tax that needs to be deducted, and/or the amount that needs to be deducted for insurance plans, pension plans, unions fees, and other similar fees and optional plans. If you need to determine the amount of income tax that needs to be withheld, you will be given a table that you can use to determine the correct withholding. For example, a problem might state "Sarah is paid on a weekly basis, and she made $750 this week. Based on the table below, how much income tax will be withheld from Sarah's check if she is single and claims 2 exemptions?"

You would then be provided with a withholding table (see example on following page). In order to determine the correct answer to this particular question, you simply need to find the correct line on the table. This means that the amount of income tax withheld from Sarah's check would be $78 because she made *at least* $750 for the week but *less than* $760, and she claimed two exemptions, which are also known as allowances.

Single Persons Paid Weekly

If the wages are –		And the number of withholding allowances claimed is –					
At least	But less than	0	1	2	3	4	5
700	710	95	80	70	60	50	40
710	720	97	81	71	62	52	42
720	730	100	83	73	63	53	43
730	740	102	85	74	64	54	44
740	750	105	87	76	66	56	46
750	760	107	90	77	68	58	48
760	770	109	94	79	69	59	49
770	780	111	96	80	70	60	50
780	790	114	98	82	71	61	51
790	800	116	101	84	74	64	54

If you need to determine the amount that needs to be deducted for the Social Security Tax, which is also known as the Federal Insurance Contribution Act Tax or FICA Tax, you will need to determine whether the individual has already reached the Social Security limit for the year or not. This is because the FICA Tax actually consists of a Social Security Tax and a Medicare Tax that are combined into one joint tax, and an individual only has to pay both parts of the FICA Tax before he or she earns a certain amount each year. As of 2008, the limit is $102,000, so you would need to determine if the individual has made over $102,000 for the year already or not. If the amount that the individual has made for the year totals less than $102,001, then you can determine the amount that will be deducted from the individual's check for the FICA Tax by multiplying the amount that the individual made for the week by the FICA Tax rate, which as of 2008 is 7.65%. If the amount that the individual has made for the year totals over $102,001, then you can determine the amount that will be deducted from the individual's check for the FICA Tax by multiplying the amount that the individual made for the week by the Medicare Tax, which as of 2008 is 1.45%.

If the amount that the individual has made for the week will bring the individual over the yearly Social Security limit, you must determine how much of that amount is earned before the limit and how much of that amount is earned after the limit. For example, you might see a problem that states "Sarah has made a total of $101,500 so far this year. Based on the FICA Tax for 2008, which consists of a 6.2% Social Security Tax that is assessed on all earnings equal to or less than $102,000 and a 1.45% Medicare Tax that is applied on all earnings, how much will be deducted from her check for the FICA Tax if she made $750 this week?" In order to solve this problem, you need to determine the amount that is below $102,001 and the amount that is over $102,000. You can determine the amount that is over a $102,000 by adding the amount that Sarah made this week to the total that she made for the year and subtracting $102,000 from that number. This means that Sarah *only* needs to pay the Medicare Tax on $101,500 + $750 - $102,000 or $250. You can then determine the amount on which Sarah needs to pay the full FICA Tax by subtracting the amount over $102,000 from the amount she made for the week, which means that Sarah must pay the full tax on $750 - $250 or $500. In order to determine the FICA Tax that will be deducted, you must multiply the full FICA Tax rate (7.65%) by the amount under $102,001 ($500) and add that amount to the Medicare Tax rate (1.45%) multiplied by the amount over $102,000 ($250.) In other words, the total amount deducted from Sarah's check for the FICA Tax would be .0765 * $500 + .0145 * $250 or $41.88 (rounded to the nearest cent.)

It is important to note that you will be given all of the necessary information related to the FICA Tax and the FICA tax limits if you are required to determine the amount that an individual must pay for the FICA Tax. In other words, you don't need to memorize the tax rates or tax limits in order to answer any of the questions on the exam because each problem will give you all of the information that is necessary to calculate the answer. It is also important to note that some of the questions related to the FICA tax may only require you to determine the tax before the tax limit or determine the total tax that an individual paid for the entire year rather than a week. As a result, the problems on the actual exam may be much simpler than the problem in the example above because some of the questions on the exam will not require you to calculate the Medicare tax. However, it is always a good idea to look at the information and the options that are provided so that you can try to determine what the question is looking for before you try to solve the problem.

If you need to determine the total amount that has been deducted from an individual's pay check for a particular pay period, the total amount that has been deducted for a particular deduction other than the FICA Tax or Income Tax, or the total amount that an individual will take home after deductions, you will be given the amount of each deduction or information about how each deduction is calculated. For example, you might see a problem that states "Matt receives a weekly salary of $775 before taxes and deductions. If $111 is withheld for federal taxes, $59.29 is deducted for the FICA Tax, $38.75 is withheld for state taxes, 5% of his gross pay is deducted for his Employee Stock Purchasing Program, and 10% of his gross pay is deducted for his 401K plan, what is Matt's weekly net pay?" The problem in this particular example may seem relatively complicated because it contains a lot of different numbers. However, this problem is actually relatively simple to solve as all you need to do in order to solve this problem is determine the amount deducted for the employee stock purchasing program, determine the amount deducted for the 401k plan, add all of the deductions together, and subtract the total deductions from Matt's weekly salary.

According to the information provided in the problem, the amount deducted for the employee stock purchasing program is equal to Matt's gross pay of $775 * 5% or $38.75. The amount deducted for Matt's 401k is equal to Matt's gross pay of $775 * 10% or $77.50. The total amount deducted from Matt's paycheck each week is therefore equal to $111 (Federal Income Taxes) + $59.29 (FICA Tax) + $38.75 (State Income Tax) + $38.75 (Employee Stock Purchasing Program) + $77.50 (401k) or $325.29. You can then determine the answer to the question in the problem by subtracting the total amount deducted each week, which is $325.29, from Matt's gross pay of $775, which means that Matt's weekly net pay is $449.71.

Is it a Profit or a Loss?

The profit and loss questions in the arithmetic reasoning section of the TEA Exam will present you with information related to the costs, the discounts offered, the prices, the profits, and/or the losses associated with the sale of a particular item. Each of these questions will then require you to determine the cost of the item, the amount of profit earned from selling the item, the amount lost from selling the item, the total discount applied to the price of an item, or the selling price of the item. In order to answer most of these questions you should only need to perform some simple addition, subtraction, multiplication, and/or division. However, you will need to use one of several different formulas in order to determine the correct answer to each problem.

Selling Price, Cost Price, Profit, and Loss

If a problem asks you to determine the amount of profit earned from the sale of a particular item or the amount lost from the sale of a particular item, you can determine the profit or loss by using the formula profit or loss = selling price – cost price. For example, you might see a problem that states "Jack purchased a book from a local bookstore for $5.00. After reading the book, Jack sold the book on the internet for $3.50. How much was Jack's profit or loss?" You can determine the answer to this problem by subtracting the price Jack **purchased** the book for, which is known as the cost price, from the price Jack **sold** the book for, which is known as the selling price. Jack sold the book for $3.50 and purchased the book for $5.00, which means that Jack lost $3.50 - $5.00 or $1.50. This is considered a loss because Jack paid more to purchase the book than he earned from selling the book. If, on the other hand, Jack had purchased the book for $3.50 and sold it for $5.00, Jack would have made a profit of $5.00 - $3.50 or $1.50 because he earned more from selling the book than he paid to purchase the book. In other words, if you subtract the cost of the item from the price that the item is sold at and the answer is negative, it is considered a loss. If, on the other hand, you subtract the cost from the price of the item and the answer is positive, it is considered a profit.

With this all in mind, it is important to note that you may see a question on the exam that asks you to determine the profit or loss as a percentage instead of a specific amount of money. In other words, some of the profit and loss questions on the exam will ask you to determine the percentage of profit or the percentage of loss associated with the sale of a particular item instead of the specific amount of money gained or the specific amount of money lost from selling that item. This type of question takes the process above one step further and asks you to determine the percentage gained or the percentage lost based on either the selling price or the cost price.

If a question asks you to determine the percentage of the cost gained (percentage of profit) or the percentage of the cost lost (percentage of loss), you can determine the answer by dividing the amount gained or the amount lost by the cost. For example, you might see a modified version of the problem from the above paragraph that states "Jack purchased a book from a local bookstore for $5.00. If Jack sold the book on the internet for $3.50 after reading it, what percentage of the cost did Jack lose?" In order to solve this problem, you need to find the amount that Jack lost, which as you know from the example above is $1.50 ($3.50 - $5.00), and divide it by the cost. This means that the percentage of the cost lost on the sale of the book is equal to $1.50 / $5.00, which is equal to .03 or 30%.

If a question asks you to determine the percentage of the selling price gained or the percentage of the selling price lost, you can determine the answer by dividing the amount gained or the amount lost by the selling price. For example, you might see another version of the problem from the paragraph above that states "Jack purchased a book from a local bookstore for $5.00. If Jack sold the book on the internet for $3.50 after reading it, what percentage of the selling price did Jack lose?" In order to determine the answer to this question, you must take the amount that Jack lost, which is $1.50 ($3.50 - $5.00), and divide it by the price that the item sold for. This means that the percentage of the selling price lost on the sale of the book is equal to $1.50 / $3.50, which is equal to 42.86% (rounded to nearest hundredth.)

Some of the profit and loss problems on the exam may provide you with the profit or loss and ask you to determine the selling price or the cost price. If a problem asks you to determine the selling price, you can solve the problem by using the formula selling price = cost price + profit or loss. For example, you might see a problem on the exam that states "Jill just purchased a used car for $2,000 that she plans to fix up and sell. How much will Jill have to sell the car for in order to make a $3000 profit? This problem is asking you to determine the price that Jill would need to sell the car for to make a $3,000 profit, so you need to add the amount of profit that Jill wants to make to the amount that Jill had to pay to purchase the car. This means that the amount that Jill must sell her car for in order to earn a $3,000 profit is equal to the cost of purchasing the car ($2,000) plus the amount of profit Jill needs to earn ($3,000) or $5,000.

If a problem asks you to determine the cost price, you can solve the problem by using the formula cost price = selling price – profit if the vendor earned a profit from the sale of the item or the formula cost price = selling price + loss if the vendor incurred a loss. For example, you might see a problem on the exam that states "Jill just sold a used car for $5,000. If Jill lost $2,000 when she sold the car, how much did Jill originally pay for the car?" This problem is asking you to determine the cost price that Jill originally paid to purchase the car, so you need to add the price that she sold the car for to the amount that she lost from selling the car. This means that the amount that Jill originally paid to purchase the car is equal to the price that she sold the car for ($5,000) plus the amount that she lost from selling the car ($2,000) or $7,000. However, if Jill had made a profit instead of incurring a loss, you would need to subtract the profit from the selling price instead of adding it to the selling price, which means that the amount Jill must have paid to purchase the car is equal to $5,000 - $2,000 or $3,000.

Now, after looking at these examples, you may have noticed that the selling price and cost price questions are pretty easy to answer. However, it is important to realize that you may see some questions on the exam that add an extra component to the problem by providing you with the percentage of profit or the percentage of loss rather than the dollar amount of a specific profit or loss. In order to solve these problems, you will have to determine the dollar amount of the profit or loss from the percentage that the problem gives you. If a question presents you with the percentage of the cost price gained or the percentage of the cost price lost and asks you to determine the selling price, you can determine the answer by using the formula selling price = cost price + cost price * percentage of profit if the vendor earned a profit or the formula selling price = cost price - cost price * percentage of loss if the vendor incurred a loss.

For example, you might see a question on the exam that states "The owner of a toy store just purchased 15 new action figures for $5.00 each. How much would the toy store owner have to sell each toy for to make a profit of 50% of the cost price?" This question is asking you to determine how much the store owner would have to sell each toy for, so you need to use the formula to determine the selling price with a percentage of profit related to the cost, which is selling price = cost price + cost price * percentage of profit. This means that the store owner would have to sell each action figure for $5.00 + .5 * $5.00, which is equal to $5.00 + $2.50 or $7.50.

- 63 -

If a question presents you with the percentage of the selling price gained or the percentage of the selling price lost and asks you to determine the cost price, you can determine the answer by using the formula cost price = selling price + selling price * percentage of loss if the vendor incurred a loss or the formula cost price = selling price – selling price * percentage of profit if the vendor earned a profit. For example, you might see a modified version of the question from the above paragraph that states "The owner of a toy store just sold 15 new action figures for $7.50 each. How much did the toys originally cost if the toy store owner made a profit of 50% of the selling price on each toy?" This question is asking you to determine how much the toy store owner paid to acquire each toy in the first place, so you need to use the formula to determine the cost price with a percentage of profit related to the selling price, which is cost price = selling price – selling price * percentage of profit. This means that the owner of the toy store would have to purchase each action figure for $7.50 - .5 * $7.50, which is equal to $3.75.

As you can see from the examples above, answering each of these questions is usually just a matter of multiplying and adding the numbers presented in the problem. However, you may see a question on the exam that asks you to find the cost price using a percentage of profit related to the cost price or find the selling price using a percentage of profit related to the selling price. These types of questions are usually slightly more complicated than the other profit and loss questions on the exam because some of the numbers that you need to use aren't stated in the problem outright. Nevertheless, you can determine the answer to these problems without too much difficulty as long as you are dealing with a profit. In order to solve these problems, you will need to determine the percentage of the profit that the selling price or cost price represents.

If a problem presents you with the percentage of the cost price gained and the question asks you to determine the cost price, you can solve the problem by using the formula cost price = selling price / (percentage of profit + 100%.) For example, you might see a problem on the exam that states "The owner of a toy store just sold 15 new action figures for $7.50 each. How much did the toys originally cost if the toy store owner made a profit of 50% of the cost price on each toy?" This question is asking you to determine the price that the toy store owner paid to acquire each toy, so you need to use the formula to determine the cost price using a percentage of profit related to the cost price, which is cost price = selling price / (percentage of profit + 100%.) This means that the toy store owner would have to purchase each toy for $7.50 / (50% + 100%), which is equal to $7.50 / 1.5 or $5.00.

If a problem presents you with the percentage of the selling price gained and the question asks you to determine the selling price, you can solve the problem by using the formula selling price = cost price / (100% - percentage of profit.) For example, you might see a problem on the exam that states "The owner of a toy store just purchased 15 action figures for $2.50 each. How much would the store owner have to sell each toy for to make a profit of 50% of the selling price?" This question is asking you to determine the price that the toy store owner would have to sell each toy for, so you need to use the formula to determine the selling price using a percentage of profit related to the selling price, which is selling price = cost price / (100% - percentage of profit.) This means that the toy store owner would have to sell each toy for $2.50 / (100% - 50%), which is equal to $2.50 / .5 or $5.00.

After reading the information above, you may be thinking "Alright, these questions are relatively straightforward if you need to find the cost price with the percentage of profit related to the cost price or if you need to find the selling price with the percentage of profit related to the selling price, but what do you do if you have a question that asks you to find the cost price with the percentage of loss related to the cost price or a question that asks you to find the selling price using the percentage of loss related to the selling price?" The answer is, as far as the TEA Exam is concerned,

- 64 -

that you probably won't need to. This is because the profit and loss questions that *typically* appear on the TEA Exam will not ask you to determine the cost price with the percentage of loss related to the cost price or the selling price with the percentage of loss related to the selling price. However, if you happen to come across a question that doesn't appear to be "typical," you can determine the cost price using the percentage of the cost price lost with the formula cost price = selling price - percentage of loss * selling price. If you encounter an atypical question where you need to determine the selling price with the percentage of the selling price lost, you can use the formula selling price = cost price / (100% + percentage of profit) to solve the problem.

Discounts

In addition to the profit and loss questions that ask you to determine the profit, loss, cost price, or selling price, you may see a question on the exam that asks you to determine the total discount applied to a particular item. These questions will present you with the list price and a single discount rate or a group of discount rates that you must apply to the list price in order to determine the total discount or the selling price of the item after all the discounts have been applied. If you are given a single discount and you need to find the total discount applied and/or the selling price, you can determine the answer to the problem by using the formula Discount = list price * discount rate or $D = l * r$. For example, there might be a problem on the exam that states "An electronics store that offers a 10% discount to members of their preferred buyer's club is selling a brand new computer that is listed at $650.00. How much would a member of the store's preferred buyer's club have to pay for the new computer?" This question is asking you to find the selling price after all of the discounts have been applied so you will need to use the formula $D = l * r$ to find the discount and subtract that amount from the list price. This means that the total discount that a member of the store's preferred buyer's club will receive is equal to $650.00 * 10%, which is equal to $650.00 * .1 or $65. Since this particular question is asking for the selling price after the discounts have been applied, you can then determine the answer to the question by subtracting the discount ($65) from the list price ($650.00), so the price that a member of the preferred buyer's club would have to pay to purchase the new computer is $585.00.

If you are given a group of discounts and you need to find the total discount applied and/or the selling price, you can determine the answer to the problem by using the formula to find a single discount for each discount rate. You can then add the discount applied for each discount rate together to determine the total discount. For example, you might see a variation of the example in the above paragraph that states "An electronics store is selling a brand new computer listed at $650.00 with a number of different discounts available. The discounts that the store is offering for this particular computer include a 20% off sale, a 10% discount to members of the store's preferred buyer's club, and a 5% manufacturer's discount. If an individual was a member of the store's preferred buyer's club and was eligible to receive all three discounts, how much would that individual have to pay for the new computer?" This question is asking you to find the selling price after all of the discounts have been applied, so you will need to use the formula $D = l * r$ to find the discount at each discount rate, add each of the discounts together, and subtract the total discount from the list price. This means that the total discount that a member of the store's preferred buyer's club will receive is equal to $650.00 * 20% + $650.00 * 10% + $650.00 * 5%, which is equal to $650.00 * .2 + $650.00 * .1 + $650.00 * .05 or $130 + $65 + $32.50 or $227.50. Since this question is asking for the selling price after the discounts have been applied, you can determine the answer to the question by subtracting the total discount ($227.50) from the list price ($650.00), so the price that a member of the store's preferred buyer's club would have to pay to purchase the new computer is $422.50.

- 65 -

Important Note: If you've carefully read all of the information above, you may have noticed that a loss is actually a negative number. However, all of the formulas described in this section are designed to deal with a loss in terms of a positive number. As a result, you will only need to be concerned with whether a number is negative or not when you are attempting to determine whether an individual incurred a loss or made a profit. This means that you should ignore the negative sign when you are plugging a loss into the formula to find the cost price or the selling price.

Is This Proportional to That?

The proportion questions in the arithmetic reasoning section of the TEA Exam will present you with a word problem that identifies a specific ratio, or in other words, a specific relationship between two different amounts in the problem. Each of these questions will then require you to find a ratio that is equal to the ratio presented. In other words, these questions are written in the format if this amount is equal to that amount, then how much is this amount equal to? These questions are usually written in a relatively straightforward way, so they are typically less confusing than some of the other questions in the arithmetic reasoning section of the exam. However, these questions can still be tricky because it is very easy to setup an equation incorrectly, which makes it much easier for you to make a mistake and arrive at the wrong answer. As a result, there are several things that you should keep in mind when you are attempting to answer one of the proportion questions on the exam.

First, it is important to have a basic idea of the different ways that a proportion can be written. This is important because you may see a proportion written in one of several different formats on the exam, and you won't be able to answer a proportion question if you don't understand what the question is trying to say. Therefore, you may want to keep the three different ways of writing a proportion in mind. The first way that you may see a proportion written on the exam is in the format $x:y = a:b$. For example, you might see a proportion written on the exam as $3:6 = 4:8$. The second way to write a proportion is in the format $x/y = a/b$. For example, you might see the proportion above written as $3/6 = 4/8$. The final way of writing a proportion is in the format x is to y as a is to b. For example, you might see the proportion above written on the exam as 3 is to 6 as 4 is to 8. With these three formats being stated, it is important to note that most of the proportions questions on the exam will be written in the format x is to y as a is to b. However, it is still important to be able to recognize the other formats as well as you may see the other formats on the exam.

Second, almost all of the proportion questions on the exam will present you with three numbers that belong in a specific proportion, and you will be asked to find the fourth number. The most important thing to remember about this type of question, or any other type of proportion question on the exam for that matter, is that you must write the proportion correctly in order to determine the correct answer. This is because each of these problems can be solved through some simple multiplication and/or division if you know which numbers to multiply and/or divide. Unfortunately, it is very easy to end up using the wrong number in your multiplication or division if you don't have the proportion setup correctly. As a result, you must make sure that you place each number from the problem into the correct part of the proportion.

The best way to ensure that you set up a proportion correctly is to look at the information presented in the problem and write the proportion in the format $x/y = a/b$ so that the first amount stated in the problem is written as the top of the first ratio and the amount that is directly related to that amount is written as the top of the second ratio. For example, you might see a problem on the exam that states "The manager of a small pharmacy needs to order 2 boxes of plastic bags for every

50 customers that are expected to make a purchase. How many boxes should the manager order if the pharmacy expects 250 customers to make purchases?" You would then set up the proportion so that the 2 boxes are written as the top of the first ratio and the 50 customers are written as the top of the second ratio. Once you have established the placement of the first two numbers, you can place the third number under the number that is described in the same units. In other words, in this particular example, you can place the 250 customers below the 50 customers because they are both describing the number of customers involved. This means that the ratio should be written as $2/y = 50/250$, and y represents the number of customers that you need to find.

Finally, in order to solve any of the proportion problems on the exam, you will need to know what should be multiplied and what should be divided. This is because answering each of these questions is simply a matter of multiplying and dividing the appropriate numbers. However, it may be extremely difficult to determine which numbers should be multiplied if you don't understand how to solve the proportion that you have written. This is especially true if you have set up the proportion incorrectly as it will be impossible to multiply the correct numbers if the numbers are not written in the right locations. As a result, it is essential for you to be able to write the proportion correctly, identify the numbers that should be multiplied, and identify the number that you should divide the product of those two numbers by in order for you to find the correct answer.

This means that in order for you solve the problem correctly you should multiply one of the numbers in the equation by the number diagonally opposite it. You should then divide the number you arrive at by the third number in the proportion. For instance, if you take the example above that states "The manager of a small pharmacy needs to order 2 boxes of plastic bags for every 50 customers that are expected to make a purchase. How many boxes should the manager order if the pharmacy expects 250 customers to make purchases?" you know that the proportion in the problem can be written as $2/y = 50/250$. You also know from the question presented in the problem that you are attempting to find the amount that the y in the formula represents. In order to solve this particular problem, you need to multiply the 2 boxes by the 250 customers and divide by 50. Therefore, the manager of the pharmacy would have to order 250 customers * 2 boxes / 50 boxes or 10 boxes in order to make sure that there were enough bags for 250 customers.

If this process seems confusing, try writing the equation from the above example on a piece of paper with the 2 over the y and the 50 over the 250. The number at the top of the first ratio, which is the number 2, and the number at the bottom of the second ratio, which is the number 250, are diagonally opposite each other, so you should multiply them. Then, since you don't know what y represents until you solve the problem, there is only one other number in the proportion that you can use, which is the 50 at the top of the second ratio, so that is the number you divide by in order to determine the answer.

Ratio Ready

The ratio questions in the arithmetic reasoning section of the TEA Exam are very similar to the proportion questions in the arithmetic reasoning section of the exam as each ratio question will provide you with a word problem that identifies a specific ratio. However, each of these questions will ask you to simplify the ratio presented in the problem or determine how a specific amount should be split based on the ratio presented in the problem instead of asking you to identify a specific ratio that is equal to another ratio. These questions usually appear to be much more confusing than they actually are because a ratio can be written in several different ways. As a result, there are a few things about the ratio questions on the exam that you may want to keep in mind.

First, it is important to have a basic idea of the different ways that a ratio can be written. This is important because you may see a ratio written in one of several different formats on the exam, and you won't be able to answer a ratio question if you don't understand what the question is trying to say. Therefore, you may want to keep the three different ways of writing a ratio in mind. The first way that you may see a ratio written is in the format x/y. For example, you might see a ratio written as 5/8. The second way that you may see a ratio written on the exam is in the format x:y. For example, you might see the ratio above written as 5:8. The third and final way of writing a ratio is in the format x to y. For example, you might see the ratio above written as 5 to 8. It is important to note that it doesn't matter which format a ratio is written in because 5/8 means the same thing as 5:8 or 5 to 8, so you may see a ratio written in any of these three ways.

Second, some of the ratio questions on the exam will present you with an amount that you will need to split based on a specific ratio. If a question asks you to split a certain amount, or in other words, determine how much each person, group, object, etc. gets according to a specific ratio, you should add each of the numbers in the ratio together. Once you have added all of the numbers in the ratio together, you should divide the amount to be distributed by the sum of all of the numbers in the ratio. This will give you the amount that is to be distributed for a single portion. You can then multiply that amount by each of the numbers in the ratio to determine how much each person, group, object, etc. will receive.

For example, you might see a problem that states "Sarah, Joe, Matt, and Christine have purchased 3 pizzas that they are attempting to divide amongst each other. After a lot of discussion, the group decided that they should divide the pizzas so Sarah gets 1 slice to every 2 slices Matt gets to every 4 slices Joe gets to every 5 slices Christine gets. How many slices of pizza will each person get if there are 24 slices in total?" This question is asking you to use the ratio that is established in the problem to split the total number of slices of pizza amongst the four people described in the problem, so you need to add the numbers in the ratio together, which gives you 1 + 2 + 4 + 5 or 12. You then need to determine how many slices make up a single portion according to the ratio by dividing the total number of slices, which is 24, by the sum of all of the numbers in the ratio, which is 12. Therefore, a person receiving a single portion according to the ratio would receive 24/12 or 2 slices. You can then determine the answer to the problem by multiplying each number in the ratio by the number of slices an individual receives for a single portion. This means that Sarah would receive 2 slices * 1 portion or 2 slices, Matt would receive 2 slices * 2 portions or 4 slices, Joe would receive 2 slices * 4 portions or 8 slices, and Christine would receive 2 slices * 5 portions or 10 slices. Therefore, the answer to the problem would be that Sarah would get 2 slices, Matt would get 4 slices, Joe would get 8 slices, and Christine would get 10 slices.

Finally, you may see a question on the exam that asks you to simplify a ratio that doesn't use whole numbers. In other words, some of the ratio questions on the exam will ask you to simplify a ratio that refers to the relationship between two decimals, fractions, or percentages. In order to answer each of these questions, you will need to write each number as a fraction and divide the two fractions. This means that if you have a decimal or a percentage, you must determine the fraction that the decimal or percentage is equal to before you try to solve the problem. For example, .75 or 75% is equal to ¾ so you would need to write .75 or 75% as ¾ before you start making calculations. Once you have written each number as a fraction, you can divide the two fractions in order to find the answer.

This type of problem may sound as if it's extremely complicated, especially if you're not familiar with how to multiply or divide fractions, but it is actually easier than it looks. This is because you can divide two fractions simply by inverting the second fraction, multiplying the top two numbers of each fraction together, and multiplying the bottom two numbers of each fraction together. For example, you might see a problem that states "Joe and Sarah have decided to open a business together with Sarah handling a large amount of the responsibility. In order to make sure that Sarah and Joe each receive a share of the profits based on the amount of work they do, they have decided to use a ratio where Joe gets 40% of the profits for every 80% of the profits Sarah gets. Simplify the ratio between the profits Joe will receive and the profits Sarah will receive." This question is asking you to simplify a ratio that is describing two percentages so you will need to convert the percentages to fractions and divide the fractions in order to find the correct answer. This means that 40% should be written as 40/100 or 2/5, and 80 percent should be written as 80/100 or 4/5.

Once you have written each number as a fraction, you can then divide the two fractions by inverting the second fraction, which means that 4/5 would become 5/4, and multiplying the first fraction by the inverted second fraction. In other words, 2/5 divided by 4/5 is equal to 2/5 * 5/4. You can then determine the first number of the ratio by multiplying the top number of the first fraction by the top number of the second fraction, which means that the first number in the ratio is equal to 2 * 5 or 10. You can then determine the second number in the ratio by multiplying the bottom number of the first fraction by the bottom number of the second fraction, which means that the second number in the ratio is equal to 5 * 4 or 20. This means that the ratio that Sarah and Joe are using to split the profits can be expressed as 10 to 20, but this ratio can actually be simplified further. This is because 10 to 20 or 10/20 is equal to ½, which means that Joe and Sarah are splitting the profits based on a ratio of 1 to 2. Therefore, if this was actually a question on the exam, you would need to choose the option that indicated 1:2, ½, or 1 to 2.

It is important to note that you may see a question on the exam that asks you to simplify a ratio that shows the relationship between a fractional number and a whole number. In other words, there may be a question on the exam that asks you to simplify a ratio with a whole number and a decimal, fraction, or percentage instead of asking you to simplify a ratio with two decimals, two fractions, two percentages, or two whole numbers. If you need to simplify a ratio that has a fractional number and a whole number, you will need to write the whole number as a fraction and divide the two fractions as you normally would. For example, you might see a problem that states "Matt and Jay pooled their money to purchase season tickets for their favorite football team. However, Jay put in more money than Matt, so the two guys decided that Matt should get ½ a ticket for every 2 tickets Jay gets. Simplify the ratio between the number of tickets Matt should get and the number of tickets Jay should get." This question is asking you to simplify a ratio that is describing a fraction and a whole number, so you need to convert the whole number to a fraction and divide the fractions in order to determine the correct answer. This means that the whole number 2 should be written as 2/1.

Once you have made sure that each number is written as a fraction, you can then divide the two fractions by inverting the second fraction, which means that 2/1 would become ½, and multiplying the first fraction by the inverted second fraction. This means that you would multiply the top of the first fraction by the top of the second fraction and the bottom of the first fraction by the bottom of the second fraction so the first number in the ratio is equal to 1 * 1 or 1 and the second number in the ratio is equal to 2 * 2 or 4. Therefore, the correct answer would be that Matt and Jay are splitting the tickets using a ¼, a 1:4, or a 1 to 4 ratio.

Avoiding Tax Troubles

The tax questions in the arithmetic reasoning section of the TEA Exam will provide you with information related to the amount that an individual or group must pay taxes on, the tax rate, the total amount of taxes collected, and/or information related to any surtaxes that an individual or group must pay. Each of these questions will then require you to find the total tax that the individual or group owes, the tax rate that is necessary for an individual or business to pay a certain amount of taxes on a certain amount of money, or the amount of money that must be taxed to earn a certain amount of taxes at a certain rate. The tax questions on the TEA Exam are usually pretty simple as most of these questions can be answered by plugging the appropriate numbers into the appropriate formula. However, as you may have guessed, you need to know what those formulas are and how to apply each formula in order to determine the correct answer.

First, if a question asks you to calculate the total tax that an individual owes and there is **only one** tax involved, you can use the formula total tax = amount taxable * tax rate or $T = b * r$ (it is important to note that the amount taxable is also referred to as the tax base, so the amount taxable is represented by the b in the formula). For example, you might see a problem on the exam that states "Megan just purchased a new DVD player for $200.00. If there is a 5% sales tax, how much will Megan have to pay in taxes on the DVD player?" This question is asking you for the amount of sales tax that Megan will have to pay on the purchase of the DVD player, so you need to use the formula to determine the total tax, which is $T = b * r$. This means that Megan will have to pay $200.00 *.05 or $10 in taxes.

Second, if a question asks you to calculate the total tax that an individual owes and there is a tax **and a surtax** involved, you can use the formula tax = amount taxable * tax rate or $T = b * r$ to determine the amount of tax owed at each tax rate. You can then add the amount of tax for each tax rate together to determine the total tax. For example, you might see a problem on the exam that states "A cigar shop that made $50,000 in sales this year has to pay a flat 5% income tax on its earnings and a 7% surtax on the sale of any tobacco product. Assuming that all of the store's sales for the year are tobacco-related, how much does the cigar shop owe in taxes?" This question is asking you to find the total tax that the store would owe on $50,000 in sales, so you need to determine the amount of tax that the store owes for the flat 5% income tax and the amount that the store owes for the 7% tobacco tax. In order to determine the amount that the store owes for each tax, you simply need to multiply the amount that is taxable by each tax rate, so the store owes $50,000 * .05 or $2,500 for the flat income tax and $50,000 * .07 or $3,500 for the tobacco surtax. This means that the cigar shop will owe $2,500 + $3,500 or $6,000 in taxes this year.

Third, you may see a question that asks you to determine the total tax that an individual owes, but the rate is described in terms of a certain tax per amount. If a question asks you to determine the tax owed and the rate is described in terms of a certain tax per amount, you should divide the amount taxable by the per tax amount. This will give you the amount on which the individual or group is, in effect, paying taxes once the per tax amount is taken into consideration. Once you have determined the amount that an individual is, in effect, paying taxes on, you can use the formula tax = amount taxable * tax rate or $T = b * r$ to determine the tax as you normally would. For example, you might see a modified version of the question above that states "A cigar shop that made $48,000 in sales this year has to pay $12 in taxes per every $100 in tobacco sales. Assuming that all of the store's sales for the year are tobacco related, how much does the cigar shop owe in taxes?" This question is asking you to find the total tax that the store would owe on $50,000 in sales, but the tax rate is a certain tax per each amount of money, so you need to divide the amount taxable by the certain tax per amount. This means that the amount that is actually taxable once you take the per tax amount into consideration is equivalent to $48,000 / $100 or $480. You will then need to plug the amount that is effectively taxable into the tax formula to determine the tax owed. Therefore, the tax that the cigar shop will owe on $48,000 is equal to $480 / $12 or $40.

Fourth, if a question asks you to determine the tax rate that an individual had to pay as a percentage, you can use the formula tax rate = tax paid / amount taxable or $r = T / b$. For example, you might see a question on the exam that states "A group of politicians have drafted a bill to implement a new healthcare program. However, in order for the politicians to fund their new program, they will need to implement a new annual tax to collect approximately $350 from each person working in the country. Assuming that the average person makes $35,000 a year, determine the tax rate that the politicians will need to set in order to fund the new healthcare program." This question is asking you to find the tax rate that will yield a tax of $350 on $35,000 so you need to use the formula $r = T / b$. This means that the tax rate will have to be equal to $300 / $35,000 or 1% in order to fund the new healthcare program.

Fifth, you may see a tax question that asks for the tax rate in terms of a certain tax per each amount of money rather than a specific percentage rate. If a question asks you to determine the tax rate in terms of a certain tax per amount, you should divide the amount taxable by the per tax amount. This will give you the amount that the individual or group is, in effect, paying taxes on once the per tax amount is taken into consideration. Once you have determined the amount that the individual or group is, in effect, paying taxes on, you can use the formula tax rate = tax paid / amount taxable or $r = T / b$ to determine the tax rate as you normally would. For example, you might see a modified version of the example from the above paragraph that states "A group of politicians have drafted a bill to implement a new healthcare program. However, in order for the politicians to fund their new program, they will need to implement a new annual tax to collect approximately $350 from each person working in the country. If the average person earns $35,000 a year, how much will the new tax have to charge per every $100 of income in order to fund the program?" This question is asking you to find the tax rate per every $100 that will yield a tax of $350 on $35,000, so you need to divide the amount taxable by the per tax amount. This means that the amount that is actually taxable once you take the per tax amount into consideration is equivalent to $35,000 / $100 or $350. You will then need to plug the amount that is effectively taxable into the tax rate formula to determine the tax rate so the tax rate per $100 is equal to $350 / $350 or $1. Therefore, the new tax will have to be $1 per every $100 of income in order to fund the new program.

Finally, if a question asks you to determine the amount that must be taxed in order to yield a certain tax at a certain rate, you can use the formula taxable amount = tax / tax rate or $b = t / r$. For example, you might see another version of the example above that states "A group of politicians have drafted a bill to implement a new healthcare program. However, in order for the politicians to fund their new program, they will need to implement a new annual tax to collect approximately $350 from each person working in the country. If the politicians decide to set the new tax at a rate of 2%, how much will each person need to make in order to fund the program?" This question is asking you to find the taxable amount that each person would need to earn in order to pay $350 with a tax rate of 2%, so you need to use the formula $b = t / r$. This means that the amount that would need to be taxed to earn $350 from a 2% tax rate is equal to $350 / .02 or $17,500. Therefore, each person would have to earn $17,500 in order to fund the new program with a 2% tax.

How much work will get the Job done?

The work/time required questions in the arithmetic reasoning section of the TEA Exam will present you with information related to the number of people working, the speed at which each individual is working, the amount of work that needs to be performed, and/or the time frame in which the work must be performed. Each of these questions will then ask you to determine the length of time that it will take for a specific group of workers to complete a particular job, the amount of work that a particular group of workers can perform in a specific amount of time, or the number of workers that will be required to complete a specific job in a certain length of time. These questions often seem more confusing than they actually are because they usually contain a large amount of information that you don't really need in order to answer the question. As a result, you may need to sift through each problem to find the information you need to solve the problem, which can make these questions more confusing than some of the other questions on the exam. However, once you have identified the information you need, answering each question is really just a matter of some simple addition, subtraction, multiplication, and division.

In order to answer each of the work/time required questions in the arithmetic reasoning section of the TEA Exam, there are several things that you should keep in mind. First, it is important to remember that each of these problems can usually be solved through some simple logic. This is because each question is based on the real-life relationship between the number of people working, the amount of work that needs to be performed, and how long it takes to perform a particular job. As a result, it may be easier for you to answer each question if you remember three simple rules.

The first rule that you should keep in mind is that the amount of work a group of workers is able to perform will **increase** as the number of workers **increases** and *decrease* as the number of workers *decreases*. In other words, a larger group of people will be able to perform more work than a smaller group of people. The second rule that you should keep in mind is that the amount of time that is necessary to complete a particular job will **increase** as the amount of work **increases** and *decrease* as the amount of work *decreases*. In other words, it takes longer to complete a big job than it takes to complete a smaller job. The third rule that you should keep in mind is that the amount of time that is necessary to complete a particular job will **decrease** as the number of workers **increases** and *increase* as the number of workers *decreases*.

These three rules will help you to understand the basic underlying concepts that you can use to solve any of the problems in this section. However, it is important to note that each of these rules will only work if the speed of each worker remains constant. This is because it is possible to have fewer workers performing the same amount of work if each worker is working more quickly. As a result, it is important to keep these rules in mind because they will help you to understand the relationship between the amount of work performed, the time, and the number of workers. However, you must also remember that the speed at which each worker is working will affect the amount of work that can be performed and/or the amount of time that it will take for a specific amount of work to be performed.

Workers working at the Same Speed

Second, if a question asks you to find the amount of work performed, the time until completion, or the number of workers required and each worker works at the **same speed**, you will be able to answer the question simply by plugging the appropriate numbers into the appropriate formula. If a question asks you to determine the length of time it will take for a single person to complete a certain amount of work and the worker is working at the **same speed** as the other workers in his or her group, you can use the formula time until completion for a single person = time until completion for the entire group * the number of workers in the group or $s = g * n$ where s is the time it takes a single person to complete the job, g is the time it takes the group to complete the job, and n is the number of workers in the group. For example, you might see a question that states "Alex works in a warehouse in which the shipping and receiving department is separated into teams. Alex's team can usually unload an entire 18-wheeler in 2 ½ hours. If there are four people in Alex's team who all work at the same speed, how long would it take Alex to unload an entire 18-wheeler by himself?" This question is asking you to determine the length of time that it would take for a single person to complete the job that a group completed, so you can find the answer to the problem by using the formula $s = g * n$. Therefore, Alex could unload the entire 18-wheeler in 2 ½ hours * 4 workers or 10 hours.

If a question asks you to determine the length of time it will take for a group of people to complete a certain amount of work and each member of the group is working at the **same speed** as a single worker described in the problem, you can use the formula time until completion for the entire group = time until completion for a single person / the number of workers or $g = s / n$. For example, you might see a variation of the example from the above paragraph that states "If Alex can usually unload an entire 18-wheeler in 9 hours by himself, how long would it take 3 people working at the same speed as Alex to unload the entire 18-wheeler?" This question is asking you to determine the length of time that it would take an entire group to complete the job that a single person completed, so you can solve the problem by using the formula $g = s / n$. This means that the time it would take the group to unload the entire 18-wheeler is equal to 9 hours / 3 people or 3 hours.

If a question asks you to determine the length of time that it will take for a group of people to complete a certain amount of work and each member of the group is working at the **same speed** as the members of another group, you can use the formula the time until completion for the first group = the time until completion of the second group * the number of people in the second group / the number of people in the first group or $g_1 = g_2 * n_2 / n_1$. For example, you might see a question on the exam similar to the questions above that states "Alex and Steve work in a warehouse in which the shipping and receiving department is separated into teams. Alex's team consists of 4 workers who can unload an entire 18-wheeler in 3 hours. How long will it take Steve's team to complete the job if there are 3 workers on Steve's team, and all of the workers are working at equal rates?" This question is asking you to determine the length of time that it would take an entire group to complete the job that another group completed, so you can solve the problem by using the formula $g_1 = g_2 * n_2 / n_1$. This means that the time it would take for Steve's group to unload the entire 18-wheeler is equal to 4 * 3 / 3, which is equal to 12 / 3 or 4 hours.

If a question asks you to determine the amount of work that a person or group can perform in a specific amount of time, you can use the formula amount of work completed = rate * time or $w = r * t$. For example, you might see a question on the exam that states "If Alex can unload 4 entire trucks in 2 days, how many trucks can Alex unload in 5 days?" This question is asking you to determine the amount of work that Alex can perform in 5 days, so you need to use the formula $w = r * t$. However, in order to use this formula, you must put the rate in terms of a single unit of time, which in this case is one day, so you need to divide the 4 trucks by the 2 days to find the rate that Alex is working at for each day. This means that the rate Alex is working at is equal to 4 trucks unloaded / 2 days or 2 trucks unloaded per day and the amount of work that Alex will be able to complete in 5 days is equal to 2 trucks unloaded per day * 5 days or 10 trucks unloaded.

If a problem presents you with the number of workers required to complete a specific job and the question asks you to determine the number of workers that would be required to complete the same job in less time, you can use the formula number of workers required = the number of workers typically required to complete the job * time required to typically complete the job / time allowed for the new job or $n_1 = n_2 * t_2 / t_1$. For example, you might see a question that states "Four workers can unload 2 18-wheelers in 6 hours. How many workers would be required to unload 2 18-wheelers in 2 hours?" This question is asking you for the number of workers required to complete the job in less time, so you need to use the formula $n_1 = n_2 * t_2 / t_1$. This means that the number of workers required to unload 2 18-wheelers is equal to 4 workers * 6 hours / 2 hours or 12 workers.

Workers working at Different Speeds

Finally, it is important to remember that different people can work at different speeds. This is important because you may see a question on the exam that asks you to determine the amount of work that an individual from a group of people working at **different** speeds can perform or the amount of time that it will take for an individual from a group of people working at **different** speeds to perform a particular job. If a question asks you to determine the length of time it will take for a single individual to perform the same job as a group of people working at different speeds, you will need to determine how many workers working at the slowest speed can perform the amount of work that the entire group performed. Once you have identified the number of workers that the fast and slow workers would be equivalent to if everyone was working at the same speed, you can determine the time it would take for a single slow worker to complete the job. You can then determine the length of time that the individual will require to complete the job by dividing the amount of time that is required for a single slow worker to complete the job by the number of the slowest workers that the individual is equivalent to in speed. For example, you might see a question that states "Alex, James, Steve, and Ted work together in an electronics warehouse loading and unloading trucks. Alex and James have been working at the warehouse for some time while Steve and Ted have just started. As a result, Alex and James each work twice as fast as Steve or Ted. If it takes Alex, James, Steve, and Ted 3 hours to unload a truck when the four of them work together, how long will it take Alex to unload a truck by himself?" This question is asking you to identify the length of time that it will take for a single individual to perform the same job as a group of people working at the same speed, so you need to determine how many slow workers are equivalent to all of the workers in the group. In this particular case, since Alex and James each work twice as fast as Steve or Ted, Alex can complete the work of two Steves or two Teds and James can complete the work of two Steves or two Teds, so the group can unload the truck in the same time that it would take 2 slow workers + 2 slow workers + 1 slow worker + 1 slow worker or 6 Steves or 6 Teds to complete the job.

You can then determine the length of time that it would take for a single slow worker to complete the job by multiplying the number of slow workers that are equivalent to the group in the problem, which is 6 slow workers, by the number of hours it took the group to complete the job, which is 3 hours, so a single slow worker could complete the job in 6 slow workers * 3 hours or 18 hours. You can then determine the answer to the problem by dividing the length of time it would take for a single slow worker to complete the job, which is 18 hours, by the number of slow workers that the individual is equivalent to in speed. This means that Alex could unload a truck by himself in 18 hours / 2 slow workers or 9 hours. This type of problem is relatively straightforward as you will be able to find the answer to the problem simply by adding, multiplying, and dividing. However, it is important to note that this particular process will only work if it easy to compare the speed of each worker.

If a question asks you to determine the length of time that it would take for a group of people working together to complete a job and it is **not** easy to compare the speed of each worker, you will have to determine how much each worker can complete in a single unit of time in order to answer the question. In other words, you will need to determine the amount of work that each worker can complete in a single minute, hour, day, week, month, or year to answer a question in which the speeds of each worker are not easily comparable. Determining the amount of work that each worker can perform in a single unit of time may sound like a lot of work, but it is actually much easier than it seems. This is because you can determine the amount of work that an individual has performed in a single unit of time simply by writing the time it takes to complete a particular job as a fraction and then inverting the fraction. You can then add the amount of work that each worker can complete in a single unit of time together to calculate the total amount of work that the group can complete in a single unit of time. Once you have added the amount of work that each worker can complete in a single unit of time together, you can solve the problem by inverting the total amount of work that the group completed in a single unit of time.

For example, you might see a problem that states "Alex, James, and Ted work together in an electronics warehouse loading and unloading trucks. Alex can typically load a truck in 3 hours, James can typically load a truck in 4 hours, and Ted can typically load a truck in 5 hours. How many hours would it take Alex, James, and Ted to load a truck if they worked together?" This question is asking you to determine the length of time that it would take for a group of people to complete a specific job, and the speeds of each worker are difficult to compare, so you need to write each speed as a fraction and invert the fraction. This means that Alex can load a truck in 3/1 hours or 1/3 of a truck in an hour, James can load a truck in 4/1 hours or 1/4 of a truck in an hour, and Ted can load a truck in 5/1 hours or 1/5 of a truck in an hour. Each of these inverted fractions refers to the amount of work that each worker can complete in a single unit of time, which in this particular case is one hour. You can then add each of these inverted fractions together to determine the total amount of work that the group could perform in a single unit of time so 1/3 + 1/4 + 1/5 is equal to 20/60 + 15/60 + 12/60 or 47/60. Once you have added each of the inverted fractions together, you can invert the sum of all of the inverted fractions to solve the problem, so Alex, James and Ted could unload a truck in 60/47 hours or 1 hour and 13/47 of an hour.

If a question asks you to determine the length of time that it will take for a single individual to complete a job, and the problem gives you the length of time that it will take for one or more other individuals to complete the job as well as the length of time that it will take for the entire group to complete the job, you will have to determine how much each worker can complete in a single unit of time before you make any calculations. You can determine the amount of work that each worker can complete in a single unit of time by using the same method that is described above, which means that you need to write the amount of time that it takes for each worker to complete the job as a fraction and invert the fraction. You can then add each of the inverted fractions together to calculate the total amount of work that the known individuals can complete in a single unit of time. Once you have added each of the inverted fractions together, you can write the total length of time that it takes for all of the workers working as a group to complete the job as a fraction and invert the fraction. You can then subtract the total amount of work that the known individuals can complete from the total that all of the workers can complete working as a group. This will give you a fraction that you can invert to determine the length of time that it would take for the individual that completed an unknown amount of work to complete the job alone.

For example, you might see a problem that states "Alex, James, and Ted work together in an electronics warehouse loading and unloading trucks. Alex can typically load a truck by himself in 2 hours and James can typically load a truck by himself in 3 hours. If Alex, James, and Ted can typically load a truck in 1 hour when they are working together, how long does it typically take Ted to load a truck?" This question is asking you to determine the length of time that it would take for a single individual to complete a specific job based on how long it takes each of the other individuals to complete the job and on the length of time that it takes for the group to complete the job, so you need to write each speed as a fraction and invert the fraction. This means that Alex can load the truck in 2/1 hours or 1/2 of a truck in an hour and James can load the truck in 3/1 hours or 1/3 of the truck in an hour.

You can then add each of the inverted fractions together to determine the total amount of work that the group can perform in a single unit of time if they worked without Ted so 1/2 + 1/3 is equal to 6/12 + 4/12 or 10/12. Once you have added each of the inverted fractions together, you can then write the length of time that it takes Alex, James, and Ted to load a truck when they are working together as a fraction and invert the fraction. You can then subtract the total amount of work that the group can perform in a single unit of time without Ted from the length of time that it takes Alex, James, and Ted to load a truck as group so 1/1 – 10/12 is equal to 12/12 – 10/12, which is equal to

2/12 or 1/6. Then, in order to determine the answer to the question, you must invert the fraction you arrived at when you subtracted so 1/6 becomes 6/1. Therefore, Ted can load 1/6 of a truck in an hour or an entire truck in 6/1 hours, which means that the answer to the question is that Ted can load a truck by himself in 6 hours.

How do I Answer the Problems for Investigation Questions?

The problems for investigation section of the TEA Exam consist of 30 multiple-choice questions that are designed to test your ability to analyze and use different types of information related to a particular situation. In other words, the questions in this section of the exam are designed to test your critical thinking skills. These questions assess your critical thinking skills by asking you to identify a statement that indicates that a particular piece of information is true, to identify a specific type of statement, to identify a statement that provides a piece of information that is reliable and/or useful, or to identify a statement that provides a piece of information that is unreliable and/or useless. These questions are somewhat similar to the verbal reasoning questions on the exam as you will have to use the information that you read in the passage and the information that you read in the statements to answer each question. However, you will usually be required to perform a deeper analysis of each piece of information in the problems for investigation section than you would for the information in the verbal reasoning section. As a result, there are several things that you should keep in mind.

First, it is always a good idea to read the passage and the series of statements that are associated with a given set of questions before you try to answer any of the questions. This is because the statements in this section of the exam are actually expanding on the information that is provided in the passage. Therefore, you will need a basic understanding of the situation presented in each passage in order to understand each of the statements that are associated with that passage and to understand each of the questions associated with those statements. It is, however, important to note that this does not necessarily mean that you should analyze each passage and statement before you read the questions but instead, that you should read each question through once quickly. In other words, you should read everything in this section of the exam, but you shouldn't focus on anything for too long because you will only have 60 minutes to answer all of the questions in the problems for investigation section.

Second, it is important to remember that this section of the exam is testing your critical thinking skills and not your knowledge of any specific set of law enforcement or investigation procedures. This is important to remember because you may encounter statements in this section of the exam that contain information that was inappropriately collected or information that seems to indicate that the investigation is proceeding down the wrong path. This can be a problem if you have a background in or even a basic knowledge of law enforcement or criminal investigation because you may be tempted to throw out statements that were inappropriately collected or statements that seem to indicate that someone other than the person you suspect committed the crime. However, you should avoid the temptation to throw out statements based on your knowledge of procedure or your impressions of the situation. This is because the exam is not testing you on how the information was collected, but rather on how the information can be *used* in an investigation, so you may encounter information that seems useless but is actually essential to proving an individual's guilt or innocence.

Third, while you are attempting to answer a question, you should focus your attention on the five statements or five statement pairs that are provided as options. These statements are the only statements that will provide the information that will answer the particular question that you are looking at, so you don't need to look at any of the other statements *unless* the question is related to a specific statement. This means that you can save a lot of time by rereading each of the statements provided as options rather than rereading the entire list or statements for every question. However, some of the questions that you see on the exam may be related to a specific statement, so you will have to read the statement in order to determine which option is the correct answer to the question. For example, a question might ask you "Which of the following statements along with statement 7 proves that John Ciles had an opportunity to steal the gem?" In order to answer this question, you would have to read statement 7 in addition to all of the options provided because the information in statement 7 is related to the information in the correct answer.

Fourth, while you are reading each question, you should pay close attention to the way that the question is worded. This is important because these questions use a lot of negating words such as "no and "not," a lot of negating prefixes such as "in" or "un," and a lot of words that have similar spellings and/or similar sounds to words used in other questions that have drastically different meanings such as "indicate," "implicate," and "intimidate." This means that it is very easy to misread the questions in this section because the presence of a single word or the lack of a single word may change the meaning. As a result, you will need to read each question quickly, but carefully in order to determine the correct answer in the time allowed.

Finally, if you are having difficulty identifying the statement that correctly answers a particular question, look at each statement, and try to eliminate any of the statements that appear to be unrelated to the question or any of the statements that seem to identify the opposite of what the question is asking you to identify. For example, if you are presented with the question "Which of the following statements may indicate that John Ciles was in the jewelry store when the crime took place?" you can eliminate a statement such as "John Ciles said that he was at a local movie theatre at the time the crime took place" because the statement indicates the opposite of what the question is asking you to prove. You can also eliminate a statement such as "A witness said the thief caught her by surprise because she was a regular at the jewelry store and she had never had a problem before" because the statement has nothing to do with the question and probably nothing to do with the investigation. Eliminating these options allows you to look at only the statements that may be correct rather than the statements that are irrelevant or the statements that provide information that indicates the opposite of what the question is asking you to indicate.

Problems for Investigation Terminology

The following section discusses a number of simple techniques that you can use to answer the questions in the problems for investigation section of the TEA Exam and some of the ways that the exam's designers may try to trick you in this section. However, you will need to know some of the basic terminology related to an investigation in order to understand all of the information covered in this section of the exam. This is because knowing these basic terms will help you to understand the passages, statements, and questions on the exam. As a result, you may want to be at least somewhat familiar with the following terms:

Access: Access is the physical ability of a suspect to enter a crime scene.

Alibi: An alibi is a piece of information that shows that the suspect was at a location other than the crime scene at the time of the crime.

Circumstantial Evidence: Circumstantial evidence is a piece of information that seems to indicate that a particular action has been taken, but does not definitely prove it.

Collusion: criminal act in which two or more individuals work together to commit a crime. Collusion is usually used to refer specifically to cases of fraud.

Conspiracy: a criminal act in which two or more individuals work together to commit a crime. Conspiracy may refer to a case of fraud or any other type of crime in which two or more individuals are involved.

Corroborating evidence: a piece of information that verifies or helps to verify the accuracy of a specific conclusion or a separate piece of information.

Crime scene: the location at which a crime took place.

Hearsay: a piece of information that an individual did not hear or witness first-hand as in "I heard that Jack was the thief." In other words, hearsay is something that an individual hears from someone else and then repeats.

Motive: reason for the commission of a criminal act. In other words, a motive is the underlying motivation that caused a particular individual to commit a crime.

Opportunity: ability of a suspect to enter a crime scene at the time of the crime.

Social commentary: statement that provides an individual's opinion on the cause of a specific situation rather than specific facts related to the actual cause of the situation.

Verifying the Facts

Some of the questions in the problems for investigation section of the TEA Exam will require you to identify a statement that indicates that a specific piece of information is true. These questions are usually easier to answer than the other questions in the problems for investigation section as they are simply looking for a statement that seems to indicate that a particular event has occurred, that a particular person has committed a specific act, that a certain event occurred prior to or after another event, that a certain individual was in a certain place at a certain time, or that another similar piece of information is true. However, it is important to realize that these questions, like many of the other questions on the exam, are designed to trick you. As a result, you need to know how to avoid some of the common tricks that the exam's designers will try to use.

First, most of the options for the fact verification questions in the problems for investigation section of the exam are designed to look as if they prove something to be true or sound as if they are at least related to the fact that you are attempting to prove even though they don't actually prove what the question is asking you to prove. In other words, you may see a statement that proves something similar to what the question is asking you to prove, but the statement doesn't actually verify the fact that the question is asking you to confirm. For example, you might see a question that states "Which of the following statements indicates that John Ciles was at the scene of the crime?" and a statement that states "John Ciles stated that he went to a local movie theatre while the crime was taking place, but the employees at the movie theatre said that they have never seen John Ciles before." This statement seems to indicate that John Ciles was not at the movie theatre and that he lied about his whereabouts, so it is possible that he was at the scene of the crime. However, this statement doesn't actually indicate that John Ciles was ever at the crime scene but rather that he wasn't where he said he was supposed to be during the crime, so this statement is not the correct answer for this particular question. This means that you will have to read the question and each statement very carefully in order to find the correct answer.

Second, if you have read the introduction at the beginning of this section on how to answer the problems for investigation questions on the exam, you know that some of the options for these questions will provide you with statements that prove the opposite of what the question is asking you to prove. This fact is especially important to keep in mind for the fact verification questions on the exam as these questions will almost always have at least one option that indicates the opposite of what the question is asking for, but the option seems correct because it looks similar to the question. This means that you may see a statement that seems to answer the question, but it is actually proving the complete opposite of what you are attempting to prove. As a result, you may want to reread the question after you have chosen an answer to make sure that you have actually answered the question that you were supposed to be answering.

Is this Evidence Reliable or Unreliable/Useful or Useless?

Some of the questions in the problems for investigation section of the TEA Exam will require you to identify a statement that is reliable and/or useful or a statement that is unreliable and/or useless. These questions are usually more difficult to answer than the other questions in the problems for investigation section of the exam as you will need to determine how each statement can be used in an investigation or a court case. In other words, most of the questions in the problems for investigation section will simply require you to identify a particular fact or type of statement. However, in order to answer the evidence reliability/usefulness questions on the exam, you will have to think about how a particular piece of information could be applied in an actual investigation or in an actual court case if the situation presented in the problem had actually taken place. As a result, there are a few things that you may want to keep in mind while you are attempting to answer the evidence reliability/usefulness questions on the exam

First, when you are asked to identify a statement that is reliable or unreliable, consider the source of the statement. This is because the individual that actually provided the information in the first place plays a large role in whether that statement should be considered accurate or not. If the statement is from a trustworthy source such as a police officer investigating the crime, a witness that saw the incident first-hand, or another similar individual, it is usually safe to assume that the statement is reliable. On the other hand, if the statement is from an untrustworthy source such as an individual suspected of committing a crime, an individual that may have been involved in the crime or involved in covering up the crime, or any other individual that may have some reason to protect the criminal or provide false information, it is usually safe to assume that the statement is unreliable.

Secondly, when you are asked to identify a statement that is reliable or unreliable, you should consider the circumstances of the situation in which the individual is making the statement. This is because the situation itself can influence a particular individual's truthfulness. For example, a statement such as "Marie Anderson said that she intervened when she saw a tall, slender man with a medium build attacking a smaller man lying motionless on the ground" could be a reliable statement. However, that same statement may be unreliable if there is reason to believe that the individual who intervened may have been threatened by the attacker. This means that the information presented in the question and the information presented in the initial passage that describes the situation can be extremely important.

Third, when you are asked to identify a statement that is reliable or unreliable, you should consider where the individual got the information. This is because the information contained in a statement is only as reliable as its initial source, and the information will be less reliable if it has gone through several people before it has reached an investigator. This means that if a statement indicates that the individual making the statement witnessed the act first-hand, that the individual making the statement was the first individual to find the victim or find evidence of the crime, that the individual making the statement heard someone screaming, or that the individual making the statement has received the information first-hand, the statement may be reliable. On the other hand, a statement

- 79 -

from an individual who overheard a conversation between two intoxicated individuals, a statement from an individual who heard from his or her best friend that the crime took place at a certain time, a statement from an individual who heard a rumor about the crime, or any other similar statement from an individual who did not receive the information first-hand should be considered unreliable.

Fourth, if you need to identify the statement that is the most useful or the least useful for proving a particular case, you should consider whether the information provided in the statement actually indicates something of importance or not. For example, a statement such as "Michael Karenson said that he saw a tall, slender man with a blood-covered knife leaving the area of the crime scene around the time of the crime" may be useful because it indicates the physical characteristics of a specific individual that may be responsible for the crime. However, a statement such as "Michael Karenson saw a tall, slender man in a business suit walking out of an office building near the crime scene" is probably not very useful because the statement doesn't make it clear whether the individual is simply working in the area or involved in the crime.

Finally, if you need to identify the statement that is the most useful or the least useful for proving a particular case, you should consider whether the information is reliable or not and whether the information can be verified or not. If a statement is reliable and the statement indicates something of importance, then the statement will probably be useful in court. This is also usually the case for a statement that can be verified because a verified statement will be useful in court as long as it provides an important piece of information. On the other hand, it is important to note that the reverse is true for a statement that is unreliable or a statement that is difficult to verify because an unreliable or unverified statement will almost always be useless in court even if the information indicates something of importance.

What type of statement is this anyway?

Some of the questions in the problems for investigation section of the TEA Exam will require you to identify a specific type of statement. These questions are usually relatively easy to answer if you are familiar with some of the basic terminology used in law enforcement. However, in order to answer the statement type identification questions on the exam, you will have to be able to tell the difference between different types of evidence and other information. As a result, there are certain things that you may want to keep in mind about each type of statement that the exam may ask you to identify.

First, if a question asks you to identify a statement that indicates that an individual had **access or opportunity**, the question is looking for a statement that indicates that the individual had a realistic opening in which he or she was physically able to commit the crime. This means that the key thing that you should look for in any statement that may prove opportunity is the ability of the individual to get to the crime scene and actually commit the crime during the period that the crime took place. For example, a statement that states "Sarah Archer said that she saw John Ciles in the vicinity of the crime scene on the night the gem was stolen" would indicate that John Ciles had an opportunity to steal the gem. On the other hand, a statement that states "Natalie Russ said that John Ciles was in Hawaii with her on the night the gem was stolen from the Gems Galore Jewelry Store in New York" would indicate that John Ciles did not have an opportunity to steal the gem because he was nowhere near the jewelry store. It is important to note that a statement must indicate that there was a *realistic* opening **and** that the suspect was *physically able* to commit the crime in order for the statement to indicate opportunity and/or access. In other words, a statement such as "Sarah Archer said that she saw John Ciles sitting in a wheelchair in the vicinity of the crime scene" may not necessarily indicate opportunity if the thief had to have significant physical strength to make his or her way into the jewelry store.

- 80 -

Second, if a question asks you to identify a statement that appears to provide a reasonable **alibi**, the question is looking for a statement that indicates that the individual was *not* at the crime scene at the time of the crime because he or she was somewhere else. This means that the key thing that you should look for in any statement that may provide a reasonable alibi is a phrase that describes the individual in a place other than the crime scene at the time of the crime. For example, a statement that states "Natalie Russ said that John Ciles was in Hawaii with her on the night the gem was stolen from the Gems Galore Jewelry Store in New York" would be an alibi because the statement indicates that John Ciles was somewhere else when the gem was stolen. As you may have noticed, this example is the same statement that is used as an example in the above paragraph of a statement that does not indicate opportunity. This is because a reasonable alibi will almost always indicate that an individual *did not* have an opportunity to commit the crime.

Third, if a question asks you to identify a statement that appears to indicate that there was an act of **collusion** or **conspiracy**, the question is looking for a statement that indicates that more than one individual was involved in the crime. This means that the key thing that you should look for in any statement that may indicate collusion or conspiracy is a phrase that indicates that a specific person helped the criminal *or* that the criminal must have had help in committing the crime. For example, a statement that states "Sarah Archer said that she saw Nathalie Russ driving away in a blue station wagon with John Ciles in the passenger seat near the Gems Galore Jewelry Store in New York just after the crime had taken place" may indicate that Nathalie Russ and John Ciles had conspired to commit the crime together. It is important note that an individual does not necessarily have to be at the crime scene at the time of the crime in order to be involved in a conspiracy. This is because any individual that helps a criminal plan the crime, escape, or cover-up the crime is considered to be involved in a criminal conspiracy.

Fourth, if a question asks you to identify a statement that should be considered **hearsay**, the question is looking for a statement that does not provide first-hand information. This means that the key thing that you should look for in any statement that may be considered hearsay is a phrase such as "My best friend told me," "heard through the grapevine," "heard a rumor," "heard that she was doing this," "heard that he was doing that," or any other phrase in which the individual providing the statement wasn't actually the individual that witnessed or gathered the information that the individual is providing. For example, a statement such as "Jackie Doe said that she heard that John Ciles had been bragging about stealing the gem from the jewelry store" is hearsay because Jackie Doe did not actually see or hear John Ciles brag about stealing the gem but rather heard from another individual that John Ciles was bragging about it.

Finally, if a question asks you to identify a statement that appears to indicate that an individual may have had a **motive**, the question is looking for a statement that indicates that an individual may have had a reason to commit the crime. This means that the key thing that you should look for in any statement that may indicate a motive is a phrase that describes what may have caused the individual to commit that particular crime. For example, a statement such as "John Ciles was an employee at the Gems Galore Jewelry Store in New York until his employment was terminated when he accidently gave a customer a ring valued at nearly $1,000 more than the ring the customer had actually bought" may indicate a motive if the store was robbed because it suggests that John Ciles may have robbed the store to punish his former employer for firing him.

A Final Note on What Happens after the Exam

If you've read through this entire guide, you should be pretty well-prepared to pass the Treasury Enforcement Agent Exam. However, it is important to note that passing the TEA Exam will not necessarily guarantee you a position within the Bureau of Alcohol, Tobacco, and Firearms, the

Immigrations and Customs Enforcement Agency, the Internal Revenue Service, the U.S. Marshals Service, the United States Secret Service, or any other agency. This is because passing the TEA Exam is only one of the requirements involved in the application process that each of these federal bureaus and agencies uses, and each agency or bureau only has a limited number of positions available. As a result, you will have to find an open position, apply for that position, and compete with other applicants for that position after you have passed the TEA Exam.

It is also important to note that you may be required to go through an intensive training program that is specifically designed for the position that you are taking. This is because each position has its own distinct rules, responsibilities, and procedures, and you will have to learn these rules and procedures in order to remain in a particular position after you have been hired. In other words, what this all basically means is that most of the positions within these bureaus and agencies will require you to take the TEA Exam, but there is more to obtaining a position within one of these agencies than simply passing the exam.

Special Report: TEA Secrets in Action

Sample Math Question:

Three coins are tossed up in the air. What is the probability that two of them will land heads and one will land tails?

    A. 0

    B. 1/8

    C. 1/4

    D. 3/8

Let's look at a few different methods and steps to solving this problem.

1. Reduction and Division

Quickly eliminate the probabilities that you immediately know. You know to roll all heads is a 1/8 probability, and to roll all tails is a 1/8 probability. Since there are in total 8/8 probabilities, you can subtract those two out, leaving you with $8/8 - 1/8 - 1/8 = 6/8$. So after eliminating the possibilities of getting all heads or all tails, you're left with 6/8 probability. Because there are only three coins, all other combinations are going to involve one of either head or tail, and two of the other. All other combinations will either be 2 heads and 1 tail, or 2 tails and 1 head. Those remaining combinations both have the same chance of occurring, meaning that you can just cut the remaining 6/8 probability in half, leaving you with a 3/8ths chance that there will be 2 heads and 1 tail, and another 3/8ths chance that there will be 2 tails and 1 head, making choice D correct.

2. Run Through the Possibilities for that Outcome

You know that you have to have two heads and one tail for the three coins. There are only so many combinations, so quickly run through them all.

You could have:

    H, H, H

    H, H, T

    H, T, H

    T, H, H

    T, T, H

    T, H, T

    H, T, T

    T, T, T

Reviewing these choices, you can see that three of the eight have two heads and one tail, making choice D correct.

3. Fill in the Blanks with Symbology and Odds

Many probability problems can be solved by drawing blanks on a piece of scratch paper (or making mental notes) for each object used in the problem, then filling in probabilities and multiplying them out. In this case, since there are three coins being flipped, draw three blanks. In the first blank, put an "H" and over it write "1/2". This represents the case where the first coin is flipped as heads. In that case (where the first coin comes up heads), one of the other two coins must come up tails and one must come up heads to fulfill the criteria posed in the problem (2 heads and 1 tail). In the second blank, put a "1" or "1/1". This is because it doesn't matter what is flipped for the second coin, so long as the first coin is heads. In the third blank, put a "1/2". This is because the third coin must be the exact opposite of whatever is in the second blank. Half the time the third coin will be the same as the second coin, and half the time the third coin will be the opposite, hence the "1/2". Now multiply out the odds. There is a half chance that the first coin will come up "heads", then it doesn't matter for the second coin, then there is a half chance that the third coin will be the opposite of the second coin, which will give the desired result of 2 heads and 1 tail. So, that gives 1/2*1/1*1/2 = 1/4.

But, now you must calculate the probabilities that result if the first coin is flipped tails. So draw another group of three blanks. In the first blank, put a "T" and over it write "1/2". This represents the case where the first coin is flipped as tails. In that case (where the first coin comes up tails), both of the other two coins must come up heads to fulfill the criteria posed in the problem. In the second blank, put an "H" and over it write "1/2". In the third blank, put an "H" and over it write "1/2". Now multiply out the odds. There is a half chance that the first coin will come up "tails", then there is a half chance that the second coin will be heads, and a half chance that the third coin will be heads. So, that gives 1/2*1/2*1/2 = 1/8.

Now, add those two probabilities together. If you flip heads with the first coin, there is a 1/4 chance of ultimately meeting the problem's criteria. If you flip tails with the first coin, there is a 1/8 chance of ultimately meeting the problem's criteria. So, that gives 1/4 + 1/8 = 2/8 + 1/8 = 3/8, which makes choice D correct.

Sample Verbal Question:

Mark Twain was well aware of his celebrity. He was among the first authors to employ a clipping service to track press coverage of himself, and it was not unusual for him to issue his own press statements if he wanted to influence or "spin" coverage of a particular story. The celebrity Twain achieved during his last ten years still reverberates today. Nearly all of his most popular novels were published before 1890, long before his hair grayed or he began to wear his famous white suit in public. We appreciate the author but seem to remember the celebrity.

Based on the passage above, Mark Twain seemed interested in:

1. maintaining his celebrity
2. selling more of his books
3. hiding his private life
4. gaining popularity
5. writing the perfect novel

Let's look at a couple of different methods of solving this problem.

<u>1. Identify the key words in each answer choice.</u> These are the nouns and verbs that are the most important words in the answer choice.

> A. maintaining, celebrity
>
> B. selling, books
>
> C. hiding, life
>
> D. gaining, popularity
>
> E. writing, novel

Now try to match up each of the key words with the passage and see where they fit. You're trying to find synonyms and/or exact replication between the key words in the answer choices and key words in the passage.

> A. maintaining – no matches; celebrity – matches in sentences 1, 3, and 5
>
> B. selling – no matches; books – matches with "novels" in sentence 4.
>
> C. hiding – no matches; life – no matches
>
> D. gaining – no matches; popularity –matches with "celebrity" in sentences 1, 3, and 5, because they can be synonyms
>
> E. writing – no matches; novel – matches in sentence 4

At this point there are only two choices that have more than one match, choices A and D, and they both have the same number of matches, and with the same word in the passage, which is the word "celebrity" in the passage. This is a good sign, because the exam will often have two answer choices that are close. Having two answer choices pointing towards the same key word is a strong indicator that those key words hold the "key" to finding the right answer.

Now let's compare choice A and D and the unmatched key words. Choice A still has "maintaining" which doesn't have a clear match, while choice D has "gaining" which doesn't have a clear match. While neither of those have clear matches in the passage, ask yourself what are the best arguments that would support any kind of connection with either of those two words.

"Maintaining" makes sense when you consider that Twain was interested in tracking his press coverage and that he was actively managing the "spin" of certain stories.

"Gaining" makes sense when you consider that Twain was actively issuing his own press releases, however one key point to remember is that he was only issuing these press releases after another story was already in existence.

Since Twain's press releases were not being released in a news vacuum, but rather as a response mechanism to ensure control over the angle of a story, his releases were more to *maintain* control over his image, rather than *gain* an image in the first place.

Furthermore, when comparing the terms "popularity" and "celebrity", there are similarities between the words, but in referring back to the passage, it is clear that "celebrity" has a stronger connection to the passage, being the exact word used three times in the passage.

Since "celebrity" has a stronger match than "popularity" and "maintaining" makes more sense than "gaining," it is clear that choice A is correct.

2. Use a process of elimination.

A. maintaining his celebrity – The passage discusses how Mark Twain was both aware of his celebrity status and would take steps to ensure that he got the proper coverage in any news story and maintained the image he desired. This is the correct answer.

B. selling more of his books – Mark Twain's novels are mentioned for their popularity and while common sense would dictate that he would be interested in selling more of his books, the passage makes no mention of him doing anything to promote sales.

C. hiding his private life – While the passage demonstrates that Mark Twain was keenly interested in how the public viewed his life, it does not indicate that he cared about hiding his private life, not even mentioning his life outside of the public eye. The passage deals with how he was seen by the public.

D. gaining popularity – At first, this sounds like a good answer choice, because Mark Twain's popularity is mentioned several times. The main difference though is that he wasn't trying to gain popularity, but simply ensuring that the popularity he had was not distorted by bad press.

E. writing the perfect novel – Though every author of fiction may strive to write the perfect novel, and Mark Twain was a famous author, the passage makes no mention of any quest of his to write a perfect novel.

TEA Practice Test

Arithmetic Practice 1

1. 25% of 400 =
    a. 100
    b. 200
    c. 800
    d. 10,000

2. 22% of $900 =
    a. 90
    b. 198
    c. 250
    d. 325

3. Which of these numbers is a factor of 21?
    a. 2
    b. 5
    c. 7
    d. 42

4. (9÷3) x (8÷4) =
    a. 1
    b. 6
    c. 72
    d. 576

5. Once inch equals 2.54 cm, how many centimeters tall is a 76- inch man.
    a. 20 cm
    b. 29.92 cm
    c. 193.04 cm
    d. 300.04 cm

6. What is the reciprocal of 6?
    a. ½
    b. 1/3
    c. 1/6
    d. 1/12

7. A room measures 11 ft x 12 ft x 9 ft. What is the volume?
    a. 1188 ft³
    b. 32 ft³
    c. 120 ft³
    d. 1300 ft³

8. A roast was cooked at 325 °F in the oven for 4 hours. The internal temperature rose from 32 °F to 145 °F. What was the average rise in temperature per hour?

    a. 20.2 °F/hr
    b. 28.25°F/hr
    c. 32.03°F/hr
    d. 37°F/hr

9. You need to purchase a textbook for nursing school. The book cost $80.00, and the sales tax where you are purchasing the book is 8.25%. You have $100. How much change will you receive back?

    a. $5.20
    b. $7.35
    c. $13.40
    d. $19.95

10. You purchase a car making a down payment of $3,000 and 6 monthly payments of $225. How much have you paid so far for the car?

    a. $3225
    b. $4350
    c. $5375
    d. $6550

11. Your supervisor instructs you to purchase 240 pens and 6 staplers for the nurse's station. Pens are purchase in sets of 6 for $2.35 per pack. Staplers are sold in sets of 2 for 12.95. How much will purchasing these products cost?

    a. $132.85
    b. $145.75
    c. $162.90
    d. $225.05

12. Which of the following percentages is equal to 0.45?

    a. 0.045%
    b. 0.45%
    c. 4.5%
    d. 45%

13. A vitamin's expiration date has passed. It was suppose to contain 500 mg of Calcium, but it has lost 325 mg of Calcium. How many mg of Calcium is left?

    a. 135 mg
    b. 175 mg
    c. 185 mg
    d. 200 mg

14. You have orders to give a patient 20 mg of a certain medication. The medication is stored 4 mg per 5-mL dose. How many milliliters will need to be given?

    a. 15 mL
    b. 20 mL
    c. 25 mL
    d. 30 mL

15. In the number 743.25 which digit represents the tenths space?

    a. 2
    b. 3
    c. 4
    d. 5

16. Which of these percentages equals 1.25?

    a. 0.125%
    b. 12.5%
    c. 125%
    d. 1250%

17. If the average person drinks 8, (8oz) glasses of water per day, a person who drinks 12.8 oz of water after a morning exercise session has consumed what fraction of the daily average?

    a. 1/3
    b. 1/5
    c. 1/7
    d. 1/9

18. If y = 3, then $y^3 (y^3-y) =$

    a. 300
    b. 459
    c. 648
    d. 999

19. 33% of 300 =

    a. 3
    b. 9
    c. 33
    d. 99

20. You need 4/5 cups of water for a recipe. You accidentally put 1/3 cups into the mixing bowl with the dry ingredients. How much more water in cups do you need to add?

    a. 1/3 cups
    b. 2/3 cups
    c. 1/15 cups
    d. 7/15 cups

21. ¾ - ½ =

    a. ¼
    b. 1/3
    c. ½
    d. 2/3

22. You cannot find your 1 cup measuring cup. You can only locate your ¼ measuring cup. Your recipe calls for 2 ½ cups of flour. How many times will you need to fill your ¼ measuring cup with flour for the recipe?

    a. 4
    b. 6
    c. 8
    d. 10

23. You are financing a computer for $5000. You are required to put down a 15% down payment. How much money do you need for your down payment?

    a. $500
    b. $650
    c. $750
    d. $900

24. You are traveling in Europe, and you see a sign stating that London is 3 kilometers away. If 1 kilometer is equal to 0.625 miles, how many miles away is London from where you are?

    a. 0.208 miles
    b. 1.875 miles
    c. 2.75 miles
    d. 3 miles

25. You need exactly a 1680 ft³ aquarium for your fish. At the pet store you see four choices of aquariums, but the volume is not listed. The length, width, and height are listed on the box. Which of the following aquariums would fit your needs?

    a. 12 ft x 12 ft x 12 ft
    b. 13 ft x 15 ft x 16 ft
    c. 14 ft x 20 ft x 6 ft
    d. 15 ft x 16 ft x 12 ft

26. You invested $9,000 and received yearly interest of $450. What is your interest rate on your investment?

    a. 5%
    b. 6%
    c. 7%
    d. 8%

27. In your class there are 48 students, 32 students are female. Approximately what percentage is male?

    a. 25%
    b. 33%
    c. 45%
    d. 66%

28. If w = 82 +2, and z = 41 (2), then:

    a. w<z
    b. w>z
    c. w-z = 1
    d. w=z

29. After talking with his girlfriend on the telephone long distance, a student calculates the amount of money he spent on the call. The first 20 minutes were 99 cents, and each additional minute was 10 cents. He calculated that his phone call cost $ 5.49. How long was his call?

    a. 40 minutes
    b. 45 minutes
    c. 65 minutes
    d. 75 minutes

30. You are teaching a community education class on fire safety to children. There are 6 first graders, 7 second graders, and 5 third graders. What percentage of the class are second graders?

    a. 28%
    b. 33%
    c. 39%
    d. 48%

31. One slice of bread is 80 calories. Approximately how many calories are in 2 ½ slices of bread?

    a. 140 calories
    b. 200 calories
    c. 220 calories
    d. 240 calories

32. $7x = 3a + 2a$. If $a = 7$, then $x =$

    a. 5
    b. 7
    c. 9
    d. 12

33. Infant Dose Calculations using Fried's Rule is:

$$\text{Infant's dose} = \frac{\text{Child's age in months}}{150} \times \text{adult dose}$$

If the adult dose of medication is 15 mg, how much should be given to a 2 year-old child?

    a. 1.2
    b. 2.4
    c. 3.6
    d. 4.8

34. What is the area of a triangle if the base is 6 cm and the height is 8 cm.

    a. 18 cm³
    b. 20 cm³
    c. 22 cm³
    d. 24 cm³

35. 7 ½ - 5 3/8 =

    a. 1 ½
    b. 1 2/3
    c. 2 1/8
    d. 3 ¼

36. The school's softball team won 15 games, but lost 10. What was ratio of wins to losses?
    a. 2:1
    b. 3:1
    c. 3:2
    d. 4:1

37. 35 is 20% of what number?
    a. 175
    b. 186
    c. 190
    d. 220

38. 6 x 0 x 5=
    a. 30
    b. 11
    c. 25
    d. 0

39. 7.95 ÷ 1.5=
    a. 2.4
    b. 5.3
    c. 6.2
    d. 7.3

40. If x = 4, then 2x + 7x =
    a. 24
    b. 27
    c. 35
    d. 36

41. 7/10 equals:
    a. .007
    b. .07
    c. .7
    d. 1.7

42. 4/8 equals:
    a. .005
    b. .05
    c. .5
    d. 1.5

43. 8/24 equals:
    a. 1/6
    b. 1/4
    c. 1/8
    d. 1/3

44. 83,000 equals:

    a. 83.0×10^5
    b. 8.3×10^4
    c. 8.3×10^{-4}
    d. 83.0×10^{-3}

45. .00875 equals:

    a. 8.75×10^1
    b. 8.75×10^{-3}
    c. 8.75×10^3
    d. 87.5×10^4

46. –32 + 7 equals:

    a. –25
    b. 25
    c. –26
    d. 26

47. –37 + -47 equals:

    a. 84
    b. –84
    c. 10
    d. –10

48. 41% equals:

    a. 4.1
    b. .41
    c. .041
    d. .0041

49. $22(5x) =$

    a. $110x$
    b. $4.4\ x$
    c. $110x^2$
    d. $4.4\ x^2$

Verbal/Investigation Practice 1

50. John prefers _____ art to the classics.

    a. Contemporary
    b. Contemperary
    c. Contemparary
    d. Conteporary

51. Allen told Steve that he would give him the _____ version of his morning when he had time.

    a. Unabridgged
    b. Unabriddged
    c. Unabbridged
    d. Unabridged

52. Lisa was known for having _____ relationships.
    a. Promiscous
    b. Promicuous
    c. Promiscuous
    d. Promicious

53. The new tax was passed for _____ the waterfront district.
    a. Revitallizing
    b. Revitalizzing
    c. Revitelizing
    d. Revitalizing

54. The increased _____ to the class fund allowed for an end of the year party.
    a. Revenuee
    b. Revenue
    c. Revanue
    d. Revanuee

55. The teenager _____ some candy from the grocery store.
    a. Pillferred
    b. Pilferred
    c. Pillfered
    d. Pilfered

56. Being from a small town, some of Dean's views were _____.
    a. Parochial
    b. Perochial
    c. Porochial
    d. Parochiel

57. All of the students dreaded the quizzes the professor gave since he tested on _____ material.
    a. Obscere
    b. Obscore
    c. Obbscure
    d. Obscure

58. The judge sued the newspaper for ___.
    a. Libel
    b. Labal
    c. Lobel
    d. Libbel

Identify the key word/words that complete the statements.

59. The _____ of the rainbow were _____ against the bright blue sky.
    a. Textures, Clear
    b. Hues, Vivid
    c. Alabaster, Bright
    d. Line, Dark

60. The president has a ____ of ____ around him when he makes public appearances.
    a. Catalyst, Individuals
    b. Barrier, Contrast
    c. Hedge, Protection
    d. Derrick, Protection

61. A small selection of terms was found at the back of the textbook. It was a:
    a. Glossary
    b. Preface
    c. Diction
    d. Kefir

62. The horror movie frightened the children. It was:
    a. Melancholy
    b. Dramatic
    c. Ghastly
    d. Tragedy

63. After practice, the girl's softball team stated, "We're famished!" Famished means:
    a. Fatigued
    b. Hungry
    c. Excited
    d. Ready

64. The newborn baby was enamored with the rattle. Enamored means:
    a. Fascinated
    b. Happy
    c. Unsure what to do
    d. Aggravated

65. When having a problem, it is best to dissect the situation then act.
Dissect means

    a. Cut apart
    b. Talk about
    c. Ignore
    d. Analyze

66. The books subject matter was ____ to the ____, and it did not sell.
    a. Attractive, Masses
    b. Limited, People
    c. Loathsome, Masses
    d. Colorful, Individual

67. The kitten was soaked to the ____ from the ___.
    a. Skin, Abyss
    b. Skin, Craven
    c. Skin, Storm
    d. Hide, Abyss

68. The bouncer's countenance discouraged brawls.

Countenance means

    a. Message
    b. Presence
    c. Expression
    d. Strength

69. The child apprized her father's authority and behaved herself in church.

Apprized means:

    a. Appreciated
    b. Compromised
    c. Defied
    d. Noted

Identify the appropriate error in the following sentences.

70. David was known for belching; and telling inappropriate jokes in public.
    a. Capitalization
    b. Punctuation
    c. Spelling
    d. Grammar

71. Graduation from High School is considered by many a momentous occasion.
    a. Capitalization
    b. Punctuation
    c. Spelling
    d. Grammar

72. Nurses plays a vital role in the healthcare profession.
    a. Capitalization
    b. Punctuation
    c. Spelling
    d. Grammar

73. After having his tonsels removed, the child was listless for a few days.
    a. Capitalization
    b. Punctuation
    c. Spelling
    d. Grammar

74. The park was serine at twilight.
    a. Capitalization
    b. Punctuation
    c. Spelling
    d. Grammar

75. The patient's mind was lucid during the evaluation?
    a. Capitalization
    b. Punctuation
    c. Spelling
    d. Grammar

Questions 76 – 81 pertain to the following passage:

Reading 1

Most brides and grooms over spend when they plan their wedding. They choose the most expensive items and do not set a realistic budget. Most couples forget that it is only one day in their life. Here are a few tips on how you can avoid the wedding money mistake that most couples make.

Wedding budgets can range from one hundred dollars to a life long debt that may never be retired. Your job is to set a firm budget and stick with it. If you spend more in one area, you must cut in another one.

Once you decide your budget, here are a list of items and percents of the budget that they will take. Wedding and engagement rings will require 15 percent of your budget. The wedding apparel will cost approximately 6 percent of your expenditures. The reception, food, and wedding cake will take 42 percent of your budget. Invitations and decorations including flowers will eat up 17 percent. The officiant, limousine rental, photographer and videographer will cost another 13 percent of your budget. The wedding party gifts, rehearsal dinner, and pre-wedding parties will take up the rest.

Do not make the same mistake many naive brides do by placing wedding debt onto their credit card. If your credit card debt is the same each month or increasing with every month, it may take 40 years for you to pay off your wedding especially if you have an 18% APR. This is also exclusively your debt; you are stuck with the bill if your ex-fiancé decides to skip town the night before the wedding.

Assess your current cash reserves. Do not count on gifts to cover the cost of your wedding. If you need to cash in CD's, bonds, or stocks to pay for your wedding, cash them in well in advance. Most service-oriented companies like to have their cash in hand before the big day.

Set up a separate checking account for your wedding so that you will not overdraw your personal account and spend more than you intended. With that in mind, put ten percent more than you intended to use on your budget into that checking account. In the event that you do go over budget, you will not be hit with insufficient funds fees.

Stay away from short-term loans offered by many financial institutions. The fees are often hidden and can quickly accumulate to more than you borrowed. These loans are very difficult to repay in the short amount of time given. If one payment is missed, you will have a substantial late fee tacked on top of your loan balance.

To save money after the wedding, be sure to have someone responsible for returning all rental items before their due date. Some companies have substantial late fees that can be the equivalent to the cost of the rental. They feel that if you do not return it then they cannot rent it.

- 97 -

Remember that this is one day of your life. Ask yourself if the debt you accumulate is worth the stress on your new marriage.

76. This passage is mainly about:
    a. Coping with marriage problems
    b. Saving money for your wedding
    c. Avoiding marriage pitfalls
    d. Budgeting for your wedding

77. We may infer from the article that a wedding is not:
    a. Worth going into lots of debt
    b. The joyful occasion it is usually thought to be
    c. An expensive party
    d. That costly

78. The article states that the wedding party gifts, rehearsal dinner, and pre-wedding parties will take up the rest. What is this sentence stating?
    a. These items will use up the rest of the budget
    b. These are necessary parts of a complete wedding
    c. These events and items will be the most costly part of your wedding
    d. These do not need to be included in the budget

79. What percent do the above stated items take up of the budget?
    a. 4%
    b. 5%
    c. 7%
    d. 8%

80. The article states that most brides and grooms "do not set a realistic budget." Realistic means:

    a. Significant
    b. Practical
    c. Firm
    d. Ideal

81. We may infer from the article that many weddings:
    a. Are budgeted
    b. Go over budget
    c. Are exactly what the bride want
    d. Do not have to cost more than one hundred dollars

Questions 82 – 87 pertain to the following passage:

Reading 2

Dogs are amazing creatures designed with a unique blend of senses. These senses are similar to humans but are found in different concentrations in dogs.

A dog's sense of sight can detect movement at greater distances than humans can. This occurs because their eyes are wider apart than human eyes, but they have

- 98 -

difficulty seeing closer objects. They are able to see in dimmer light that helps them with night hunting. Dogs see few colors and can only distinguish between a few of them.

Dogs are known for their sense of smell. A dog can follow a trail that is weeks old. They are able to smell scents that are one-millionth the concentration that humans require to detect an odor. This trait makes them beneficial as police dogs. They can be trained to detect drugs, locate dead bodies, or find lost children.

A dog's sense of hearing is amazing; dogs can hear approximately four times better than humans can. Dogs similar to humans have a wide range of vocalizations that include whimpers, moans, whines, and barks.

Dogs have less taste buds than human have. Dogs are willing to eat or chew on about anything. They are omnivores since they eat both meat and plant material.

Moreover, dogs' sense of touch is similar to a human's touch. They enjoy being petted, groomed, and played with by their owners.

Dogs have the same senses as human, but they are found in different concentrations.

82. Which of these titles would describe best this passage?
    a. "Making Sense of a Dog's Senses"
    b. "A Dog's Life"
    c. "Dogs Save Lives with Their Senses"
    d. "Canine's Plight"

83. We can infer from the article that a dog could hear:
    a. Better than a cat
    b. The same as a human
    c. Worse than a human
    d. Better than a human

84. The dog is able to smell what concentration of an odor compared to a human?
    a. One-tenth
    b. One-thousandth
    c. One-millionth
    d. One-billionth

85. What sense that a dog has would be most beneficial to the police department.
    a. Sight
    b. Taste
    c. Touch
    d. Smell

86. The article states that "Dogs see few colors and can only distinguish between a few of them." Distinguish means:
    a. Make important
    b. Design
    c. Concern
    d. Differentiate

87. As described in the article, which is the best statement to describe what dogs eat?

    a. Dogs eat meat and vegetables
    b. Dogs are solely carnivores
    c. Dogs exclusively eat plant material
    d. Dogs eat only meat

Questions 88 – 93 pertain to the following passage:

Reading 3

Frank Tower, have you ever heard of him? He is the questionable figure who supposedly survived three doomed ships in the 1900's. Some consider him one of the luckiest men alive.

He was touted to be a middle-aged fireman in the engine room. Some considered him an ordinary, hardworking person, but he had the ability to avoid dying in some of the most horrendous ocean liner accidents ever recorded.

He was said to have once been a crewmember on the Titanic at the time that the ship hit the iceberg. Two years later, he was working on the Empress of Ireland when she collided with the Storstad. Over one thousand people died in that disaster. He was then employed in May of 1915 on the Lusitania when it was hit by a U-20 torpedo. He apparently lived through that without a scratch as well.

If you are beginning to doubt this man's existence, you are probably not to far from the truth. No records have been found ever listing a man by Frank Towers working on any of the three ships.

The legend of Frank Towers seems to be another case of an urban folk tale, humanity's desire to see triumph over a tragic situation. Fact or fiction, Frank Towers is one of the multiple characters that help color the history books.

88. According to the article, the Lusitania is a?

    a. Airplane
    b. Torpedo Boat
    c. Ship
    d. Train

89. In this statement from the article, "He was touted to be a middle-aged fireman in the engine room." Touted means?

    a. Publicized
    b. Demeaned
    c. Set-up
    d. Sighted

90. This passage sheds doubt on:

    a. The fact that three ships sank
    b. The thought that America was at war with other countries
    c. Frank Towers causing the ships to sink
    d. Urban folk tales are not always based on real people

91. The title of this article could be:

    a. "Frank Towers, a Man of Mystery"
    b. "Surviving the Impossible"
    c. "The Legend of Frank Towers Debunked"
    d. "How to Survive Doomed Ships"

92. According to this passage, which of the following phrases best captures the intent of the article.

    a. A stitch in time saves nine
    b. Don't believe everything you read
    c. Seeing is believing
    d. There are many layers of an onion

93. The article states that urban folk tales are created because

    a. They are fun to hear
    b. Humanity likes to see someone triumph over tragedy
    c. They trick people into believing lies
    d. People do not remember details clearly

Questions 94 – 99 pertain to the following passage:

Reading 4

Medical documentation standards vary between state and federal organizations. Hospitals and insurance companies have policies that regulate medical documentation and terminology. Health care professionals must adhere to these standards to support the level of treatment and the care plan administered. Medicare is the leader in determining what is required in medical documentation to support delivery of services. The other major insurance companies look to Medicare for leadership with medical documentation and medical terminology.

Medical documentation and terminology are used to allow a continuity of care between health care professionals. This terminology is universal and is the language of health care providers. Appropriate medical terminology allows a health care practitioner to clearly identify a colleague's opinion and determine delivery of services. If an error is present in medical documentation and terminology, the patient will suffer the consequences. For example, if a vascular surgeon identifies the need for a below knee amputation (BKA) on the right lower extremity and an orthopedic doctor performs an above knee amputation (AKA) on the right lower extremity, a malpractice suit will most certainly follow.

Medicare also sets standards of care that require appropriate documentation for reimbursement purposes. Inappropriate medical documentation and terminology does not support the proper delivery of services and payment to the hospital or clinic will not be forth coming. Consequently, hospitals will go broke if multiple claims are denied, because of inappropriate medical documentation and terminology.

- 101 -

94. The main idea of this passage is?

    a. The importance of proper medical documentation and terminology
    b. Documentation standards are universal
    c. Health care professionals are allowed to document however they want
    d. Medical documentation does not effect reimbursement

95. Considering the information in this passage, you might suspect that hospitals would teach their employees

    a. How to maximize reimbursement with their documentation skills
    b. How to document pre-operatively
    c. A standardized set of medical abbreviations
    d. All of the above

96. According to the article, what could be the end result of poor documentation?

    a. Claims denied
    b. Patients injured
    c. Hospital goes out of business
    d. All of the above

97. What organization sets the standards for medical documentation according to this article?

    a. The medical profession
    b. The healthcare professionals
    c. Medicare
    d. The hospital

98. The article states that health care professionals must adhere to these standards. Adhere means?

    a. Obtain
    b. Comply
    c. Include
    d. Remember

99. Readers of this passage might expect the author to proceed to discuss

    a. Other benefits of proper medical documentation
    b. How to document properly
    c. The relationship between medical terminology and documentation
    d. Programs to implement for better documentation in hospitals

Questions 100 – 105 pertain to the following passage:

Reading 5

When Title IX came into effect in 1972, it challenged colleges to offer increased sport opportunities for women. Since 1972, the number of women participating in college sports has increased five fold. Colleges were required to offer improved ratios of scholarships for women sports and to obtain sex equality in sports.

Generally, colleges compare the ratio of women in athletics to the ratio of women in their undergraduate programs to determine compliance with Title IX. The (CHE) Chronicle of Higher Education report in July 2002, stated that 45 colleges are in compliance with Title IX. Thousands of colleges still have challenges to become compliant with Title IX according to the CHE. Ohio State, Syracuse and Texas Tech are three of the schools in compliance with Title IX according to the CHE.

Many colleges have begun cutting back on the opportunities for men sports and increasing the opportunities for women to be compliant with these new guidelines. Sports such as wresting and gymnastics for men are being cut at colleges, and sports such as golf and rowing are being offered to women. Colleges have a set amount of money to dedicate to athletics and smaller men's sports are being cut to allow sports like football and baseball to continue.

College women have been offered new chances for scholarships and funding for college. Many colleges are desperately seeking women for rowing, soccer, and golf teams to reach equality ratios. College females, who need extra money for college and have even a small amount of athletic ability, will be considered for these positions. If a high school senior has kept in shape and likes working out, then rowing in college may be close to a free ride. If a high school senior has played golf several times, they may qualify for women's college team at a small school.

Currently, some male college athletes are crying foul play and charging discrimination, if their sport program is being cut. However, colleges are trying to balance the books and comply with Title IX. Changes are probably coming to Title IX; however, the precedent of increased women participation in sports has already been determined.

100. What is the main idea of this article?
   a. How female students can get free money
   b. Discrimination of male athletes
   c. How increasing compliance with Title IX by colleges affect males and females
   d. Changes to Title IX

101. Which of the following statements are supported by the article?
   a. Men's sports are being completely eliminated for women's sports
   b. Mediocre women athletes may be able to win scholarships at small schools
   c. All colleges are compliant with Title IX
   d. Men's Gymnastics is not a sport that is being cut by some schools for Title IX

102. Title IX is best described as:
   a. An act that encouraged schools to increase funding of female sports determined by the ratio of women enrollees to the number of sports opportunities
   b. An act that eliminates some male sports for women's sports
   c. An act that is being followed by the majority of universities in the United States
   d. An act that dictates that schools must be compliant with the standards given by the CHE for college sports equality

103. According to the article which of the following schools was not mentioned as being compliant with Title IX.
   a. Texas Tech
   b. Syracuse
   c. Tennessee State
   d. Ohio State

104. According to the article, participation in women's sports has increased how much since Title IX was implemented.

    a. 3 times
    b. Five fold
    c. Twice as much
    d. One fifth as much

105. The article states that some male college athletes are crying foul play. In this statement, foul play means

    a. Bird
    b. Unfair
    c. Necessary
    d. Fossick

Arithmetic Practice 2

106. 75% of 500

    a. 365
    b. 375
    c. 387
    d. 390

107. 45% of 600

    a. 250
    b. 260
    c. 270
    d. 280

108. $(7 \times 5) + (8 \times 2) =$

    a. 51
    b. 57
    c. 85
    d. 560

109. $(8 \div 2) (12 \div 3) =$

    a. 1
    b. 8
    c. 12
    d. 16

110. Which of the following numbers is a prime number?

    a. 12
    b. 25
    c. 27
    d. 31

111. Which number is a factor of 36?
    a. 5
    b. 7
    c. 8
    d. 9

112. 75 x 34 =
    a. 1200
    b. 2050
    c. 2550
    d. 3100

113. x + 372 = 853, x =
    a. 455
    b. 481
    c. 520
    d. 635

114. Convert .25 into fraction form.
    a. ¼
    b. ½
    c. 1/8
    d. 2/3

115. 60 grains are equal to 1 dram. How many grains are in 15 drams?
    a. 900
    b. 1020
    c. 1220
    d. 1300

116. A pitcher holds 7 ½ cups water. How many cups will 5 pitchers hold?
    a. 34 ¼
    b. 35 ½
    c. 37 ½
    d. 38 ¼

117. If a = 3, b= 4, c=5, then $(a + b + c)^2 + (a - b - c) =$
    a. 124
    b. 136
    c. 138
    d. 150

118. 0.85 =
    a. 13/15
    b. 17/20
    c. 18/19
    d. 19/22

119. Which fraction is closest to 2/3 without going over?

    a. 6/13
    b. 7/12
    c. 11/16
    d. 9/12

120. A puddle of water contained 72 pints of water. A rainstorm added 21% more water to the puddle. Approximately, how many pints of water are now in the puddle?

    a. 76
    b. 87
    c. 92
    d. 112

121. If $x = 2$ then $x^4 (x + 3) =$

    a. 72
    b. 80
    c. 96
    d. 114

122. A circle graph is used to show the percent of patient types that a hospital sees. How many degrees of the circle should the graph show if 1/3 of the patient type is pediatric?

    a. 90 degrees
    b. 120 degrees
    c. 220 degrees
    d. 360 degrees

123. A traveler on vacation spent $ 25 at the grocery store the first week of school; the next two weeks he spent $ 52; and the last week he spent $34. What was his average food expenditure while he was on vacation?

    a. $37.00
    b. $38.25
    c. $40.75
    d. $52.00

124. 437.65 – 325.752 =

    a. 111.898
    b. 121.758
    c. 122.348
    d. 133.053

125. 43.3 x 23.03 =

    a. 997.199
    b. 999.999
    c. 1010.03
    d. 1111.01

126. How many nonoverlapping 2-inch x 2-inch squares are contained in a 8-inch x 24- inch rectangle?

    a. 32
    b. 44
    c. 48
    d. 52

127. After going on diet for two weeks, you have lost 6% of you weight. Your original weight was 157 lbs. What do you weigh now?

    a. 132 lbs
    b. 135.48 lbs
    c. 144.98 lbs
    d. 147.58 lbs

128. In order for a school to allow a vending machine to be placed next to the cafeteria, 65% of the school's population must ask for it. If 340 of the school's 650 students have requested the vending machines, how many more are needed to get the vending machines?

    a. 75
    b. 83
    c. 89
    d. 99

129. After purchasing a book that has a no return policy, the book goes on sale at the bookstore for 15% less. You realize that you spent an extra $12.75 on the book. What amount did you pay for the book originally?

    a. $65
    b. $75
    c. $85
    d. $95

130. Which of the following fractions have the largest value?

    a. 8/15
    b. 7/12
    c. 6/13
    d. 9/16

131. Round this number to the nearest hundredths 390.24657

    a. 400
    b. 390.247
    c. 390.25
    d. 390.2

132. To get 1 as an answer, you must multiply 4/5 by

    a. 5/4
    b. ½
    c. 1
    d. ¼

133. z = 4, z + 6 – (z+4)=

    a. 2

    b. 4

    c. 6

    d. 8

134. While working, patient's sodium intake was 300 mg on Monday, 1240 mg on Tuesday, 900 mg on Wednesday and Friday, and 1500 on Thursday. What was the average intake of sodium while the patient was at work?

    a. 476 mg

    b. 754 mg

    c. 968 mg

    d. 998 mg

135. Which of the following numbers is correctly rounded to the nearest tenth?

    a. 3.756 rounds to 3.76

    b. 4.567 rounds to 4.5

    c. 6.982 rounds to 7.0

    d. 54.32 rounds to 54.4

136. 4.2% of 328 =

    a. 12.7

    b. 13.8

    c. 14.2

    d. 15.5

137. Which of the following fraction equal 0.625

    a. 3/4

    b. 5/6

    c. 5/8

    d. 2/3

138. Which of the following illustrates the distributive property of multiplication?

    a. 2x + 5(z – 3) = 10x + 5z -15

    b. 2x + 5(z – 3) = 2x + 5z - 3

    c. 2x + 5(z – 3) = 2x + 5z - 15

    d. 2x + 5(z – 3) = 2z + z – 15

139. Which of the following is the square root of 80

    a. $4\sqrt{5}$

    b. 8

    c. $5\sqrt{4}$

    d. 16

Questions 140 - 143 refer to the following information:

> A school has a 50 x 60 yard rectangular playground. There are 3 classes playing on it. 15 students are from Mrs. Red's class, 12 are from Miss White's class, and 17 are from Ms. Brown's class.

140. How many square yards does the playground cover?

    a. 110
    b. 300
    c. 3,000
    d. 30,000

141. How many students are playing on the playground?

    a. 15
    b. 22
    c. 36
    d. 44

142. If both sides of the playground are increased by 10%, what would the area be in square yards?

    a. 121
    b. 1210
    c. 3,000
    d. 3,630

143. Ms. Brown's class raised $400 to help put a fence around the playground. The fence cost $15 a yard. How much more money per student would Ms. Brown's class have to raise to completely fence in the playground?

    a. $165.12
    b. $170.59
    c. $183.57
    d. $220.25

144. 160%=

    a. 5/6
    b. 6/5
    c. 8/5
    d. 9/6

145. A 6% (by volume) solution of bleach in water is required for cleaning a bathroom. How many milliliters of the solution can be made from 50 milliliters of pure bleach?

    a. 833
    b. 952
    c. 1054
    d. 2000

146. 8.7 x 23.3 equals:

    a. 202.71
    b. 2027.1
    c. 212.71
    d. 2127.1

147. 134.5 Divided by 5 equals:
     a. 26.9
     b. 25.9
     c. 23.9
     d. 22.9

148. 5.30 x 10^{-4} equals:
     a. .000053
     b. .00053
     c. 53,000
     d. 5,300,000

149. 23/3 =
     a. 6 2/3
     b. 7 1/3
     c. 7 2/3
     d. 8 1/3

150. 33/100 =
     a. .0033
     b. .033
     c. .33
     d. 3.3

151. $45^x/5^x$ =
     a. 9^x
     b. 9
     c. 11^x
     d. 11

152. 24x/3 =
     a. 8x
     b. 8
     c. 7x
     d. 7

153. 52x(4y) =
     a. 13xy
     b. –13xy
     c. $208x^{-y}$
     d. 208xy

154. 4500 + 3422 + 3909 =
     a. 12,831
     b. 12,731
     c. 11,831
     d. 11,731

Verbal/Investigation Practice 2

155. Susan's _____ of darkness prevents her from leaving her house at night. means
    a. Abhorance
    b. Abhorence
    c. Abhorrence
    d. Abhorrance

156. The girl displayed _____ behavior when she found out her puppy was injured.
    a. Destraught
    b. Distaught
    c. Distraught
    d. Distrauht

157. The French exchange student spoke English as if it were her first language. She was
    a. Dandy
    b. Fluent
    c. Caustic
    d. Talented

158. The prescription plan did not cover name brand drugs if there was a _____ substitute available.
    a. Generic
    b. Reasonable
    c. Compatible
    d. Complete

159. The _____ crowd mourned the loss of their leader.
    a. Sember
    b. Somber
    c. Sombar
    d. Sombor

160. The southern _____ girl was known for her behavior.
    a. Gentell
    b. Ganteel
    c. Genteal
    d. Genteel

161. The mother attempted to _____ her son with toys.
    a. Molifey
    b. Mollify
    c. Molify
    d. Mollifey

162. The car accident caused a sliver of glass to cut the passenger's optic nerve. The passenger lost his

    a. Arm
    b. Movement
    c. Smell
    d. Vision

163. Some people accused John of thinking too much. He would sometimes ___ on a subject for months at a time.

    a. Pondar
    b. Pondder
    c .Ponnder
    d. Ponder

164. The young artist had an _____ passion for watercolors.

    a. Unbradled
    b. Unbriddled
    c. Unbridled
    d. Unbridlled

165. The _____ kept the students cool while they sat outside studying.

    a. Zephyir
    b. Zepheyer
    c. Zepyr
    d. Zephyr

166. The pianist played his rendition of a _____.

    a. Sonata
    b. Sonatina
    c. Sonate
    d. Sonete

167. The entertainer had no _____ about performing in front of two thousand screaming fans.

    a. Qulams
    b. Quelms
    c. Qualms
    d. Qualmes

168. The ___ still enjoyed being around its mother but was acting more independent each day.

    a. Yearling
    b. Yeerling
    c. Yearlling
    d. Yearlinng

169. The financial planner had reached the top of his career; he felt he was at his

    a. Performance
    b. Stress level
    c. Limit
    d. Zenith

170. The siblings found _____ in each other as they _____ the good times with their father.

    a. Happiness, Prepared
    b. Sorrow, Committed
    c. Solace, Remembered
    d. Sorrow, Limited

171. The young boy sat _____ as the principal yelled at him.

    a. Passivly
    b. Pasively
    c. Passivelly
    d. Passively

172. The teenage was accused of killing his father and mother. He was accused of:

    a. Sobriety
    b. Misguidance
    c. Misgamy
    d. Parricide

173. Brian's secret to studying success relied on a system designed to assist with the recollection of terms. His secret was the use of:

    a. Syllables
    b. Memorabilia
    c. Mnemonics
    d. Puzzles

Identify the appropriate error in the following sentences.

174. The bachalor never married. Most people thought it was because of misogyny.

    a. Capitalization
    b. Punctuation
    c. Spelling
    d. Grammar

175. The intricacy of the mathematical equation, drove the student crazy trying to solve it.

    a. Capitalization
    b. Punctuation
    c. Spelling
    d. Grammar

176. The hybrid tomatoes is immune to most common diseases.

    a. Capitalization
    b. Punctuation
    c. Spelling
    d. Grammar

177. The professor was humiliated when his students reported him to the Dean for verbal abuse.

    a. Capitalization
    b. Punctuation
    c. Spelling
    d. Grammar

178. The con artist hoodwinked the old lady when he sold her fradulent insurance.

    a. Capitalization
    b. Punctuation
    c. Spelling
    d. Grammar

179. The movie star was accused of a misdemeanor, when she stole 15 dollars worth of merchandise from the store.

    a. Capitalization
    b. Punctuation
    c. Spelling
    d. Grammar

180. The congregation sang a comtemporary hymn.

    a. Capitalization
    b. Punctuation
    c. Spelling
    d. Grammar

Questions 181 – 186 pertain to the following article:

Reading 1

The SOAP format is used in most medical schools and allied health schools. SOAP stands for Subjective, Objective, Assessment and Plan. Each of these sections require the basic understanding of medical terminology to allow continuity of care. The SOAP format requires medical terminology that is considered appropriate by the facility where you are working. Each facility should have a listed set of appropriate medical abbreviations and surgical abbreviations. The "S" includes the patient's goal, patient's pain complaint, medical history and social history. The "O" includes the clinician data collection of strength, range of motion, skin integrity and organ system function. The "A" includes the clinician's opinion about the presented case, prognosis, diagnosis and goals. The "P" includes the plan to progress to the goals set in the "A" and the interventions that are necessary.

Some schools and are trying to get away from the SOAP format and going to a problem based documentation plan. Basically, under this new plan only changes in status need to be documentation with problem based documentation, other than vitals sign and critical medical information. The problem with the SOAP format is that is unclear when a clinician should stop documenting. As a result, SOAP notes can turn into complete medical reassessments with a single treatment.

A clinician's documentation standards should be set high. Too often, medical terminology and documentation are ambiguous. Clinicians often use arrows, their own abbreviations and paraphrasing that is not professional. Paraphrasing and inappropriate use of medical terminology can result in the firing of a clinician with strong patient care skills. Hospitals and clinics are a business. If they are losing money over poor documentation, changes will be made. Medicare has made information available about frequent medical documentation errors. Moreover, hospitals are trying to bring staff up to speed on these issues. Overuse of abbreviations can lead to sentences that are unclear; therefore, medical errors may have increased occurrence.

A medical professional will not be able to remember the definition of every medical term. Medical terminology could fill volumes of dictionaries. However, a medical professional can learn the prefixes, suffixes and word roots that allow for an understanding of most medical terms.

181. Which of the following could be a title of this article?

a. "SOAP Notes Exposed"
b. "Medical documentation Condensed"
c. "The relationship of Medical Terminology and SOAP NOTES"
d. "SOAP Notes and the Palliative Implications"

182. The "O" in the SOAP note stands for?

a. Operational
b. Objective
c. Organization
d. Operations

183. Which of the following is considered a problem with SOAP notes?

a. When to document
b. When to stop documenting
c. When to abbreviate with medical terminology
d. When to reiterate the main points

184. Which of the following statements is not supported in the above text?

a. SOAP notes require proper medical terminology
b. SOAP notes can become complete reassessments of medical care
c. Good clinicians have been fired over poor documentation
d. Medical documentation must be reviewed by administration

185. According to the article, the effects of poor medical terminology use have not resulted in which of the following?

a. Firing of clinicians
b. Medical errors
c. Poor documentation
d. SOAP note format changes

186. Future changes in medical documentation that may be inferred from this article are:

a. Medical terminology will continue to change in the future
b. Medical documentation errors will continue to increase in the future
c. SOAP notes may require more structured text and format in the future
d. SOAP notes will continue to require skilled clinicians

Questions 187 – 192 pertain to the following article:

Reading 2

Many scams of college freshman revolve around quick cash schemes. Some involve working at home, mailing letters, and offering services to others that are invisible. Some profitable quick cash schemes are selling plasma, typing papers, providing transportation, and selling back books.

- 115 -

Various blood-related organizations will pay 30-60$ for platelets provided, if a student can give platelets. Normally, giving platelets requires several hours hooked up to IV tubing, and a minimal body weight. In addition, students with certain rare blood conditions may be able to make profitable quick cash in just a few hours.

Typing papers has always been the reliable college job through out the years. Normally, students put up flyers in student study hot spots and wait for business. Any rate can be charged, however if it isn't reasonable, no one will call the listed phone number. Last minute students often try and use this kind of service. The typist may be asked to fill in missing phrases or transitional words in the provided paper, but the typist should remember, who should be doing the work. Many typists require at least half of the money up front and the other half would be paid upon completion of the paper. Consequently, students that disappear off the radar prior to payment will loose their initial investment. $10-15 an hour is a reasonable price, but you may charge extra if you have a tight timeline.

If you have a car on campus, friends will probably ask for a ride frequently. If you have a fuel-efficient car you may be able to make a few dollars by charging a flat fee for transportation expenses. Limit the number of free rides around campus and consider posting a small visible sign inside your vehicle requesting payment. Be extremely wary of providing rides to strangers, and people that you don't really know. Criminal minds abound on campus so don't become a victim, and use sound judgement. Make sure your insurance is kept current in the event of an accident.

Selling books back to the bookstore is another good way to make money. Books in good condition will have more value upon return, than books in poor condition with multiple entries in the margins. A student that has a little time to raise quick cash may consider putting up flyers advertising books for resell. In general, a student will make more money selling directly to another student, then selling back to the bookstore. The bookstore may run out of used books quickly, consequently the only available books to buy may be unused full price books. Check out the bookstore to determine if this is the case. Be sure and post a flyer close to the bookstore to pick up any potential customers going to the bookstore.

Be wary of schemes to work in Alaska, folding envelopes, and being a sales agent on campus for a business with a P.O.Box address. Many students try going to Alaska during the summer to work on fishing boats. However, summer conditions off the coast of Alaska are not fun. Ten to twenty foot seas can be the normal conditions of the day. A student would be required to work in all weather conditions and operate on minimal amounts of sleep. Also many a student has lost a finger, or had a traumatic injury working on fishing boats.

Folding envelopes is a slow tedious process that offers poor rewards on time and return. Often money from the envelope's company is slow in coming and short on the investment of time. Businesses without a P.O. Box are often times businesses without a permanent addresses and location. Scam artists attempting to separate a college student from their money run some of these businesses.

187. In this article the author focuses on:

   a. The relationship between quick cash and college funding.
   b. The relationship between quick cash and academic freedom
   c. The relationship between college and scholarships.
   d. The relationship between cost and college

188. Which of the following was not considered a scheme to make money in college in the article?

   a. Selling plasma
   b. Selling back books
   c. Typing papers
   d. Working full-time

189. Which of the following was not considered a possible mechanism of action used by scam artists?

   a. Folding envelopes scheme
   b. Questionable business addresses
   c. Selling vacations
   d. Alaska opportunities

190. The article implies that selling back books is:

   a. A difficult and complicated process.
   b. Harder if selling to underclassmen directly: however, it may be more profitable.
   c. An easy way to earn a small amount of money in a hurry.
   d. Profitable

191. In this article, the author reports that typing papers is:

   a. A difficult and complicated process
   b. Always profitable
   c. Harder if typing for upperclassmen
   d. Sometimes a last minute business

192. According to the passage, boats in Alaska:

   a. May operate in 10-20 foot seas
   b. Offer comfortable quarters
   c. Provide good medical care
   d. Offer good food

Questions 193 – 198 pertain to the following article:

Reading 3

Generally, an applicant must be hired by a police department and then be sent to the police officer academy for further training. Consequently, the selection process for the police officer academy occurs primarily with a specific police department. Once you have meet all of the necessary requirements and have been hired, the police department that you work for will set up officer training. Smaller police departments in rural settings do not run their own police officer academies. They rely on regional academy for officer training. Most of these regional academies are in urban areas.

- 117 -

Most of the time, urban police officers make more money than rural police officers. The urban environment offers a large tax base than can support higher salaries. These higher salary positions are often much more selective than rural police because the rural police department may less applicants due to poorer salaries. Higher salary positions in the urban police officer force may require additional hurdles to becoming a patrol officer. Sometimes, police officers are required to participate in the local corrections department, until a patrol officer position opens up. Consequently, patrol officer positions may be at a premium.

Moreover, new graduates or junior officers are often assigned the major holidays and patrols at night. These patrols are tough because of holiday activity, and the criminal element likes the cover of darkness to operate under. Be prepared to be distant from family and friends as a junior officer during holidays.

According the Bureau of Labor and Statistics, the 2000 median annual earnings for police patrol officers was $39,790 nationwide. In 2000, median earnings were broken down as follows:

State:	$44,400
Local:	$39,710
Federal:	$37,760

According to the International City-County Management Association's annual Police and Fire Personnel, Salaries and Expenditures Survey in 2000 the following data was concluded:

	Min. Pay	Max. Pay
Police Chief	$62,640	$78,580
Deputy Chief	$53,740	$67,370
Police Captain	$51,580	$64,230
Police Lieutenant	$47,750	$57,740
Police Sergeant	$42,570	$50,670
Police Corporal	$35,370	$43,830
Police Officer	$31,410	$43,450

It should be noted that whenever a city or town increases police officer pay, there is sometimes a surge in applicants. Consequently, a hiring freeze may occur following a hiring surge. Potential police officers should decide quickly following a pay increase if they are committed enough to join the police force.

193. The main idea of this passage is:
    a. Law Enforcement Training and Pay
    b. The Criminal Element
    c. Urban Police Officers
    d. Hiring surges in Law Enforcement Jobs

194. According to the article, which profession would a Law Enforcement Agent hold if they made 44,000 a year?

   a. Police Officer
   b. Police Corporal
   c. Police Sergeant
   d. Police Captain

195. According to the article, which of the following is a true statement?

   a. Urban police officers make less than rural officers
   b. Most officers desire local correctional department jobs
   c. During holidays, most police departments have their most experience staff on duty
   d. Federal police officers make less money than state police officers on average

196. According to the article, urban areas are able to offer higher pay because

   a. Of a larger tax base
   b. They require less police forces
   c. They pay their fire department less
   d. They have less expenditures

197. Which of the following statements is supported by the article?

   a. Once you become a police officer, you will not have a pay increase
   b. Most rural areas do not have their own training facilities
   c. Police Captains are the lowest paid of the law enforcement officials
   d. Rural police officers make more money than urban police officers

198. According to the article, a junior officer may work difficult shifts. They should expect

   a. Better pay than senior officers
   b. To be away from their families at night and on holidays
   c. To be training rurally
   d. To be transferred to another shift

Questions 199 – 204 pertain to the following article:

Reading 4

Ask an interviewer what the number one attribute they are looking for in an interviewee and you'll invariably get the same response – Attitude. The most important impression you want to leave your interviewer with is that you have the right attitude for the school. Other characteristics are important, such as intelligence and experience, but they aren't as significant to your success in the interview as your attitude.

Every potential applicant has their qualifications all polished up and displayed proudly on their application. But those accomplishments are all in the past. An interviewer has to look at you in the present to determine how successful they think you will be in the future. The attitude you display is fundamental to their perception of your future success. Almost every employer would rather have a team player with a great attitude working at 100%, rather than a flashy superstar working at 50%. Regardless of your usual personality, remember that you're only in the interview for

30 minutes on average. In that short amount of time, do whatever it takes to wear a smile, remain positive, and exude a positive attitude.

It is easy to blame others for your mistakes or shortcomings. If an interviewer asks a question about something that you may be embarrassed about, don't immediately become negative and blame other people or situations. Accept responsibility for your actions and your past but make sure that anything negative does not remain the focus. Turn negatives into positives. For example, suppose an interviewer asks, "I see on your application that you show you dropped out of high school. Could you explain what happened?"

"As a teenager, I made my share of mistakes. That time in my life was the best thing that ever happened to me. I needed to grow-up, and I did. I learned to take responsibility for my actions. I earned my GED and have since held the same job for over two years. I have learned that I want to better myself, and I have been extremely active in working with troubled youths. My own background has offered an excellent background for this type of community service. I work to discourage them from what appears to be the easy way out which in the end turns out to be much harder."

Whatever you do; do not constantly shift the blame to others. It is okay to have had shortcomings in your past. The key in an interview is to show how you've learned from those experiences and have moved on and overcame them.

199. The best title for this selection is:
    a. "How to Maximize Your Interview"
    b. "Turning Bad into Good"
    c. "Presenting a Polished Image"
    d. "Covering Your Mistakes"

200. According to the article the number one most important attribute a person needs to display in an interview is:
    a. Arousing the interviewers interest
    b. Apologetic about mistakes
    c. Calmness
    d. A positive attitude

201. According to the article, if you went to prison, you should:
    a. Deny that it happened
    b. Own up to your mistake and describe what you have learned from it
    c. Explain how it was not your fault
    d. Express your sorrow and say how you cannot get pass the experience

202. If a teacher had to select among the following student applicants, which would he select according to the article?
    a. A super star working at 50%
    b. A perfectionist
    c. A hard worker with a positive attitude
    d. A underachiever

203. Which of the following statements should you not make during an interview?

a. "If you give me a chance, I will prove to you what a positive asset I can be to your program"
b. "The community service that I had to do as a juvenile delinquent helped me develop into the hard working person I am today"
c. "I wouldn't even have a record if my parents hadn't turned me in"
d. "I have overcome my drug problem; I learned so much about myself from the personal development classes I attended in rehab"

204. According to the article, all accomplishments that you have had so far in life are:

a. Unimportant
b. In the past
c. Determine your future
d. Shape what type of applicant you will be

Questions 205 – 210 pertain to the following article:

Reading 5

Fishing with live bait is not as popular as it used to be. The majority of bass fishermen use artificial lures. Even with this being the case, the record book show that live bait may be the way to go. The second largest bass weighed 21 pounds, 3 ounces and was taken on a crawfish. The third largest bass weighed 20 pounds, 15 ounces and was caught on a night crawler.

Different weather and water conditions affect how a bass reacts to live bait. Clear water conditions make an artificial lure easy for a bass to identify. Largemouth bass prefer live bait after a cold front or when their optimal feeding temperature is above or below normal. Slow-moving bass prefer slow-moving bait. Most artificial lures just do not look real when moving at a slow pace. Live bait on light line has a very realistic and tempting movement especially when it is dragged slowly along the bottom of the chosen body of water.

Another commonly used technique is adding live bait to a lure. This gives the lure a natural movement and works well with jigs, spinners, or spinnerbaits. The most often used bait for this technique is worms and minnows.

Largemouth bass will strike on a variety of live bait since they eat a wider variety of native foods than most fish. Some of the most popular live bass bait includes waterdogs, frogs, crawfish, shrimp, golden shiners, and night crawlers.

205. Which of the following would be an appropriate title for the article:

a. Champion Fishing
b. Fishing for Bass with Live Bait
c. Waterdogs and How to Use Them
d. Popular Bass Bait

206. According to the article, live bait looks more realistic than artificial bait in:

a. Saltwater
b. Freshwater
c. Clear water
d. Dark water

207. According to the article, which types of live bait work well when added to an artificial lure?

    a. Waterdogs and frogs
    b. Shrimp and crawfish
    c. Minnows and worms
    d. Golden shiners and night crawlers

208. Which of the following is a true statement according to the article?

    a. Two of the three largest bass were caught with live bait
    b. Jigs and spinnerbaits do not function well with live bait
    c. Artificial bait looks as real as live bait when used at a slow pace
    d. The majority of fishermen use live bait

209. When using live bait which type of line should you use?

    a. Heavy weight
    b. 40 lbs weight
    c. Medium weight
    d. Light weight

210. The article states when their optimal feeding temperature is above or below normal. Optimal means:

    a. Perfect
    b. Fastest
    c. Slowest
    d. Worst

Answer Key and Explanations

Arithmetic Practice 1

1. A: 25% of 400 is 100. To find a percentage of a whole number, first convert the percentage to a decimal by dividing it by 100. This can be done through the normal process of division or by simply shifting the decimal point two places to the left. So, in this problem, 25% becomes 0.25. This should make sense, since 25% means "25 out of a 100" and 0.25 means "25 hundredths." Then multiply the decimal by the whole number: $0.25 \times 400 = 100$.

2. B: 22% of $900 is 198. Again, find the percentage of a whole number by converting the percentage to a decimal and then multiplying by the whole number. Do not be confused by the use of dollars in this problem: a dollar is simply a whole unit of money, while cents are expressed to the right of the decimal point. This problem is sets up as $0.22 \times 900 = 198$.

3. C: 7 is a factor of 21. Factors are all of the numbers that can be divided into a given number evenly (with no remainder). 21 has 4 factors: 1, 3, 7, and 21. In mathematics, there is a distinction between prime numbers and composite numbers. Prime numbers have only two factors: 1 and the number itself. 5, 11, 13, and 17 are all prime numbers. Composite numbers have more than two factors. 8, for instance, is a composite number because it has four factors: 1, 2, 4, and 8.

4. B: $(9 \div 3) \times (8 \div 4) = 6$. This problem requires an understanding of the order of operations, or the sequence in which the various functions in a problem should be solved. The order of operations is as follows: parentheses, exponents, multiplication, division, addition, subtraction. Many people use a mnemonic (memory aid) like "Please Excuse My Dear Aunt Sally" to remind them of the order of operations. Problem 4 is a little tricky, because one might assume that the multiplication should be performed before the division (after all, multiplication precedes division in the order of operations). However, the division problems are within parentheses, and therefore should be performed first. This yields $3 \times 2 = 6$.

5. C: A 76-inch man is 193.04 cm tall. This problem requires you to make a unit conversion. The best way to do this is to set up the following equation: $1/2.54 = 76/x$. This equation states: 1 is to 2.54 as 76 is to x. In other words, if one inch equals 2.54 cm, then 76 inches equals x cm. The first step in solving the equation is to cross-multiply. $1 \times x = x$ and $2.54 \times 76 = 193.04$, so $x = 193.04$. This means that a 76-inch man is 193.04 cm tall.

6. C: The reciprocal of 6 is 1/6. The reciprocal of a number is the number that, if multiplied by the given number, would yield 1. The reciprocal of any whole number x is $1/x$. So the reciprocal of 6 is 1/6 and the reciprocal of 5 is 1/5. Finding the reciprocal of a fraction is easy as well: just switch the numerator and denominator. So, the reciprocal of 1/2 is 2/1, and the reciprocal of 2/3 is 3/2. Returning to whole numbers, it might help to remember that a whole number is equivalent to that number over one, and therefore the obvious reciprocal is one over that number. In other words, $6 = 6/1$, so the obvious reciprocal of 6 is 1/6.

7. A: If a room measures 11 ft × 12 ft × 9 ft, the volume is 1,188 ft³. The volume of a rectangular prism, like a box or a room, is calculated by multiplying the length, width, and height. So, this problem is solved $V = 11\text{ft} \times 12\text{ft} \times 9\text{ft} = 1,188$ ft³. Because the units are multiplied together three times, the resulting unit of volume is cubed.

8. B: The average rise in temperature was 28.25°F per hour. To solve this problem, begin by determining the total rise in temperature. This is done by subtracting the original temperature from

- 123 -

the final temperature: 145 – 32 = 113. The roast's internal temperature increased 113 degrees over four hours. To find the average hourly increase, divide total temperature change by number of hours: 113 degrees ÷ 4 hours = 28.25 degrees per hour.

9. C: If you use $100 to pay for an $80 book with 8.25% sales tax, you will receive $13.40 in change. The first step in this problem is to determine the total price of the book. To find the value of the sales tax, multiply the price of the book by the sales tax expressed as a decimal: 80 × 0.0825 = 6.6. So, the value of the sales tax is $6.60. Add this to the price of the book to find the total cost: 80 + 6.60 = 86.60. Then subtract this amount from the amount presented for payment: 100 – 86.60 = 13.40.

10. B: If you purchase a car with a down payment of $3,000 and 6 monthly payments of $225, you have paid $4,350 so far for the car. Find the total value of the monthly payments by multiplying a single payment by the number of months paid: 225 × 6 = 1,350. So, you have thus far made $1,350 in monthly payments. Add this to the down payment to find the total amount paid to this point: 3,000 + 1,350 = 4,350.

11. A: If you must purchase 240 pens in 6-packs that cost $2.35 and 6 staplers in 2-packs that cost $12.95, you will spend $132.85. First, determine the number of packs of pens that must be purchased by dividing the required number of pens by the number of pens in each pack: 240 ÷ 6 = 40. Then find the total cost of pens by multiplying the number of packs required by the price per pack: 40 × 2.35 = 94. Perform the same operation for the staplers: 6 ÷ 2 = 3 and 3 × 12.95 = 38.85. Add the price of the pens to the price of the staplers to determine total price: 94 + 38.85 = 132.85.

12. D: 45% is equal to 0.45. A percentage can be converted to a decimal simply by shifting the decimal point two places to the left. Although 45% does not display a decimal point, there is an implied point after the 5, since 45% = 45.0%.

13. B: If a vitamin had 500 mg of Calcium and loses 325 mg of Calcium, it has 175 mg of Calcium left. This is a subtraction problem. Take the original amount of Calcium and subtract the amount lost to determine the amount remaining: 500 – 325 = 175.

14. C: If you must give a patient 20 mg of a medication that has 4 mg for each 5 mL dose, you will need to give 25 mL. This problem can be set up as an equation: $5/4 = x/20$. This equation essentially states, "If a dose of 5 milliliters contains 4 mg of medication, how many milliliters are required to yield 20 mg?" Solve for x by cross-multiplying (5 × 20 and 4 × x) to yield $100 = 4x$, and then divide both sides by 4 to yield $25 = x$.

15. A: In the number 743.25, 2 is in the tenths place. The tenths place is the first place value to the right of the decimal point. There is no "oneths" place.

16. C: 125% is equal to 1.25. A decimal or whole number can be converted into a percentage by shifting the decimal point two places to the right. So, for instance, the number 8 is equal to 800%. It may seem odd that a small-looking number like 1.25 is equal to 125%, but remember that 125% is merely stating one-and-a-quarter units, with the units being ones.

17. B: If the average person drinks eight 8-ounce glasses of water per day, a person who drinks 12.8 ounces of water after a morning exercise session has consumed 1/5 of the daily average. Begin by determining the total number of ounces the average person consumes during the day: 8 × 8 = 64 ounces. The person described has consumed 12.8 of the 64 ounces, or 12.8/64. To make this a workable fraction, you must convert the numerator into a whole number by multiplying by five (this number is chosen because 5 is the lowest number that can be multiplied by 8 to generate a

product ending in zero). The denominator must be multiplied by five as well for the sake of consistency: $(12.8 \times 5)/(64 \times 5) = 64/320$. Both numerator and denominator should then be divided by the greatest common factor, 64, to yield 1/5. Another way to solve this problem would be to divide 12.8 by 64, which yields 0.2. This decimal is equal to 2/10, which can be simplified to 1/5 by dividing numerator and denominator by 2.

18. C: If $y = 3$, then $y^3(y^3 - y) = 648$. The first step here is to substitute the given value for y: $3^3(3^3 - 3)$. 3^3 is the same as $3 \times 3 \times 3$, which equals 27. So the problem is now $27(27 - 3)$. Multiply the initial 27 across the parentheses to yield $729 - 81 = 648$.

19. D: 33% of 300 is 99. The best way to solve a problem of this type is to convert the percentage into a decimal (33% = 0.33) and multiply by the other number: $0.33 \times 300 = 99$.

20. D: If you need 4/5 cup of water for a recipe and accidentally put 1/3 cup into the mixing bowl with the dry ingredients, you still need to add 7/15 cup. This problem is essentially asking you to find the difference between 4/5 and 1/3. To perform subtraction involving fractions, you must find a common denominator. The lowest common denominator for these fractions will be the lowest common multiple of 5 and 3. The multiples of 5 are 5, 10, 15, 20... The multiples of 3 are 3, 6, 9, 12, 15... So, 15 is the lowest common multiple of 5 and 3. To give both fractions 15 as a denominator, you will have to perform some multiplication. The denominator of 4/5 must be multiplied by 3 to become 15, so the numerator must be multiplied by 3 as well: $4/5 \times 3/3 = 12/15$. A similar operation is performed for the second fraction: $1/3 \times 5/5 = 5/15$. Now you can subtract: $12/15 - 5/15 = 7/15$. Seven and fifteen do not have any common factors, so the fraction cannot be simplified.

21. A: $3/4 - 1/2 = 1/4$. To perform subtraction involving fractions, you must find a common denominator. The lowest common multiple of 4 and 2 is 4, so it will not be necessary to convert 3/4. To give 1/2 the right denominator, however, both top and bottom should be multiplied by 2: $1/2 \times 2/2 = 2/4$. Now it is possible to subtract: $3/4 - 2/4 = 1/4$. This fraction cannot be simplified.

22. D: You will have to fill your 1/4 measuring cup 10 times to get 2 1/2 cups of flour. This is a division problem. You are being asked how many fourths are in 2 1/2. To perform this operation, you must convert the mixed number 2 1/2 to an improper fraction by multiplying the denominator by the coefficient and adding the product to the numerator: 2 1/2 becomes 5/2. Fraction division is performed by inverting (that is, turning upside-down) the second term and then multiplying numerator by numerator and denominator by denominator. So, 5/2 1/4 becomes $5/2 \times 4/1$ and the problem is solved $(5 \times 4)/(2 \times 1) = 20/2 = 10$.

23. C: If you are financing a \$5,000 computer, a 15% down payment will amount to \$750. The amount of the down payment can be determined by first multiplying the price by the percentage expressed as a decimal $(5,000 \times 0.15 = 750)$ and then adding the down payment to the original price: $5,000 + 750 = 5,750$.

24. B: Three kilometers is equal to 0.625 miles. This is a conversion problem, which can be solved by setting up the equation $1/0.625 = 3/y$, or "1 kilometer is to 0.625 miles as 3 kilometers is to y miles." Then cross-multiply: $y = 1.875$.

25. C: If you need an aquarium with a volume of 1,680 feet³, you should purchase the one with the dimensions 14 feet × 20 feet × 6 feet. One way to approach this problem is through trial and error. In other words, multiply out the given dimensions until you find the one that is equal or closest to 1,680 feet³. If you do this for answer choice C, you will find that an aquarium with dimensions of 14 feet × 20 feet × 6 feet is equal to 1,680 feet³.

- 125 -

26. A: If you invest $9,000 and receive yearly interest of $450, your interest rate is 5%. The interest rate is the percentage of the initial investment that will be counted as interest in one year. In other words, you are being asked to determine what percentage of 9,000 is 450. This can be done by dividing 450 by 9,000. To do this, you will have to express 450 as 450.00.

27. B: If there are 48 students in your class and 32 of them are female, 33% of the students in the class are male. First, determine the number of male students by subtracting the number of female students from the total number of students: 48 – 32 = 16. There are sixteen male students. Then express the number of male students as a fraction: 16/48. To convert this to a percentage, divide the numerator by the denominator: 16 ÷ 48. It may help to simplify the fraction first. The greatest common factor of 16 and 48 is 16, so 16/48 = 1/3. The division problem would then be 1 ÷ 3.

28. B: If $w = 82 + 2$ and $z = 41(2)$, then $w > z$. To solve this problem, calculate the values of w and z. $w = 82 + 2 = 84$ and $z = 41(2) = 82$. Therefore, of the answer choices, the only true statement is that w is greater than z.

29. C: If a phone call costs 99 cents for the first twenty minutes and ten cents for each additional minute, a phone call that lasts 65 minutes will cost $5.49. To calculate this cost, add the value of the first twenty minutes to the value of the remaining 45 minutes: 0.99 + 45(0.10). The order of operations indicates that the multiplication must be performed first, leaving you with 0.99 + 4.50 = 5.49.

30. C: If a class of students has 6 first-graders, 7 second-graders, and 5 third-graders, 39% of the class is second-graders. Begin by finding the total number of students: 6 + 7 + 5 = 18. Then create a fraction with the number of second-graders over the total number of students: 7/18. Divide 7.0 by 18. This will yield 0.3888, with the 8 repeating infinitely. To make a nice even percentage, round the hundredths place up to 9 and shift the decimal point two places to the right. Second-graders make up 39% of the class.

31. B: If one slice of bread is 80 calories, there are approximately 200 calories in 2 1/2 slices of bread. One way to solve this problem is through multiplication: 2 1/2(80). You can then either convert 1/2 into the decimal 0.5 or convert the mixed number 2 1/2 into an improper fraction by multiplying the denominator by the coefficient and adding this product to the numerator. This process yields 5/2, which can then be multiplied by 80/1. The result would be 400/2, or 200.

32. A: Given $7x = 3a + 2a$, if $a = 7$ then $x = 5$. Substitute the given value a: $7x = 3(7) + 2(7)$. Solve for x by first performing the multiplication on the right side of the equation, yielding $7x = 21 + 14$. Then add the numbers on the right side together: $7x = 35$. Finally, eliminate the 7 by dividing both sides of the equation by it $7x/7 = 35/7$, or $x = 5$.

33. B: Using Fried's rule for infant dose calculations, a two-year-old should receive 2.4 mg if an adult would receive 15 mg. To solve this problem, substitute the given values into the equation for Fried's rule: Infant's Dose = (24/150) × 15. Remember that the age must be given in months, and since there are 12 months in a year, a two-year-old is 24 months old. Take care of the division first, yielding 0.16 × 15 = 2.4.

34. D: The area of a triangle with a base of 6 cm and a height of 8 cm is 24 cm². The formula for the area of a triangle is $A = 1/2bh$. So, substituting in the given values, we have $A = ½(6)(8)$. The multiplication can be performed in any order to yield 24 cm².

35. C: 7 1/2 – 5 3/8 = 2 1/8. To complete this problem, you must find a common denominator for the fractions. The lowest common denominator of 2 and 8 is 8. The first fraction needs to have both

numerator and denominator multiplied by 4, which yields 4/8. The problem can now be written 7 4/8 – 5 3/8. Because the numerator in the first term is larger than the numerator in the second term, the problem can be completed by subtracting the fractions and whole numbers separately: 7 – 5 = 2 and 4/8 – 3/8 = 1/8, so the answer is 2 1/8. If the numerator in the first term had been smaller, it would be necessary to convert both mixed numbers to improper fractions, subtract, and then if necessary, convert the difference back into a mixed number.

36. C: If a softball team won 15 games and lost 10, the ratio of wins to losses was 3:2. A ratio expresses a proportion. As given in the problem, the ratio of wins to losses is 15:10. However, ratios can be simplified in the same way as fractions, by dividing both terms by the greatest common factor. In this case, the greatest common factor of 15 and 10 is 5. When both terms are divided by 5, the result is 3:2.

37. A: 35 is 20% of 175. One way to solve a problem of this type is to set up a proportional equation. In this case, you are trying to answer the following question: 35 is to what number as 20 is to 100? In equation form, this can be expressed $35/x = 20/100$. Solve by cross-multiplying, to yield 3500 = 20x, and then dividing both sides by 20.

38. D: $6 \times 0 \times 5 = 0$. Indeed, any number or group of numbers multiplied by 0 is equal to 0. Remember what multiplication expresses. When we say 6×5, we are essentially saying six 5s. Therefore, when we multiply 0 by anything, for instance 10, we are essentially saying no 10s.

39. B: $7.95 \div 1.5 = 5.3$. To complete a division problem involving decimals, it is essential that the divisor (the number by which the dividend is being divided) be a whole number. In this problem, 1.5 is the divisor. To go on with the calculation, we must shift the decimal point in 1.5 a single place to the right, making it 15. To keep the problem balanced, the decimal point in 7.95 must also be shifted one place to the right, making it 79.5. Now you can divide 79.5 by 15. Remember that the decimal point in the quotient should go directly above the decimal point in the dividend.

40. D: If $x = 4$, then $2x + 7x = 36$. Substitute the given value for x into the equation: $2(4) + 7(4)$. According to the order of operations, multiplication must precede division, so you will end up with $8 + 28 = 36$.

41. C: 7/10 equals 0.7. The fraction 7/10 can be verbalized as seven tenths, which suggests how it will look as a decimal. The fraction can be converted to a decimal simply by placing a seven in the tenths place.

42. C: 4/8 equals 0.5. One way to narrow down your choices on this problem is to verbalize the various options. Common sense should suggest that the fraction "four-eighths" is not going to be close to "one-point-five," "five-hundredths," or "five-thousandths." It remains then to determine whether the fraction 4/8 is equivalent to 0.5, which as "five-tenths" can be expressed 5/10. One way to determine that these fractions are equivalent is to reduce each of them to simplest form, by dividing the numerator and denominator of 4/8 by 4 and of 5/10 by 5, respectively. The simplest form for both of these fractions is 1/2, so they are equivalent.

43. D: 8/24 equals 1/3. To find the simplest form of a fraction, divide the numerator and denominator by their greatest common factor. The factors of 8 are 1, 2, 4, and 8. The factors of 24 are 1, 2, 3, 4, 6, 8, 12, and 24. The greatest common factor then is 8. After dividing both numerator and denominator by 8, you will obtain 1/3.

44. B: 83,000 equals 8.3×10^4. This problem requires knowledge of scientific notation, the system for expressing very large and very small numbers concisely. A number in scientific notation consists

of a value greater than or equal to 1 and less than ten, multiplied by ten to a certain power. To convert a number to scientific notation, shift the decimal point until the number enters that space between 1 and 10, and then count the number of shifts. Each shift to the left represents a positive value for the exponent, while each shift to the right represents a negative one. In this case, the decimal point must be shifted 4 places to the left to convert 83,000 to 8.3, and so the scientific notation form must be 8.3×10^4.

45. B: 0.00875 equals 8.75×10^{-3}. As in problem 44, here you are asked to put a number in scientific notation. In this problem, however, you begin with a value less than zero. As indicated in the explanation to problem 4, shifting the decimal point to the right will create a negative value for the exponent. Because the decimal point must be shifted three places to the right to make 0.00875 into 8.75, the scientific notation form will be 8.75×10^{-3}.

46. A: -32 + 7 equals -25. Performing even simple operations with negative numbers can be tricky, but it can help to envision the numbers on a number line. -32, of course, will be far to the left of 0 on the number line, so much so that even adding 7 to it will not make it a positive number. -25, however, is less negative than -32, which would make sense since we have added a positive number to it.

47. B: -37 + -47 equals -84. Adding a negative number is the same as subtracting it, so it may help to write this problem as -37 - 47. Envisioning this problem on a number line, it is apparent that subtracting from a negative number will yield an even more negative difference.

48. B: 41% equals 0.41. A percentage expresses a value out of a hundred. In fact, the word *percent* comes from the Latin *per centum*, or "out of a hundred." 41% is equal to 41/100 or 0.41, a decimal that could be expressed verbally as forty-one hundredths.

49. A: 22(5x) = 110x. To solve this problem, multiply the number outside the parentheses by the coefficient 5. Since there is no given value for *x*, it is impossible to eliminate it from the problem.

Verbal/Investigation Practice 1

50. A: *Contemporary* is the most appropriate word. It means up-to-date, modern, or new. In the sentence, a contrast is being drawn with "the classics," which are older pieces of art.

51. D: *Unabridged* is the most appropriate word. It means unshortened, complete, or full length. As an example, sometimes long books are sold in an "abridged" version, meaning that they are edited and shortened. In the given sentence, Allen says he needs more time to give the story, suggesting that he means the full version.

52. C: *Promiscuous* is the most appropriate word. This word is used to describe people who have casual romantic relationships with a number of different people. It has a generally negative connotation.

53. D: *Revitalizing* is the most appropriate word. It means life-restoring or enlivening. It is apparent from the context of this sentence that the waterfront district has been moribund (depressed and dying) and that the government is attempting to stimulate the economy there through taxation.

54. B: *Revenue* is the most appropriate word. It is defined as the money earned through economic activity. A general equation for profit is revenue minus expenses. The revenue earned by the class would make it possible for them to have a party at the end of the year.

55. D: *Pilfered* is the most appropriate word. It means stolen. It seems that the teenager described in the sentence is performing some petty shoplifting at the local store.

56. A: *Parochial* is the most appropriate word. It means locally focused or innocent of the ways of the world. A parochial person is unsophisticated and perhaps naive. Being parochial is not an extremely negative thing, though the word is often used in a somewhat critical fashion. A person like Dean who grew up and continued to live in a small town might never take an interest in the doings of the world outside, and might therefore be considered parochial.

57. D: *Obscure* is the most appropriate word. It means hard to find, uncommon, or rare. Many students have experienced the dread of taking tests from a teacher who includes not just the most important information, but also the random bits of knowledge that are easy to forget.

58. A: *Libel* is the most appropriate word. A libel is a false or misleading statement that injures the reputation of another person or group. It is illegal to make or publish such statements.

59. B: The words *hues* and *vivid* complete the statements. A rainbow can only be experienced with the sense of sight, so it would not be possible to feel the texture of one. Also, a rainbow consists of light colors, through which the sky can be seen, so it is unlikely that the lines of a rainbow would be dark against the sky. Instead, it makes sense for the hues, or colors, of the rainbow to be vivid, or lively.

60. C: The words *hedge* and *protection* complete the statements. A president might be subject to assassination attempts, so it would make sense that he or she would need protection. A hedge, or small obstruction, could provide such protection. A catalyst is a substance that incites action, especially a chemical reaction, so this word does not really make sense in context. A derrick is a device used to extract oil: a president would not need one of these for protection. Finally, the phrase "barrier of contrast" does not make sense.

61. A: A small selection of terms found at the back of a textbook is a *glossary*. It is an alphabetical list of words that might be unfamiliar to a reader. A preface, on the other hand, is a short introductory essay placed before the main text. It is often written by someone other than the author of the book proper. Diction is the choice of words used by the author. Finally, kefir is a drinkable yogurt product.

62. C: A frightening horror movie is *ghastly*. This word means dreadful or terrifying. A good horror movie should aim to be ghastly. Melancholy, on the other hand, is sad or mournful. A horror movie might have some melancholy elements, but this word should not describe it in a general sense. Similarly, a horror movie might be dramatic, but this cannot be inferred from the context. Finally, a horror movie falls into a different genre than tragedy.

63. B: *Famished* means hungry. It makes sense that a softball team would be famished after a grueling practice. Of course, the team might also be fatigued (tired) after a practice. The only way to know the right answer to this question is to already know the definition of famished. Similarly, it cannot be determined from context that the softball team is not ready or excited. Sometimes, you will just have to know the definition to answer the question correctly.

64. A: *Enamored* means fascinated. Newborn babies are typically enamored of any objects that are brightly colored and capable of making a loud noise. A rattle likely fits this description. The baby would probably be happy with the rattle as well, but this is not as good of a match for enamored. *Unsure what to do* and *aggravated* would both be incorrect definitions for *enamored*.

65. D: In this context, *dissect* means analyze. A dissection is an examination of the parts of something, whether it be a problem or a dead frog. Many people have a tendency to exaggerate their problems without taking the time to calmly assess the various components. Measured and serene reflection is the best way to approach a problem. The dissection of an animal often entails cutting it apart, but this is not a necessary condition. When the dissection is being performed on something abstract, like a problem, cutting apart doesn't make sense. *Talk about* and *ignore* would both make sense in this sentence, but they are incorrect definitions for *dissect*.

66. C: The words *loathsome* and *masses* complete the sentence. *Loathsome* means unpleasant or distasteful; it makes sense that a book that was unpleasant to a large number of people would have poor sales. It makes less sense to say the book had poor sales because it was "limited to the people." Similarly, it would not make sense to attribute poor sales to the book being "colorful to the individual," since this color would be an attractive quality.

67. C: The words *skin* and *storm* complete the sentence. Three of the answer choices have skin as the initial word. The only other option, *hide*, makes sense itself but the word *abyss* (a void or hole) does not. *Craven* means greedy or corrupt, qualities which are negative but which do not soak kittens to the skin. Storms, however, do.

68. C: *Countenance* means expression. In other words, the appearance and bearing of the bouncer helped dissuade people from fighting. Simply the presence of the bouncer is not enough: he (or she) must also have an imposing and intimidating appearance to maintain order. *Message* might work in this sentence, but it is not a good definition of countenance.

69. D: *Apprized* means noted. There is no positive or negative connotation to appraisal: that is, it does not mean that the child was pleased or disappointed by her father's authority. It simply means that she assessed it. Defying her father's authority would mean misbehaving in church.

70. B: The sentence has a punctuation error. There should not be a semicolon between *belching* and *and*. Indeed, there should not be any mark of punctuation between these words, as such punctuation would interrupt a continuous statement. In some situations, it is appropriate to separate the items in a list with semicolons, but this is only when the list is introduced with a colon or the items include several words. In this sentence, the actions comprised do not really constitute a list.

71. A: The sentence has a capitalization error. The words *high school* need not be capitalized. High school should only be capitalized when it immediately follows a specific name of a school: for instance, it is capitalized in *Washington High School* but not in *the high school named after George Washington*. This rule applies to many words in English: *President Obama* but *that guy became president*; *Rocky Mountains* but *mountains near my house*; *Yale University* but *the university in New Haven, Connecticut*.

72. D: The sentence has a grammar error. Specifically, the verb *plays* does not agree with the subject *nurses*. When a subject is plural, the verb form must be plural as well. The correct verb form in this sentence would be *play*, as in *Nurses play a vital role*. Another way to correct the sentence would be to make the subject singular (*The nurse plays a vital role*), although this version seems less likely.

73. C: The sentence has a spelling error. The word *tonsels* should be spelled *tonsils*. The word *listless* means lethargic or without purpose. It would be natural for a child to be tired or aimless for a few days after a minor surgery. The use of a comma is appropriate in this sentence, as it separates the introductory clause from the main part of the sentence.

74. C: The sentence has a spelling error. The word *serine* should be spelled *serene*. This word means calm, placid, or peaceful. Twilight is known to be a rather peaceful time of day. This sentence contains no capitalization other than the initial word and no punctuation except for the period, so these two answer choices could be eliminated immediately.

75. B: The sentence has a punctuation error. The sentence should end with a period rather than a question mark. It would be possible to read this sentence as a question, for instance if someone was asking the doctor about the patient's condition. A similar phrasing might be "The patient's mind was lucid during the evaluation, yes?" However, the given phrasing is much more likely to be a declarative statement than an interrogative, and therefore should end with a period. The rest of the sentence is written correctly. The word *lucid* means clear and unclouded.

76. D: This passage is mainly about budgeting for your wedding. The other answer choices are topics covered by the author in the course of the article, but they are not the best general summation of it. For instance, the second-to-last paragraph addresses saving money for a wedding, but this subject is not mentioned in the rest of the article. When asked to find a main idea, be sure to select an answer choice that can describe the entirety of the passage.

77. A: We may infer from the article that a wedding is not worth going into lots of debt. Indeed, from the opening paragraph it is clear that the author takes a skeptical view of those who go into massive debt to fund a wedding. Instead, the author takes the sensible line that a wonderful wedding can be arranged without sending the newlyweds to the poor house. A wedding may still be a joyful occasion, and it may even be expensive or costly, if the families of the bride and groom have the means. The point of the passage is not that weddings should not be expensive, but that they should not be more expensive than the participants can afford.

78. A: This sentence is stating that the wedding party gifts, rehearsal dinner, and pre wedding parties will take up the rest of the budget. The sentence is taken from the last sentence of the third paragraph, in which the author breaks down the budget for a typical wedding. The last items to be mentioned are the gifts for the wedding party (that is, for the bridesmaids and groomsmen), the rehearsal dinner, and the pre wedding parties. Of course, contrary to answer choice D, these items would need to be included in a budget. However, the author does not state that they are necessary. Furthermore, the author does not indicate whether these will be the most costly part of the wedding, though they well might be.

79. C: The wedding party gifts, rehearsal dinner, and pre wedding parties take up 7% of the budget. This figure is derived by adding up the given percentages and subtracting the sum from 100. The listed budget allotments are as follows: rings (15%); apparel (6%); reception, etc. (42%); invitations and decorations (17%); and officiant, limousine, videographer, and photographer (13%). The total percentage is 15 + 6 + 42 + 17 + 13 = 93. 100 – 93 = 7, so there will be 7 percent of the budget left over for wedding party gifts, rehearsal dinner, and pre wedding parties.

80. B: *Realistic*, as used by the author, means practical. The author makes this statement in the second sentence of the passage. It is clear throughout that the author disapproves of couples who spend more than they can afford on a wedding. The author favors instead the composition of a budget that accounts for the respective financial situations of the bride and groom and their families.

81. B: We may infer from the article that many weddings go over budget. Indeed, the author seems to be on a crusade against couples who overspend on their wedding. Many weddings may be just what the bride wants, but this information is not mentioned in the article. Likewise, many weddings

may go over-budget, but from the author's perspective this is not the problem so much as the fact that wedding budgets are often excessive to begin with. Finally, though the author sets $100 as the lowest limit for a wedding, he or she does not imply that many weddings will only cost this much.

82. A: The title "Making Sense of a Dog's Senses" best describes this passage. Moreover, it has a nice little play on the word "sense," which can mean both order and a means of acquiring information about the world. The title "Canine's Plight" would not work, because a plight is a dire or bad situation, and this article is focused on the advantages of being a dog. "A Dog's Life" is not a terrible title, but it is not nearly as specific as the correct answer. Finally, "Dogs Save Lives with Their Senses" is technically true, but only relates to a small part of the passage. The general intent of the passage is to describe the sensory apparatus of a dog, not to praise their life-saving abilities.

83. D: We can infer from the article that a dog could hear better than a human. Indeed, in the first sentence of the fourth paragraph the author describes how a dog's sense of hearing is about four times stronger than that of a person. At no point in the article does the author compare dogs to cats.

84. C: A dog is able to smell one-millionth concentration of an odor compared to a human. This information is in the third sentence of the third paragraph. It can be hard to remember specific information from a long passage, so it is always a good idea to refer to the text for reassurance. This passage has a clear structure, with each paragraph devoted to one of the senses, that makes it easy to locate details.

85. D: A dog's sense of smell would be the most beneficial to the police department. In the third paragraph, the author mentions that their phenomenal sense of smell has led to dogs becoming police employees. Presumably, dogs are able to locate missing persons and find drugs.

86. D: The word *distinguish*, as used by the author here, means differentiate. The author is stating that dogs have a hard time telling some colors apart. Color perception is one of the areas in which a dog's senses are inferior to those of a person.

87. A: According to the article, dogs eat meat and vegetables. In the third sentence of the fifth paragraph, the author describes dogs as omnivores, meaning that they are neither exclusive carnivores (meat-eaters) nor herbivores (plant-eaters).

88. C: According to the article, the *Lusitania* is a ship. This information is not stated directly in the passage, but it can be inferred. The second sentence of the first paragraph mentions that Towers survived three shipwrecks, and goes on to mention that one of these was the *Lusitania*. It also mentions that the *Lusitania* was hit by a torpedo, which is an underwater missile. It perhaps would be possible for the *Lusitania* to have been a torpedo boat, but it is described as having been hit by a torpedo rather than as having fired one. It would not make sense for a torpedo to hit an airplane or a train.

89. A: In the given statement, *touted* means publicized. This is the first sentence of the second paragraph. The author is describing a man who may not have existed, but who is said to have described some of the most famous shipwrecks in history. So, everything the author tells us about Towers is hearsay or publicity. Towers was said to be a fireman, but this cannot be proven. Certainly, we cannot say that he was sighted as one, because the whole point of the article is that there is no direct evidence of Towers' existence. *Demeaned* means made fun of or put down, so this would not make sense in the sentence. Likewise, *set-up* would not complete the sentence in a coherent way.

90. D: This passage sheds doubt on the idea that urban folk tales are not always based on real people. The whole point of the article is that this legendary figure who was said to have had an extraordinary life may never have existed at all. Indeed, in the final paragraph the author describes some reasons why the figure of Frank Towers may have been invented, namely to satisfy the human urge to see a person thwart death over and over. As for the other answer choices, the article never suggests that Frank Towers caused the ships to sink. The ships clearly did sink and the United States was irrefutably at war with other countries.

91. C: The title of this article could be "The Legend of Frank Towers Debunked." The word *debunked* means disproved or exposed as a fraud. The author's intent is to suggest that the celebrated Frank Towers is a folk hero with no basis in reality. He perhaps could be described as a "man of mystery," but that answer choice does not address the intention of the author, which is to eliminate that mystery. Again, if Frank Towers did live he certainly survived the impossible, but the whole point of the article is that he most likely never existed. Finally, the article does not offer any advice for escaping doomed ships.

92. B: The phrase "Don't believe everything you read" best captures the intent of the article. The author is making a point about the unreliable nature of history. In a sense, the author is saying that "seeing is believing," but this phrase has less application to the historical record, since no one at this point can claim to have seen the sinking of the *Lusitania*. We must depend upon the written record, shaky as it may be at times. The expression "a stitch in time saves nine" means that a thoughtful and preventive action can save work in the future. This expression does not apply to the passage. Finally, the expression "there are many layers to an onion," which alludes to the complexity of history, does not get at the nature of the Frank Towers story.

93. B: The article states that urban folk tales are created because humanity likes to see someone triumph over tragedy. The author makes this claim in the first sentence of the last paragraph. In a sense, these folk tales are created because they are fun to hear, but answer choice B does a better job of describing exactly why they are enjoyable. Though they are technically untrue, they are not meant to trick people into believing lies. Also, they are not created because people cannot remember details clearly, though this statement is true in itself.

94. A: The main idea of this passage is the importance of proper medical documentation and terminology. The author offers several reasons why documentation and terminology are important in medicine. The competence of the doctor and the safety of the patient depend upon documentation and terminology. Documentation standards are universal, but this is hardly the main idea of the passage. It would be more appropriate to describe this statement as a supporting detail. As for the other two answer choices, health care professionals are not allowed to document however they want, and medical documentation does affect reimbursement.

95. D: Considering the information in this passage, you might suspect that hospitals would teach their employees how to maximize reimbursement with their documentation skills, how to document pre-operatively, and a standardized set of medical abbreviations. The author describes the many ways that hospitals suffer when employees fail to use the proper documentation or terminology. Injured patients and lost money are just two of the unhappy consequences. Therefore, it makes sense that hospitals would do whatever necessary to minimize errors related to documentation and terminology.

96. D: According to the article, the end result of poor documentation could be claims denied, patients injured, or a hospital going out of business. These negative consequences are found at

different points throughout the article. The author's intention is to show that poor documentation can have adverse effects in a number of areas.

97. C: Medicare sets the standards for medical documentation according to this article. This information is given in the fourth sentence of the article. Later, the author reinforces this point by describing how Medicare also establishes the standard for withholding reimbursement as a penalty for poor documentation.

98. B: In the context of the article, *adhere* means comply. This word is used in the third sentence of the first paragraph. Essentially, the author is saying that doctors most obey or abide by the standards for documentation established by Medicare.

99. A: Readers of this passage might expect the author to proceed to discuss other benefits of proper medical documentation. The intention of the article is to describe the importance of proper documentation, not to detail methods of documentation or programs that would do the job better. The author spends much of the text describing how improper documentation can have negative consequences for patients and doctors, so it would not be surprising if the text went on to talk about the benefits of proper documentation.

100. C: The main idea of this article is how increasing compliance with Title IX by colleges affects males and females. Title IX was implemented to increase the athletic opportunities for women in college. It has undoubtedly fulfilled its mission, but not without some controversy. Specifically, many male athletes charge that they have been denied access to college athletics programs to make room for women. Although female athletes do obtain valuable scholarships through Title IX, it would be crude and misguided to say that the main idea of the article is how female students can get free money. Also, though the article touches on these subjects, it does not take discrimination against male athletes or changes to Title IX as its main idea.

101. B: The article supports the statement that mediocre women athletes may be able to win scholarships at small schools. This idea is put forth in the fourth paragraph, and specifically in the third sentence, in which the author describes the low standards for athletic excellence required by many small schools. The article suggests that Title IX has increased the demand for female athletic talent beyond the supply. The other statements are not supported by the article. Men's sports are most assuredly not being eliminated in favor of women's sports. In the second paragraph, the author mentions that thousands of institutions remain out of compliance with Title IX.

102. A: Title IX is best described as an act that encouraged schools to increase funding of female sports. This is the best description because it is the most closely aligned with the intention of Title IX. The act was not meant to damage men's sports. Furthermore, the act is not at present being followed by a majority of schools in the United States, as indicated by the second paragraph of the article. Finally, the Chronicle of Higher Education merely notes compliance with Title IX; it does not establish standards.

103. C: The article does not mention Tennessee State being compliant with Title IX. The last sentence of the second paragraph states that Ohio State, Syracuse, and Texas Tech are compliant. This sort of specific detail can be difficult to recall without direct reference to the text.

104. B: According to the article, participation in women's sports has increased fivefold since Title IX was implemented. This information is given in the second sentence of the first paragraph. There, the author describes how the implementation of Title IX has dramatically expanded the opportunities for female athletes at the collegiate level.

105. B: The article states that some male college athletes are crying foul play, meaning that they are alleging unfair behavior. This phrase is used in the first sentence of the last paragraph. There, the author describes how some male college athletes complain when compliance with Title IX causes their athletic programs to be cut. The author goes on to declare that there may be some attempt to rectify the perceived imbalances caused by Title IX.

106. B: 75% of 500 is 375. To find the percentage of a whole number, convert the percentage to a decimal and multiply by the whole number. One way to make the conversion is to shift the decimal point two places to the left, so that 75% becomes 0.75. The problem is then $0.75 \times 500 = 375$. When you perform the multiplication, you will actually get a product of 375.00, but the zeroes to the right of the decimal point can be eliminated for simplification purposes.

Arithmetic Practice 2

107. C: 45% of 600 is 270. To find the percentage of a whole number, convert the percentage to a decimal and multiply by the whole number. In this problem, you will end up with $0.45 \times 600 = 270$.

108. A: $(7 \times 5) + (8 \times 2) = 51$. Remember the order of operations: parentheses, exponents, multiplication, addition, subtraction. In this problem, the first step is to solve the operations within parentheses. You will be left with $35 + 16 = 51$.

109. D: $(8 \div 2)(12 \div 3) = 16$. Solving this problem requires you to remember the order of operations: parentheses, exponents, multiplication, division, addition, and subtraction. In this problem, the division operations come before the multiplication because they are placed within parentheses. It is necessary to complete any available operations within parentheses before moving on. Performing the division first yields $4 \times 4 = 16$.

110. D: 31 is a prime number. Prime numbers have only two factors: 1 and themselves. In other words, a prime number can only be divided without a remainder by 1 or itself. And the only two whole numbers that can be multiplied to produce the prime number are 1 and the number. All of the other answer choices have more than two factors: the factors of 12 are 1, 2, 3, 4, 6, and 12; the factors of 25 are 1, 5, and 25; and the factors of 27 are 1, 3, 9, and 27.

111. D: 9 is a factor of 36. Factors are those numbers that can be divided into a given number evenly (without a remainder). Another way of putting this is that the factors of a given number are all of the numbers that can be part of multiplication problems that yield the given number as a product. So all of the factors for a number will be equal to or smaller than that number. Factors are all whole numbers. The number 36 has 9 factors: 1, 2, 3, 4, 6, 9, 12, 18, and 36. None of the other answer choices can be divided into 36 evenly.

112. C: $75 \times 34 = 2,550$. Multiplication problems are easier to solve when they are arranged vertically. When solving this problem, begin by multiplying 4 by 5 and then 7. Then place a zero in the ones place of the next line and multiply 5 and 7 by 3. Then add together the products to find the answer, 2,550.

113. B: If $x + 372 = 853$, $x = 481$. To find the value of x you must isolate it on one side of the equation. This can be done by subtracting 372 from both sides: $x + 372 - 372 = 853 - 372$, so $x = 481$.

114. A: The decimal 0.25 is equivalent to 1/4. Begin by expressing the decimal 0.25 in fraction form, as twenty-five hundredths: 25/100. Then find the greatest common factor of 25 and 100. Both 25 and 100 are divisible by 25, so the simplest form of this fraction can be found by dividing

numerator and denominator by this greatest common factor: 25 ÷ 25 = 1 and 100 ÷ 25 = 4, so 25/100 = 1/4.

115. A: If there are 60 grains in one dram, there are 900 grains in 15 drams. This problem requires some unit conversion. Perhaps the easiest way to consider a problem of this type is as an analogy: 60 grains is to 1 dram as an unknown number of grains is to 15 drams. This can be set up as the following equation: $60/1 = x/15$. To solve this equation, cross-multiply: $60 × 15 = 1 × x$, or $60 × 15 = x$. Thus, $900 = x$, and our original equation can be expressed as follows: 60 grains are to 1 dram as 900 grains are to 15 drams.

116. C: If a pitcher holds 7 1/2 cups water, five pitchers will hold 37 1/2 cups. This word problem should be converted into an equation. You are given the number of cups in 1 pitcher, and then asked to find the number of cups in five pitchers. To do this, simply multiply the number of cups in one pitcher by five: 7 1/2 × 5. There are a couple of ways to multiply a mixed number. One is to multiply the fraction and then the whole number, and then add the products together. Another is to convert the mixed number into an improper fraction by multiplying the denominator by the whole number (in this case 7 × 2), adding the product to the numerator (15/2) and then multiplying by the other whole number expressed as an improper fraction: 15/2 × 5/1 = 75/2 or 37 1/2.

117. C: If $a = 3$, $b = 4$, and $c = 5$, then $(a + b + c)^2 + (a - b - c) = 138$. Substitute the given values: $(3 + 4 + 5)^2 + (3 - 4 - 5)$. The addition and subtraction should be performed first, since it is contained within parentheses (remember the order of operations): $12^2 + (-6)$. Subtracting 4 from 3 yields -1, and then subtracting 5 more yields -6. Multiply 12 by itself and subtract 6 from the product. Adding a negative number is the same thing as subtracting a positive number.

118. B: $0.85 = 17/20$. To convert a decimal into a fraction, it helps to verbalize it. So, 0.85 is the same as 85 hundredths. This suggests a fraction form of the decimal, namely 85/100. Of course, any decimal with the smallest place in the hundredths can be converted into a fraction by placing it over a hundred. Once the decimal has been converted into a fraction, it should be simplified. This is done by dividing numerator and denominator by the greatest common factor. In this case, the greatest common factor of 85 and 100 is 5. After dividing both terms by 5, you will be left with 17/20.

119. B: The fraction 7/12 is closest to 2/3 without being over. The best way to approach this problem is to divide out each of the fractions and determine which one comes the closest without going below the quotient of 2/3 (which is 0.67). 7 divided by 12 can be rounded off to 0.58, which makes it the closest value less than 0.67.

120. B: If a puddle contained 72 pints of water and a rainstorm adds 21% more, the puddle will have approximately 87 pints of water. To answer this question, you must determine the value of 21% of 72. This is done by multiplying the percentage expressed as a decimal by the total amount of water: $0.21 × 72 = 15.12$. Because the problem asks for an approximate answer, we can round off the product to 15 and add it to 72 to derive the answer.

121. B: If $x = 2$ then $x^4(x + 3) = 80$. Substitute the given value for x: $2^4(2 + 3)$. Abiding by the order of operations, perform the addition first, yielding $2^4 × 5$. Then find the value of 2^4: $2 × 2 × 2 × 2 = 16$. Finally, multiply: $16 × 5 = 80$.

122. B: If 1/3 of the patient type is pediatric, this wedge of a circle graph should take up 120 degrees. To answer this problem, you must know that there are 360 degrees in a circle. Then you can set up a proportion equation to find the answer: $1/3 = y/360$. That is, 1 out of 3 is equal to y out of 360. To solve, cross-multiply (yielding $360 = 3y$) and then divide both sides by 3.

123. C: If a traveler on vacation spent $25 at the grocery store the first week of school, $52 the next two weeks, and $34 in the final week, he will have spent an average of $40.75 on food. An average is calculated by adding the sums from each of the three weeks and dividing by the number of weeks: $(25 + 52 + 34) \div 3 = 40.75$. Actually, when you perform the division by hand you will end up with 40 3/4. Converting this fraction to a decimal requires multiplying both numerator and denominator by 25, which produces seventy-five hundredths, or 0.75.

124. A: $437.65 - 325.752 = 111.898$. When performing subtraction involving decimals, it is important to set up the problem vertically such that the decimal points are directly above one another. In this problem, that will mean that the lower term extends one more place value to the right than does the top term. To proceed, add a zero to the top term, making it 437.650. You can then subtract as usual. Of course, you will need to begin by borrowing from the hundredths place and making the zero in the thousandths place a 10.

125. A: $43.3 \times 23.03 = 997.199$. Remember that the solution to a multiplication problem involving decimals must have a number of places to the right of the decimal point equal to the sum of the place-values to the right of the decimal points in the two terms. So, in other words, for this problem the product must extend to the thousandths place since there is one place to the right of the decimal point in 43.3 and two to the right of the decimal point in 23.03.

126. C: There are 48 nonoverlapping 2-inch by 2-inch squares in an 8-inch by 24-inch rectangle. To solve this problem, find the area for the squares and for the rectangle. Area is equal to length times width, so the area of each small square is 4 in² and the area of the rectangle is 192 in². To determine the final answer, divide the area of the rectangle by the area of each small square: $192/4 = 48$.

127. D: If you start out at 157 pounds and lose 6% of your weight, you will then weigh 147.58 pounds. Find the value of 6% of 157 by converting the percentage to a decimal and multiplying: $0.06 \times 157 = 9.42$. Then subtract this value from the original weight: $157 - 9.42 = 147.58$.

128. B: If 65% of a school's population must request a vending machine in order for it to be installed, and 340 of the school's 650 students have made this request, 83 more students must do so in order for the machine to be installed. To solve this problem, determine how many students make up 65% by multiplying the percentage expressed as a decimal by the total number of students: $0.65 \times 650 = 422.5$. Since there cannot be half a student, round up to 423. Then subtract the number of students who have so far requested from the number of students needed to find out how many students still have to request: $423 - 340 = 83$.

129. C: If a book you purchased at full price subsequently went on sale for 15% less, a difference of $12.75, then you paid $85 for the book. Set up a proportion equation: $15/100 = 12.75/y$. This equation is saying, "fifteen is to a hundred as 12.75 is to what?" Cross-multiply, yielding $1275 = 15y$, and then divide both sides by 15 to produce 85.

130. B: Of the given fractions, 7/12 has the largest value. Perhaps the easiest way to solve a problem of this type is to convert the fractions into decimals. What you are trying to do is establish a basis for comparison. If it were easy to do so, you could find a common denominator for the fractions and then compare them. However, since the given denominators (15, 12, 13, 16) are all so large and different, it makes more sense to convert the fractions into decimals. This is done by dividing the numerator by the denominator. So, as an example, for the first answer choice you would divide 8 by 15. To do this, you must write 8 as 8.0. 15 goes into 80 five times, so in your division problem you will write a five above the 0 in 8.0 (in other words, to the right of the decimal point). There will be a remainder of 5, which can be brought down and, since it is too small to divide

- 137 -

by 15, converted into 50. The end result is a quotient of 0.5333, with the three repeating infinitely. After performing the same process with the other fractions, you should be able to compare and determine which is the greatest.

131. C: The number 390.24657 rounded to the nearest hundredth is 390.25. The hundredths place is the second to the right of the decimal point. To determine how to round this number, look at the thousandths place. If it is five or greater, you must round up. If it is 4 or less, you must keep the number in the hundredths place the same. In this case, the number in the thousandths place is a six, so the four in the hundredths place should be rounded up to five.

132. A: To get 1 as an answer, you must multiply 4/5 by 5/4. This problem is a roundabout way of addressing reciprocals. The reciprocal of a number, if multiplied by that number, will equal 1. The reciprocal of any fraction is simply that fraction inverted. That is, you can find the reciprocal of any fraction by reversing the numerator and denominator. To get 1 as a product, you must multiply 4/5 by 5/4.

133. A: If $z = 4$, then $z + 6 - (z + 4) = 2$. Substitute the given value for z into the equation: $4 + 6 - (4 + 4)$. Then perform the addition inside the parentheses, leaving: $4 + 6 - 8 = 2$.

134. C: If patient's sodium intake over five days was 300 mg, 1240 mg, 900 mg, 1500 mg, and 900 mg, respectively, the patient's average intake was 968 mg. To find a daily average, add up the intakes for each respective day and then divide by the number of days: $300 + 1240 + 900 + 1500 + 900 = 4840$, and $4840/5 = 968$.

135. C: 6.982 rounds to 7.0. Because there is a number greater than four in the hundredths place, the nine in the tenths place rounds up to a zero, and the number in the ones place must be raised as well. The other answer choices are all rounded either incorrectly or to the wrong place value. 3.756 rounds to 3.76, but this is to the hundredths place rather than to the tenths. 4.567 rounds to 4.6 rather than 4.5. Finally, 54.32 rounds to 54.3 rather than 54.4.

136. B: 4.2% of 328 is 13.8. To find the value of a given percentage of a number, convert the percentage to a decimal and multiply it by the given number. The decimal 4.2% is equivalent to a decimal of 0.042. Remember that a percentage is converted into a decimal by shifting the decimal point two places to the left no matter where the decimal point begins in the percentage. Then multiply this decimal by the given number: $0.042 \times 328 = 13.776$. Because this number has a 7 in the hundredths place, its value is 13.8 when rounded to the nearest tenth.

137. C: 5/8 equals 0.625. A fraction is converted to decimal form by division. To divide 5 by 8, you must write the dividend (5) as 5.0.

138. C: The equation $2x + 5(z - 3) = 2x + 5z - 15$. This problem asks you to apply the distributive property of multiplication. In this sort of problem you must multiply the number before the parentheses by every term within the parentheses.

139. A: The number 80 is not a perfect square, so you should solve by breaking it down into factors: $80 = 4 \times 4 \times 5$. Since the square root of 4 is 2, the two 4s can be extracted and the multiplied: $2 \times 25 = 45$.

140. C: The playground covers 3,000 square yards. The area of a rectangular space is calculated by multiplying the length by the width: $50 \times 60 = 3,000$.

141. D: There are 44 students playing on the playground. There are three classes, with 15, 12, and 17 students, respectively: 15 + 12 + 17 = 44.

142. D: If both sides of the playground are increased by 10%, the new area would be 3630 square yards. To determine the new value for each side, multiply the length by 10% expressed as a decimal: 50 × 0.10 = 5 and 60 × 0.10 = 6. Then add the extra lengths to the original lengths: 50 + 5 = 55 and 60 + 6 = 66. Finally, calculate the new area: 55 × 66 = 3,630.

143. B: Ms. Brown's class would have to raise an additional $170.59 per student to completely fence in the playground. First, find the total length of fence required by calculating the perimeter of the fence. The perimeter of a rectangular space is found $P = 2l + 2w$. So for the given values, P = 2(50) + 2(60) = 100 + 120 = 220. The total cost of fencing is 220 × 15 = 3300. The class has so far raised $400, so they only need $2,900 more. There are 17 students in Ms. Brown's class (see question 36), so the additional amount required from each of them can be calculated by dividing the amount needed by the number of students: 2,900/17 = 170.59.

144. C: 160% = 8/5. One way to approach this problem is first to write 160% as a fraction: 160/100. This fraction can immediately be simplified by dividing numerator and denominator by 10, to yield 16/10. It can further be simplified by dividing the numerator and denominator by 2, to yield 8/5.

145. A: If a solution contains 6% calcium, 50 ml calcium can be used to make 833 ml of the solution. Set up a basic proportional equation: 6/100 = 50/y. This equation expresses the idea "six is to a hundred as 50 is to what number?" Cross-multiply (yielding $6y = 5000$) and divide both sides by 6.

146. A: 8.7 × 23.3 = 202.71. When multiplying decimals, remember that the product must have a number of places to the right of the decimal point equal to the sum of the places to the right of the decimal point in the two terms. In this problem, the product must have two places to the right of the decimal point because each of the terms (8.7 and 23.3) has one place value to the right of the decimal point.

147. A: 134.5 divided by 5 equals 26.9. In division, it is all right for the dividend to have numbers to the right of the decimal point, but the divisor cannot.

148. B: 5.30 × 10⁻⁴ equals 0.00053. This problem requires a knowledge of scientific notation. This is a system used to express extremely large or small values. It converts a number into a value greater than or equal to 1 and less than ten, multiplied by 10 to a given power. The exponent is equal to the number of places the decimal point must be shifted to place the number in that space greater than or equal to 1 and less than 10. If the decimal point must be shifted to the left (that is, if the number is very small), the exponent will be negative. If the decimal point must be shifted to the right (that is, if the number is very large), the exponent will be positive.

149. C: 23/3 = 7 2/3. This is at its heart a division problem. To solve, divide 23 by 3. 3 will go into 23 seven times, with a remainder of 2. The answer to a division problem can be expressed with the remainder over the divisor.

150. C: 33/100 = 0.33. The fraction 33/100 can be expressed verbally as "thirty-three hundredths," which suggests the decimal form. In any case, the fact that the denominator is 100 indicates that the decimal will need to have two places to the right of the decimal point.

151. A: $45^x/5^x = 9^x$. When dividing numbers that have the same exponent, simply divide the coefficients and leave the exponents alone.

152 A: $24x/3 = 8x$. It is impossible to solve for x in this problem, so the simplest form is achieved by dividing 24 by 3.

153. D: $52x(4y) = 208xy$. It is impossible to solve for either of the variables, so multiply the coefficients and leave the variables as they are.

Verbal/Investigation Practice 2

154. C: $4,500 + 3,422 + 3,909 = 11,831$. The best way to handle a problem of this type is to arrange it vertically. If it is helpful, add two of the terms and then add the sum to the third term.

155. C: *Abhorrence* is the most appropriate word. It means hatred or distaste. This makes sense, as a hatred or darkness would prevent one from leaving the house at night.

156. C: *Distraught* is the most appropriate word. This word means traumatized, violently emotional, or severely sad and angry. The injury of a pet would certainly be enough to make a person distraught.

157. B: *Fluent* is the most appropriate word. It means capable of speaking a language. Any student of a foreign language aspires to fluency. *Dandy* means excellent or fine. The exchange student may well have been dandy, but this word does not speak to her linguistic abilities. In the same vein, the student may have been caustic (sarcastic or bitter), but we cannot determine this from the sentence. Finally, the student is apparently talented, but this word is not specific enough about her abilities.

158. A: *Generic* is the most appropriate word. It means general or common, and is used to describe non-name brand products. Many pharmacies sell generic versions of medication in which the active ingredient and operation is exactly the same as a name brand product. These generic medications are typically cheaper. For this reason, many health insurers specify that customers obtain generic medications when they are available. Reasonable, compatible, and complete all sort of make sense in this sentence, but they are not nearly as precise as generic.

159. B: *Somber* is the most appropriate word. This word means sad or mournful. A group whose leader has died would certainly be somber.

160. D: *Genteel* is the most appropriate word. It means sophisticated, classy, or well-bred. Southern women are stereotyped as being demure, well-mannered, and classy, so genteel would be a good fit in this sentence.

161. B: *Mollify* is the most appropriate word. To mollify someone is to diminish their anger, to appease them. The parents of young children get a great deal of practice in mollifying their sons and daughters after fits and temper tantrums.

162. D: The passenger lost his vision. The optic nerve transmits information obtained through the eye to the brain. If the optic nerve is severed (cut), a person will lose his or her vision.

163. D: *Ponder* is the most appropriate word. It means think, meditate, or ruminate. In general, it is good to be a person who ponders, though excessive analysis and thinking can sometimes stand in the way of necessary action.

164. C: *Unbridled* is the most appropriate word. It means unrestrained or excessive. A bridle is used to restrain a fast horse, so an unbridled horse will run fast and loose. The word's usage has expanded to include many things besides horses.

165. D: *Zephyr* is the most appropriate word. This uncommon word means a west wind.

166. A: *Sonata* is the most appropriate word. A sonata is a piece of music written for one or two instruments.

167. C: *Qualms* is the most appropriate word. Qualms are reservations or doubts. An experienced performer might not feel any anxiety about performing before even a very large crowd.

168. A: *Yearling* is the most appropriate word. A yearling is a young horse. Although horses grow up faster than do infant humans, a year-old horse might still be scared to go out entirely on its own.

169. D: *Zenith* is the most appropriate word. The zenith is the highest point or top of something. The opposite of a zenith is a nadir or trough. In some ways the financial planner might be at his limit, but this word does not include the sense of positive performance.

170. C: *Solace* and *remembered* are the most appropriate words. Solace is consolation or an ease to suffering. From the sentence, it sounds as if the siblings' father has either gone away or died. Brothers and sisters might find happiness in one another, but the idea of "preparing the good times" does not really make sense.

171. D: *Passively* is the most appropriate word. It means inactively or without any motion or expression. Many people, not only children, will simply shut down and stop reacting when they are being criticized.

172. D: The teenager was accused of parricide. Parricide is the murder of a parent or parents. Sobriety is a lack of intoxication. Misguidance is a wandering from the intended path. Misogamy is a hatred of marriage. Each of these words could potentially be true, but they are not supported by the context.

173. C: Brian's secret was the use of mnemonics. These are tricks used to enhance the memory. For instance, many people remember the order of operations with the mnemonic "Please Excuse My Dear Aunt Sally," for parentheses, exponents, multiplication, division, addition, and subtraction.

174. C: The sentences contain a spelling error. Namely, the word *bachalor* should be spelled *bachelor*. A bachelor is an unmarried man. Misogyny is a hatred of women and could certainly be one reason for lifelong bachelorhood. The punctuation, grammar, and capitalization in these sentences are all correct.

175. B: The sentence has a punctuation error. There should not be a comma in between *equation* and *drove*. This comma divides an independent clause. Indeed, this sentence is fairly simple despite being wordy. The basic idea of the sentence could be expressed "The intricacy drove the student crazy." This idea should not be split apart by a comma.

176. D: The sentence has a grammar error. There is a disagreement in number between the subject, *tomatoes*, and the verb, *is*. *Tomatoes* is a plural verb, while *is* is a singular verb. To correct this sentence, one would change the verb to *are*: *The hybrid tomatoes are immune...* Another way to correct the sentence would be to make the subject singular: *The hybrid tomato is...*

177. A: The sentence has a capitalization error. The word *dean* should not be capitalized. Titles should not be capitalized unless they directly precede a name or position: for instance, *Secretary of the Treasury* and *Secretary Geithner* are both capitalized, but *Geithner is the secretary* would not be.

In this case, *dean* should only be capitalized when it is immediately followed by the name of the dean.

178. C: The sentence has a spelling error. The word *fradulent* should be spelled *fraudulent*. This word means intentionally fake or misleading. In the context of the sentence, it means that the insurance was not real. A con artist is a criminal who tricks people out of their money. The sentence does not contain any capitalization except for the initial word, nor any punctuation except for the period, so these two answer choices can be eliminated at once.

179. B: The sentence has two punctuation errors. There should not be a comma between *misdemeanor* and *when*, and the word *dollars* should be made possessive with an apostrophe (*dollars'*). With regard to the comma, there is no need to break up this simple sentence. Doing so almost makes it sound as if the movie star stole the merchandise after being accused of a misdemeanor. If the clauses in this sentence were reversed, however, it would be appropriate to separate them with a comma, because then the "when" clause would be serving as an introduction: *When she stole fifteen dollars' worth of merchandise from the store, the movie star was accused of a misdemeanor.* As for the other error, note that what the author is trying to express is that the movie star stole merchandise with the worth of fifteen dollars. For this reason, the word *dollars'* should have an apostrophe indicating possession.

180. C: The sentence has a spelling error. The word *comtemporary* should be spelled *contemporary*. This word means new, modern, or up-to-date. So, in the context of the sentence, the author is saying that the congregation sang a modern hymn as opposed to one of the old traditionals.

181. C: "The Relationship of Medical Terminology and SOAP NOTES" could be a title for this article. This title covers the entirety of the passage, which begins by describing SOAP notes and goes on to explain the general procedure for medical documentation and the importance of proper terminology. The article is not an attempt to discredit the use of SOAP notes, nor is it an attempt at summarizing the process of creating medical records. Finally, though the author does describe how documentation and terminology can influence quality of care, by no means is this the focal point of the passage.

182. B: The "O" in the SOAP note stands for objective. This information is given in the second sentence of the passage, in which the author states that SOAP stands for Subjective, Objective, Assessment, and Plan. It can be difficult to remember precise details from the text, so do not be reluctant to go back over what you have read before answering.

183. B: When to stop documenting is considered a problem with SOAP notes. This criticism is described in the third sentence of the second paragraph. The format is somewhat open-ended, so it can be difficult for a diligent physician to determine when to stop making notes. This can lead to unnecessary treatments and inefficiency for the hospital.

184. D: The above text does not support the statement "Medical documentation must be reviewed by administration." All of the answer choices are statements made directly by the author. Answer choice A appears in the third sentence of the passage. Answer choice B is in the last sentence of the second paragraph, as the author describes the tendency of SOAP notes to excess. Answer choice C can be found in the fourth sentence of the third paragraph.

185. D: According to the article, the poor medical terminology use has not resulted in SOAP note format changes. The other answer choices are all negative consequences of poor medical terminology. There have been some rumblings about the need to change the format of SOAP notes, but these changes have not been made as of yet.

186. C: From the article, it may be inferred that medical documentation errors will continue to increase in the future. The author describes the main problem with SOAP notes as their open-ended nature, so it would make sense for a standard structure to be imposed. Also, it is possible that hospitals and healthcare facilities will standardize terminology and abbreviations. It is certainly possible that medical terminology will change in the future, but this cannot be inferred from the article. It could also be that documentation errors will increase in the future, but the article offers nothing to support this idea. Finally, the fact that SOAP notes will continue to require skilled clinicians is probably true, but it is not a change in medical documentation so much as a continuation of the current status. For this reason, answer choice C is better.

187. A: In this article the author focuses on the relationship between quick cash and college funding. Specifically, the article describes various ways that college students try to pay their way through school. These schemes run the gamut from dependable to dangerous. The article makes no mention of academic freedom, and though scholarships are a source of funds for education, they are not mentioned in the article. Finally, although the article does have to do with the relationship between cost and college, it is more specific to say that it focuses on the quick cash schemes favored by students.

188. D: The article does not consider working full-time as a scheme to make money in college. Of course, this is one of the most straightforward ways to earn money, but it is not mentioned in the article. The article does mention selling plasma, selling old books, and typing papers as possible ways to earn some quick cash. To answer a question of this type, it may be necessary to refer to the text.

189. C: Selling vacations was not considered a possible mechanism of action used by scam artists. The article describes some of the ways in which impoverished college students can be conned. Shady businesses operating out of P.O. boxes prey on students. In addition, many students respond to envelope-stuffing operations that end up disappointing them. Finally, students should beware offers to spend the summer working in Alaska. The author suggests that the working conditions for these Alaska jobs are harsh and often dangerous.

190. B: The article implies that selling back books is harder if selling to underclassmen directly; however, it may be more profitable. The fourth sentence of the fifth paragraph describes how fellow students tend to pay more for books than do bookstores. However, it is much easier to walk into a bookstore and make a sale than to put up flyers and await a response. The article does not suggest that selling back books is a difficult or complicated process, nor does it suggest that it is a good way to earn small money in a hurry. This question is a little tricky because the article does state that selling books can be profitable. However, this information is not implied: it is stated directly. Remember that an implication is not stated outright, but can be inferred from what is written in the text.

191. D: In this article, the author reports that typing papers is sometimes a last-minute business. This information is contained in the fourth sentence of the third paragraph. It stands to reason that students who procrastinate will be more likely to need a hired typist, since they will be busy with other projects or exhausted with the mad rush to finish the project. Typing papers is not described as a difficult process, nor is it reported to be harder when performed for upperclassmen. The article does suggest that typing can be strenuous and is not especially profitable.

192. A: According to the passage, boats in Alaska may operate in ten- to twenty-foot seas. The sixth paragraph of the article discusses the perils of summer work aboard a fishing boat in Alaska. According to the author, the conditions are uncomfortable and sometimes dangerous. There is no

mention of good food or adequate health care. Instead, the author describes choppy seas, little sleep, and hazardous working conditions.

193. A: The main idea of this passage is law enforcement training and pay. Every section of the passage is in some way related to this idea. The other answer choices are touched upon at various points in the passage, but they are not relevant throughout.

194. C: According to the article, a police sergeant makes $44,000 a year. This information can be found in the second table of the article, which outlines the ranges of salary for various law enforcement professions. The range of pay for a police sergeant is $42,570 to $50,670, so $44,000 falls within it. This is the only profession for which $44,000 is somewhere between the minimum and maximum pay.

195. D: According to the article, federal police officers make less money than state police officers on average. This information can be obtained from the first table. In it, you can see that state police officers make an average of $44,400 a year, while federal police officers take home an average of $37,760 per year. The other statements are contradicted by the article. The author explicitly states that urban police officers out-earn rural ones, as a consequence of the larger tax base. The second paragraph describes how new officers are sometimes forced to work in corrections until a patrol position opens up, so it is clear that these positions are not preferred. Finally, the third paragraph of the article describes how junior officers are generally forced to work holidays, so that the more experienced officers can be with their families.

196. A: According to the article, urban areas are able to offer higher pay because of a larger tax base. This information can be found in the second sentence of the second paragraph.

197. B: The article supports the statement that most rural areas do not have their own training facilities. This information is in the fourth sentence of the first paragraph. The other statements are all contradicted by the article. The lowest paid law enforcement professionals are police officers. Police officers do receive steady increases in pay once they get a job. Finally, urban police officers on average make more per year than their rural counterparts.

198. B: According to the article, a junior officer may work difficult shifts and should expect to be away from their families at night and on holidays. By describing these shifts as difficult, the author means that they are either dangerous or inconvenient. Night shifts tend to be more perilous for law enforcement. Junior officers should not expect to receive as much pay as senior officers. They will probably not be trained in rural areas, since the article mentions that many rural communities train their employees in cities. Eventually, junior officers should expect to be transferred to another shift, but this won't happen until a vacancy opens.

199. A: The best title for this selection is "How to Maximize your Interview." The article offers a few tips for improving interview performance. The overall tone is one of encouragement and motivation. Although the article does touch on strategies for handling negative parts of your résumé, it is not exclusively focused on this subject. Likewise, the article promotes the idea of being polished, but it is more interested in how an interviewee can overcome possible problems with his or her résumé. The proposed title "Covering Your Mistakes" is similar to "Turning Bad into Good": it relates to a part of the article, but not enough to warrant being made the title.

200. D: According to the article the number one most important attribute a person needs to display in an interview is a positive attitude. This information is stated directly in the first sentence of the article. The article stresses that a potential employer or school admissions officer will be just as interested in your present and future as they are in your past. Answer choice B is incorrect because

the article stresses owning up to and even taking pride in past mistakes rather than being apologetic. According to the author, it is important to show how you have learned from the errors in your past. Being calm and interesting are both important, as well, but they are not described as the "number one most important attribute."

201. B: According to the article, if you went to prison you should own up to your mistake and describe what you have learned from it. The article suggests that it is better to acknowledge mistakes and describe how you have learned from them. An employer will be more impressed by this than if you are to evade responsibility or describe an inability to move past the experience.

202. C: The article suggests that a teacher would prefer a hard worker with a positive attitude. This answer can be gleaned from the fifth sentence of the second paragraph. There, the author states that an employer would prefer a hard-working positive person to a talented but lazy person. The author explicitly states that an employer does not want superstars working at 50 percent. Neither would an employer want a perfectionist or an underachiever.

203. C: You should not say "I wouldn't even have a record if my parents hadn't turned me in" during an interview. The problem with this statement is that it evades responsibility for past wrongdoing. To acknowledge that you committed the crime but to complain about being turned in suggests that you have not quite learned that your behavior was wrong. It suggests that you are trying to blame others for your own mistakes. The other statements would be attractive to an employer because they suggest a willingness to learn from past mistakes and move forward.

204. B: According to the article, all of the accomplishments that you have had in life so far are in the past. The article suggests that the accomplishments listed on a résumé are less important than a good attitude and a willingness to work. The article encourages interviewees to focus on how they will perform in the future, and not try to "rest on their laurels." The accomplishments of the past are important, and they are something to be proud of, but they are not as significant to an employer as the promise of excellence for the future.

205. B: An appropriate title for the article would be "Fishing for Bass with Live Bait." The article describes different types of live bait and their uses. Each paragraph pertains to this subject matter in some way. "Champion Fishing" is sort of related to the article, but does not mention live bait, which is the focal point of the article. The article briefly touches on waterdogs, but this is hardly the central topic of the article. Finally, "Popular Bass Bait" is not a satisfactory title, especially since the author says at the beginning that live bait is not as popular as it once was.

206. C: According to the article, live bait looks more realistic than artificial bait in clear water. This information is in the second sentence of the second paragraph. There, the author states that when water is clear, bass are able to identify the artificial lures. This is an indirect way of saying that live bait would look more realistic in very clear water.

207. C: According to the article, minnows and worms work well when added to an artificial lure. This information can be obtained from the last sentence of the third paragraph. The author states that adding live bait to a lure causes it to move in a lifelike manner. The other answer choices are types of live bait listed in the last sentence of the article.

208. A: According to the article, two of the three largest bass were caught with live bait. This information is in the last two sentences of the first paragraph. There, the author gives the weights and the type of bait used to catch the two largest bass on record. The other answer choices are not supported by the article. In the third paragraph, the author states that jigs and spinner baits do work well with live bait. In the second paragraph, the author declares that bass prefer slow-moving

- 145 -

bait, but that they can distinguish artificial bait when it moves slowly. Finally, the first sentence of the article indicates that the majority of fishermen do not use live bait.

209. D: When using live bait, you should use light weight line. This information can be obtained from the last sentence of the second paragraph. The advantage of light line is that it cannot be seen by the fish, so the live bait will look even more realistic. It can be hard to remember this kind of specific information after only a brief reading of the text, so do not be reluctant to look back before answering.

210. A: In the context of the article, *optimal* means perfect. This line is taken from the third sentence of the second paragraph. In this context, optimal is used to describe the feeding temperature preferred above all others by bass

How to Overcome Test Anxiety

Just the thought of taking a test is enough to make most people a little nervous. A test is an important event that can have a long-term impact on your future, so it's important to take it seriously and it's natural to feel anxious about performing well. But just because anxiety is normal, that doesn't mean that it's helpful in test taking, or that you should simply accept it as part of your life. Anxiety can have a variety of effects. These effects can be mild, like making you feel slightly nervous, or severe, like blocking your ability to focus or remember even a simple detail.

If you experience test anxiety—whether severe or mild—it's important to know how to beat it. To discover this, first you need to understand what causes test anxiety.

Causes of Test Anxiety

While we often think of anxiety as an uncontrollable emotional state, it can actually be caused by simple, practical things. One of the most common causes of test anxiety is that a person does not feel adequately prepared for their test. This feeling can be the result of many different issues such as poor study habits or lack of organization, but the most common culprit is time management. Starting to study too late, failing to organize your study time to cover all of the material, or being distracted while you study will mean that you're not well prepared for the test. This may lead to cramming the night before, which will cause you to be physically and mentally exhausted for the test. Poor time management also contributes to feelings of stress, fear, and hopelessness as you realize you are not well prepared but don't know what to do about it.

Other times, test anxiety is not related to your preparation for the test but comes from unresolved fear. This may be a past failure on a test, or poor performance on tests in general. It may come from comparing yourself to others who seem to be performing better or from the stress of living up to expectations. Anxiety may be driven by fears of the future—how failure on this test would affect your educational and career goals. These fears are often completely irrational, but they can still negatively impact your test performance.

> **Review Video: 3 Reasons You Have Test Anxiety**
> Visit mometrix.com/academy and enter code: 428468

Elements of Test Anxiety

As mentioned earlier, test anxiety is considered to be an emotional state, but it has physical and mental components as well. Sometimes you may not even realize that you are suffering from test anxiety until you notice the physical symptoms. These can include trembling hands, rapid heartbeat, sweating, nausea, and tense muscles. Extreme anxiety may lead to fainting or vomiting. Obviously, any of these symptoms can have a negative impact on testing. It is important to recognize them as soon as they begin to occur so that you can address the problem before it damages your performance.

> **Review Video: 3 Ways to Tell You Have Test Anxiety**
> Visit mometrix.com/academy and enter code: 927847

The mental components of test anxiety include trouble focusing and inability to remember learned information. During a test, your mind is on high alert, which can help you recall information and stay focused for an extended period of time. However, anxiety interferes with your mind's natural processes, causing you to blank out, even on the questions you know well. The strain of testing during anxiety makes it difficult to stay focused, especially on a test that may take several hours. Extreme anxiety can take a huge mental toll, making it difficult not only to recall test information but even to understand the test questions or pull your thoughts together.

> **Review Video: How Test Anxiety Affects Memory**
> Visit mometrix.com/academy and enter code: 609003

Effects of Test Anxiety

Test anxiety is like a disease—if left untreated, it will get progressively worse. Anxiety leads to poor performance, and this reinforces the feelings of fear and failure, which in turn lead to poor performances on subsequent tests. It can grow from a mild nervousness to a crippling condition. If allowed to progress, test anxiety can have a big impact on your schooling, and consequently on your future.

Test anxiety can spread to other parts of your life. Anxiety on tests can become anxiety in any stressful situation, and blanking on a test can turn into panicking in a job situation. But fortunately, you don't have to let anxiety rule your testing and determine your grades. There are a number of relatively simple steps you can take to move past anxiety and function normally on a test and in the rest of life.

> **Review Video: How Test Anxiety Impacts Your Grades**
> Visit mometrix.com/academy and enter code: 939819

Physical Steps for Beating Test Anxiety

While test anxiety is a serious problem, the good news is that it can be overcome. It doesn't have to control your ability to think and remember information. While it may take time, you can begin taking steps today to beat anxiety.

Just as your first hint that you may be struggling with anxiety comes from the physical symptoms, the first step to treating it is also physical. Rest is crucial for having a clear, strong mind. If you are tired, it is much easier to give in to anxiety. But if you establish good sleep habits, your body and mind will be ready to perform optimally, without the strain of exhaustion. Additionally, sleeping well helps you to retain information better, so you're more likely to recall the answers when you see the test questions.

Getting good sleep means more than going to bed on time. It's important to allow your brain time to relax. Take study breaks from time to time so it doesn't get overworked, and don't study right before bed. Take time to rest your mind before trying to rest your body, or you may find it difficult to fall asleep.

> **Review Video: The Importance of Sleep for Your Brain**
> Visit mometrix.com/academy and enter code: 319338

Along with sleep, other aspects of physical health are important in preparing for a test. Good nutrition is vital for good brain function. Sugary foods and drinks may give a burst of energy but this burst is followed by a crash, both physically and emotionally. Instead, fuel your body with protein and vitamin-rich foods.

Also, drink plenty of water. Dehydration can lead to headaches and exhaustion, especially if your brain is already under stress from the rigors of the test. Particularly if your test is a long one, drink water during the breaks. And if possible, take an energy-boosting snack to eat between sections.

> **Review Video: How Diet Can Affect your Mood**
> Visit mometrix.com/academy and enter code: 624317

Along with sleep and diet, a third important part of physical health is exercise. Maintaining a steady workout schedule is helpful, but even taking 5-minute study breaks to walk can help get your blood pumping faster and clear your head. Exercise also releases endorphins, which contribute to a positive feeling and can help combat test anxiety.

When you nurture your physical health, you are also contributing to your mental health. If your body is healthy, your mind is much more likely to be healthy as well. So take time to rest, nourish your body with healthy food and water, and get moving as much as possible. Taking these physical steps will make you stronger and more able to take the mental steps necessary to overcome test anxiety.

> **Review Video: How to Stay Healthy and Prevent Test Anxiety**
> Visit mometrix.com/academy and enter code: 877894

Mental Steps for Beating Test Anxiety

Working on the mental side of test anxiety can be more challenging, but as with the physical side, there are clear steps you can take to overcome it. As mentioned earlier, test anxiety often stems from lack of preparation, so the obvious solution is to prepare for the test. Effective studying may be the most important weapon you have for beating test anxiety, but you can and should employ several other mental tools to combat fear.

First, boost your confidence by reminding yourself of past success—tests or projects that you aced. If you're putting as much effort into preparing for this test as you did for those, there's no reason you should expect to fail here. Work hard to prepare; then trust your preparation.

Second, surround yourself with encouraging people. It can be helpful to find a study group, but be sure that the people you're around will encourage a positive attitude. If you spend time with others who are anxious or cynical, this will only contribute to your own anxiety. Look for others who are motivated to study hard from a desire to succeed, not from a fear of failure.

Third, reward yourself. A test is physically and mentally tiring, even without anxiety, and it can be helpful to have something to look forward to. Plan an activity following the test, regardless of the outcome, such as going to a movie or getting ice cream.

When you are taking the test, if you find yourself beginning to feel anxious, remind yourself that you know the material. Visualize successfully completing the test. Then take a few deep, relaxing breaths and return to it. Work through the questions carefully but with confidence, knowing that you are capable of succeeding.

Developing a healthy mental approach to test taking will also aid in other areas of life. Test anxiety affects more than just the actual test—it can be damaging to your mental health and even contribute to depression. It's important to beat test anxiety before it becomes a problem for more than testing.

> **Review Video: Test Anxiety and Depression**
> Visit mometrix.com/academy and enter code: 904704

Study Strategy

Being prepared for the test is necessary to combat anxiety, but what does being prepared look like? You may study for hours on end and still not feel prepared. What you need is a strategy for test prep. The next few pages outline our recommended steps to help you plan out and conquer the challenge of preparation.

Step 1: Scope Out the Test

Learn everything you can about the format (multiple choice, essay, etc.) and what will be on the test. Gather any study materials, course outlines, or sample exams that may be available. Not only will this help you to prepare, but knowing what to expect can help to alleviate test anxiety.

Step 2: Map Out the Material

Look through the textbook or study guide and make note of how many chapters or sections it has. Then divide these over the time you have. For example, if a book has 15 chapters and you have five days to study, you need to cover three chapters each day. Even better, if you have the time, leave an extra day at the end for overall review after you have gone through the material in depth.

If time is limited, you may need to prioritize the material. Look through it and make note of which sections you think you already have a good grasp on, and which need review. While you are studying, skim quickly through the familiar sections and take more time on the challenging parts. Write out your plan so you don't get lost as you go. Having a written plan also helps you feel more in control of the study, so anxiety is less likely to arise from feeling overwhelmed at the amount to cover.

Step 3: Gather Your Tools

Decide what study method works best for you. Do you prefer to highlight in the book as you study and then go back over the highlighted portions? Or do you type out notes of the important information? Or is it helpful to make flashcards that you can carry with you? Assemble the pens, index cards, highlighters, post-it notes, and any other materials you may need so you won't be distracted by getting up to find things while you study.

If you're having a hard time retaining the information or organizing your notes, experiment with different methods. For example, try color-coding by subject with colored pens, highlighters, or post-it notes. If you learn better by hearing, try recording yourself reading your notes so you can listen while in the car, working out, or simply sitting at your desk. Ask a friend to quiz you from your flashcards, or try teaching someone the material to solidify it in your mind.

Step 4: Create Your Environment

It's important to avoid distractions while you study. This includes both the obvious distractions like visitors and the subtle distractions like an uncomfortable chair (or a too-comfortable couch that makes you want to fall asleep). Set up the best study environment possible: good lighting and a comfortable work area. If background music helps you focus, you may want to turn it on, but otherwise keep the room quiet. If you are using a computer to take notes, be sure you don't have any other windows open, especially applications like social media, games, or anything else that could distract you. Silence your phone and turn off notifications. Be sure to keep water close by so you stay hydrated while you study (but avoid unhealthy drinks and snacks).

Also, take into account the best time of day to study. Are you freshest first thing in the morning? Try to set aside some time then to work through the material. Is your mind clearer in the afternoon or evening? Schedule your study session then. Another method is to study at the same time of day that you will take the test, so that your brain gets used to working on the material at that time and will be ready to focus at test time.

Step 5: Study!

Once you have done all the study preparation, it's time to settle into the actual studying. Sit down, take a few moments to settle your mind so you can focus, and begin to follow your study plan. Don't give in to distractions or let yourself procrastinate. This is your time to prepare so you'll be ready to fearlessly approach the test. Make the most of the time and stay focused.

Of course, you don't want to burn out. If you study too long you may find that you're not retaining the information very well. Take regular study breaks. For example, taking five minutes out of every hour to walk briskly, breathing deeply and swinging your arms, can help your mind stay fresh.

As you get to the end of each chapter or section, it's a good idea to do a quick review. Remind yourself of what you learned and work on any difficult parts. When you feel that you've mastered the material, move on to the next part. At the end of your study session, briefly skim through your notes again.

But while review is helpful, cramming last minute is NOT. If at all possible, work ahead so that you won't need to fit all your study into the last day. Cramming overloads your brain with more information than it can process and retain, and your tired mind may struggle to recall even previously learned information when it is overwhelmed with last-minute study. Also, the urgent nature of cramming and the stress placed on your brain contribute to anxiety. You'll be more likely to go to the test feeling unprepared and having trouble thinking clearly.

So don't cram, and don't stay up late before the test, even just to review your notes at a leisurely pace. Your brain needs rest more than it needs to go over the information again. In fact, plan to finish your studies by noon or early afternoon the day before the test. Give your brain the rest of the day to relax or focus on other things, and get a good night's sleep. Then you will be fresh for the test and better able to recall what you've studied.

Step 6: Take a practice test

Many courses offer sample tests, either online or in the study materials. This is an excellent resource to check whether you have mastered the material, as well as to prepare for the test format and environment.

Check the test format ahead of time: the number of questions, the type (multiple choice, free response, etc.), and the time limit. Then create a plan for working through them. For example, if you have 30 minutes to take a 60-question test, your limit is 30 seconds per question. Spend less time on the questions you know well so that you can take more time on the difficult ones.

If you have time to take several practice tests, take the first one open book, with no time limit. Work through the questions at your own pace and make sure you fully understand them. Gradually work up to taking a test under test conditions: sit at a desk with all study materials put away and set a timer. Pace yourself to make sure you finish the test with time to spare and go back to check your answers if you have time.

After each test, check your answers. On the questions you missed, be sure you understand why you missed them. Did you misread the question (tests can use tricky wording)? Did you forget the information? Or was it something you hadn't learned? Go back and study any shaky areas that the practice tests reveal.

Taking these tests not only helps with your grade, but also aids in combating test anxiety. If you're already used to the test conditions, you're less likely to worry about it, and working through tests until you're scoring well gives you a confidence boost. Go through the practice tests until you feel comfortable, and then you can go into the test knowing that you're ready for it.

Test Tips

On test day, you should be confident, knowing that you've prepared well and are ready to answer the questions. But aside from preparation, there are several test day strategies you can employ to maximize your performance.

First, as stated before, get a good night's sleep the night before the test (and for several nights before that, if possible). Go into the test with a fresh, alert mind rather than staying up late to study.

Try not to change too much about your normal routine on the day of the test. It's important to eat a nutritious breakfast, but if you normally don't eat breakfast at all, consider eating just a protein bar. If you're a coffee drinker, go ahead and have your normal coffee. Just make sure you time it so that the caffeine doesn't wear off right in the middle of your test. Avoid sugary beverages, and drink enough water to stay hydrated but not so much that you need a restroom break 10 minutes into the test. If your test isn't first thing in the morning, consider going for a walk or doing a light workout before the test to get your blood flowing.

Allow yourself enough time to get ready, and leave for the test with plenty of time to spare so you won't have the anxiety of scrambling to arrive in time. Another reason to be early is to select a good seat. It's helpful to sit away from doors and windows, which can be distracting. Find a good seat, get out your supplies, and settle your mind before the test begins.

When the test begins, start by going over the instructions carefully, even if you already know what to expect. Make sure you avoid any careless mistakes by following the directions.

Then begin working through the questions, pacing yourself as you've practiced. If you're not sure on an answer, don't spend too much time on it, and don't let it shake your confidence. Either skip it and come back later, or eliminate as many wrong answers as possible and guess among the remaining ones. Don't dwell on these questions as you continue—put them out of your mind and focus on what lies ahead.

Be sure to read all of the answer choices, even if you're sure the first one is the right answer. Sometimes you'll find a better one if you keep reading. But don't second-guess yourself if you do immediately know the answer. Your gut instinct is usually right. Don't let test anxiety rob you of the information you know.

If you have time at the end of the test (and if the test format allows), go back and review your answers. Be cautious about changing any, since your first instinct tends to be correct, but make sure you didn't misread any of the questions or accidentally mark the wrong answer choice. Look over any you skipped and make an educated guess.

At the end, leave the test feeling confident. You've done your best, so don't waste time worrying about your performance or wishing you could change anything. Instead, celebrate the successful completion of this test. And finally, use this test to learn how to deal with anxiety even better next time.

> **Review Video:** <u>5 Tips to Beat Test Anxiety</u>
> Visit mometrix.com/academy and enter code: 570656

Important Qualification

Not all anxiety is created equal. If your test anxiety is causing major issues in your life beyond the classroom or testing center, or if you are experiencing troubling physical symptoms related to your anxiety, it may be a sign of a serious physiological or psychological condition. If this sounds like your situation, we strongly encourage you to seek professional help.

Thank You

We at Mometrix would like to extend our heartfelt thanks to you, our friend and patron, for allowing us to play a part in your journey. It is a privilege to serve people from all walks of life who are unified in their commitment to building the best future they can for themselves.

The preparation you devote to these important testing milestones may be the most valuable educational opportunity you have for making a real difference in your life. We encourage you to put your heart into it—that feeling of succeeding, overcoming, and yes, conquering will be well worth the hours you've invested.

We want to hear your story, your struggles and your successes, and if you see any opportunities for us to improve our materials so we can help others even more effectively in the future, please share that with us as well. **The team at Mometrix would be absolutely thrilled to hear from you!** So please, send us an email (support@mometrix.com) and let's stay in touch.

If you'd like some additional help, check out these other resources we offer for your exam:

http://MometrixFlashcards.com/TEA

Additional Bonus Material

Due to our efforts to try to keep this book to a manageable length, we've created a link that will give you access to all of your additional bonus material.

Please visit **https://www.mometrix.com/bonus948/tea** to access the information.